Ways of Knowing in Science aneries

RICHARD DUSCHL, SERIES EDITOR

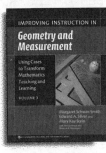

Improving Instruction in Rational Numbers and Proportionality

Using Cases to Transform Mathematics Teaching and Learning, Volume 1

Margaret Schwan Smith
Edward A. Silver
Mary Kay Stein

*with Melissa Boston,
Marjorie A. Henningsen,
and Amy F. Hillen*

Teachers College, Columbia University
New York and London

The material in this book is based on work supported by National Science Foundation grant number ESI-9731428 for the COMET (Cases of Mathematics Instruction to Enhance Teaching) Project. Any opinions expressed herein are those of the authors and do not necessarily represent the views of the National Science Foundation.

Published by Teachers College Press, 1234 Amsterdam Avenue, New York, NY 10027

Library of Congress Cataloging-in-Publication Data

Smith, Margaret Schwan.
    Improving instruction in rational numbers and proportionality / Margaret Schwan Smith, Edward A. Silver, Mary Kay Stein, with Melissa Boston, Marjorie A. Henningsen, and Amy F. Hillen.
    p. cm. — (Using cases to transform mathematics teaching and learning ; v. 1) (Ways of knowing in science and mathematics series)
    Includes bibliographical references and index.
    ISBN 0-8077-4529-4 (pbk. : acid-free paper)
    1. Mathematics—Study and teaching (Middle school)—United States—Case studies.   I. Silver, Edward A., 1948– II. Stein, Mary Kay. III. Title IV. Series.

QA13.S58 2005
513'.071'2—dc22

2004055390

ISBN 0-8077-4529-4 (paper)

Printed on acid-free paper
Manufactured in the United States of America

12   11   10   09   08   07   06   05   8   7   6   5   4   3   2   1

To the teachers in the QUASAR Project—although nearly a decade has passed since our work together ended, we continue to draw inspiration from your work. You were true pioneers in creating instructional environments that promoted mathematics learning for all students. Thank you for sharing your successes and struggles with us. We continue to learn so much from you.

Contents

Acknowledgments

The ideas expressed in this book grew out of our work on the QUASAR Project and have developed over the past decade through our interactions and collaborations with many teachers, teacher educators, and mathematicians. We would like to thank mathematicians and mathematics teacher educators Hyman Bass, John Beem, Nadine Bezuk, Kathleen Cramer, George Bright, Victoria Kouba, John Moyer, John P. Smith III, Judith Roitman, and Orit Zaslavsky, who provided feedback on early versions of the cases. Your thoughtful comments helped ensure that the cases were both sound and compelling.

We are indebted to Victoria Bill whose varied and frequent use of the cases over the past 5 years has helped us recognize the flexibility and power of the cases to promote learning in a range of situations; and to our colleagues Fran Arbaugh, Cathy Brown, Marta Civil, Gilberto Cuevas, Beatrice D'Ambrosio, Skip Fennell, Linda Foreman, Susan Friel, Judith Jacobs, Jeremy Kahan, Rebecca McGraw, Jack Moyer, Kathy Pfaendler, Elizabeth Phillips, and Judith Zawojewski, who piloted early versions of the cases, provided helpful feedback, and expanded our view regarding the possible uses of the cases and related materials.

Finally, we would like to acknowledge the contributions of Cristina Heffernan, who developed the COMET website, provided feedback on early versions of the cases and facilitation materials, and identified tasks in other curricula that corresponded to the cases; Michael Steele, who provided technological assistance in preparing the final manuscript; and Kathy Day, who provided valuable assistance in preparing figures, locating data, and copying materials.

Introduction

Teachers of mathematics in the middle grades face a difficult task. For many years, middle school mathematics teachers may have felt overlooked, as attention was paid to the secondary school because of pressure from colleges and employers, or to the primary grades because of interesting research-based initiatives related to young children's learning of mathematical ideas. In recent years, however, the spotlight has shown brightly on middle grades mathematics.

GREAT EXPECTATIONS FOR MIDDLE GRADES MATHEMATICS

Evidence of mediocre U.S. student performance on national and international assessments of mathematical achievement has sparked public and professional demand for better mathematics education in the middle grades. National organizations and state agencies have published guidelines, frameworks, and lists of expectations calling for more and better mathematics in grades K–12. Many of these give specific attention to raising expectations for mathematics teaching and learning in the middle grades. For example, *Principles and Standards for School Mathematics*, published by the National Council of Teachers of Mathematics (NCTM, 2000), calls for curriculum and teaching in the middle grades to be more ambitious. To accomplish the goals of developing conceptual understanding and helping students become capable, flexible problem-solvers, there are new topics to teach and old topics to teach in new ways.

There is some variation across the many policy documents produced in recent years regarding the teaching and learning of mathematics in the middle grades, but the essential message is the same: The mathematics instructional program in the middle grades needs to be more ambitious, setting higher expectations for middle school students and for their teachers. Compared with the situation at the beginning of the 1990s, guidelines for mathematics instructional programs in virtually every state and many local school districts in the country have been revised to reflect higher expectations for student learning of important mathematical ideas.

New Curriculum Materials

Some help in meeting higher expectations for mathematics teaching and learning in the middle grades is likely to come from new mathematics curriculum materials that reflect more ambitious demands. Some new materials have been developed along the lines suggested by the NCTM standards. In general, these curriculum materials provide teachers with carefully sequenced, intellectually challenging instructional tasks that focus on important mathematical ideas and that can be used with students to develop their mathematical proficiency.

New curriculum materials with interesting and challenging tasks are undoubtedly crucial to any effort to upgrade the quality of mathematics education, but ambitious materials will be effective only if they are implemented well in classrooms. And good implementation is a nontrivial matter since a more demanding curriculum requires that middle school teachers become effective in supporting student engagement with complex intellectual activity in the classroom. In short, new curriculum materials are unlikely to have the desired impact on student learning unless classroom instruction shifts from its current focus on routine skills and instead focuses on developing student understanding of important mathematics concepts and proficiency in solving complex problems.

Improving Teacher Preparation and Continuing Support

The success of efforts to enhance mathematics teaching and learning in the middle grades hinges to a great extent on the success of programs and practices that prepare teachers to do this work and those that continue to support them along the way. Unfortunately, the approaches typically used to prepare and support teachers in the middle grades have well-documented limitations. Many who currently teach mathematics in the middle grades received their initial preparation in programs intended for generalists rather than for mathematics specialists. In such programs, too little attention is paid to developing the specific proficiencies needed by mathematics teachers in the middle grades, where the mathematical ideas are complex and difficult for students to learn. Moreover, components of the knowledge needed for effective teaching usually are taught and learned in isolation from each other—mathematics in the mathematics department, issues of student learning in a psychology (or educational psychology) department, and pedagogy in a teacher education department. Rarely is the knowledge integrated and tied to settings where it is used by teachers. As a consequence, this fragmented, decontextualized approach often fails to build a solid foundation for effective teaching of mathematics in the middle grades. Compounding the challenge is the fact that most schools and school districts usually are not able to offer the right kinds of assistance to remedy weaknesses in preparation that their teachers may possess.

The current set of challenges facing teachers of mathematics in the middle grades call for a new approach and new tools to accomplish the work. Just as new curriculum materials can assist teachers of mathematics to meet the challenges they face, new resources can assist teacher educators and professional development specialists in their work. What is needed is an effective way to support teachers in increasing their knowledge of mathematics content, mathematical pedagogy, and student learning of mathematics, in a manner likely to affect classroom actions and interactions in ways that lead to improved student learning. The materials in this volume have been designed to help teachers of mathematics and those who prepare and support them in their work to meet the challenges that inhere in the higher public and professional expectations.

THE MATERIALS IN THIS VOLUME

This volume is divided into two parts. Part I is written primarily for teachers, prospective teachers, or other readers interested in exploring issues related to mathematics teacher and learning. Part I begins with a chapter that describes the use of cases to promote learning (Chapter 1) and includes four chapters (Chapter 2–5) that feature narrative cases of classroom mathematics lessons along with materials intended to engage readers in thinking deeply about the mathematics teaching and learning that occurred in the cases. Part II is written for teacher educators or other professional development providers who work with teachers. Part II begins with a chapter that provides general suggestions for case facilitation (Chapter 6) and includes four chapters (Chapters 7–10) that feature facilitation materials and suggestions for using the case materials in Chapters 2 through 5. Following Part II is a set of appendices that contain sample responses for selected activities presented in the case chapters in Part I. The contents of Parts I and II and the appendices are described in more detail in the sections that follow.

Part I: Using Cases to Enhance Learning

The centerpiece of Part I is a set of narrative cases of classroom mathematics lessons developed under the auspices of the NSF-funded COMET (Cases of Mathematics Instruction to Enhance Teaching) Project. The goal of COMET was to produce professional development materials for teachers based on data (including more than 500 videotaped lessons) collected on mathematics instruction in urban middle school classrooms with ethnically, racially, and linguistically diverse student populations in six school districts that participated in the QUASAR (Quantitative Understanding: Amplifying Student Achievement and Reasoning) Project (Silver, Smith, & Nelson, 1995; Silver & Stein, 1996). QUASAR was a national project (funded by the Ford Foundation) aimed at improving mathematics instruction for students attending middle schools in economically disadvantaged communities. The teachers in schools that participated in QUASAR were committed to increasing student achievement in mathematics by promoting conceptual understanding and complex problem-solving.

Each case portrays a teacher and students engaging with a cognitively complex mathematics task in an urban middle school classroom. By examining these instructional episodes, readers can wrestle with key issues of practice, such as what students appear to be learning and how the teaching supports or inhibits students' learning opportunities. The cases are based on real teachers and events, drawing on detailed documentation (videotapes and write-ups) of classroom lessons and interviews with teachers about the documented lessons. At times, cases enhance certain aspects of a lesson in order to make a particular idea salient. However, every attempt has been made to stay true to the predispositions and general teaching habits of the teacher who inspired the case. Although the names of the teachers, their schools, and their students have been changed so as to protect their anonymity, each teacher portrayed in a case gave us permission to share their stories so that others might learn from their efforts to improve mathematics teaching and learning.

Preceding the cases, Chapter 1 suggests how they can be used as a resource for professional learning. In this volume, readers are guided through a set of coordinated experiences that encourage reflection on, analysis of, and inquiry into the teaching and learning of mathematics in the middle grades. Readers of the cases also are encouraged to use the particular episodes portrayed as a base from which to generalize across cases, from cases to general principles, and from the cases to their own teaching.

Teachers of mathematics and individuals preparing to become teachers of mathematics will want to focus on this part of the volume. A teacher might learn from our materials as an individual, but, if at all possible, we encourage interaction with others around the cases. Through careful reading of the cases in this volume, accompanied by thoughtful analysis and active consideration of issues raised by the cases, readers have an opportunity to learn a great deal about mathematics teaching. Readers also have a chance to learn about student thinking because examples of student thinking about mathematical ideas are embedded in each case.

Part II: Facilitating Learning From Cases

In Part II, readers will find a facilitation chapter corresponding to each of the cases presented in Part I. The suggestions in these facilitation chapters are based on our own experiences using the cases. They reflect the lessons that we have learned about what works well and what does not with respect to preparing teachers to read the case, guiding their discussion of the case, and designing follow-up activities that will help the teachers connect the case experience to their own practice.

Each facilitation chapter begins with a short synopsis of the case. The heart of the facilitation chapter is the case analysis section, which specifies the key mathematical and pedagogical ideas embedded in the case and identifies the paragraph numbers in the case where those ideas are instantiated. Other sections of the facilitation chapters help the facilitator to prepare for activities related to the case discussions, such as the Opening Activity and the follow-up activities.

Preceding the facilitation chapters, Chapter 6 explains why we have selected narrative cases as our approach to helping middle school teachers become more thoughtful and ambitious teachers of mathematics. After a short explanation of how teachers learn from cases and what we expect teachers to learn from our cases in particular, a description of the kinds of support that can be found in each of the facilitation chapters is provided.

Part II will be of special interest to those who intend to use the materials to assist preservice and/or inservice teachers to learn and improve their practice. This group includes professionals who contribute to improving the quality of mathematics teaching and learning through their work in diverse settings: schools (e.g., teacher leaders, coaches, mentors, administrators); school district offices (e.g., curriculum coordinators, staff developers); regional intermediate units and state agencies; or colleges and universities (e.g., instructors of mathematics or methods courses).

The Appendices

The appendices following Part II contain sample responses for the Opening Activity and for the question posed in the "Analyzing the Case" section in each of the case chapters (Chapters 2–5). These sample responses are often products from our work in using the case materials in professional development settings. In some instances, the sample responses are the work of the participants in the professional development session; other times, the sample responses were generated by the case facilitator in preparation for using the case. References to the corresponding appendices are made in the case and facilitation chapters when appropriate.

Each case chapter in Part I is related to a facilitation chapter in Part II and to a set of sample responses in an appendix. The relationship between case chapters, facilitation chapters, and appendices is as follows:

- The Case of Randy Harris: Chapter 2, Chapter 7, and Appendix A
- The Case of Marie Hanson: Chapter 3, Chapter 8, and Appendix B

- The Case of Marcia Green: Chapter 4, Chapter 9, and Appendix C
- The Case of Janice Patterson: Chapter 5, Chapter 10, and Appendix D

Building on Extensive Research and Prior Experience

As noted earlier, the cases in this volume are based on research conducted in middle schools that participated in the QUASAR Project. A major finding of this research was that a teacher's actions and interactions with students were crucial in determining the extent to which students were able to maintain a high level of intellectual engagement with challenging mathematical tasks (e.g., Henningsen & Stein, 1997). More specifically, the quality and quantity of student engagement in intellectually demanding activity sometimes conformed to a teacher's intentions but often they did not (e.g., Stein, Grover, & Henningsen, 1996). Our research also showed that there were consequences for student learning when teachers were able or unable to maintain high intellectual demands (Stein & Lane, 1996). In classrooms where high-demand tasks were used frequently, and where the intellectual demands usually were maintained during lessons, students exhibited strong performance on a test assessing conceptual understanding and problem-solving. In contrast, in classrooms where intellectually demanding tasks rarely were used or where the intellectual demands frequently declined during lessons, student performance was lower.

This research also identified characteristic ways in which cognitively demanding tasks either were maintained at a high level or declined. For example, tasks sometimes declined by becoming proceduralized; in other cases, they declined due to unsystematic and nonproductive student exploration. In our first casebook (Stein, Smith, Henningsen, & Silver, 2000), we presented six cases that served as prototypes to illustrate these distinct patterns.

The materials in this volume build on that earlier work in at least two important ways. First, they make salient key instructional factors and pedagogical moves that affect the extent and nature of intellectual activity in classroom lessons involving cognitively complex mathematics tasks. For example, the cases illustrate how a teacher might uncover student thinking and use it productively to encourage students to explain and justify their thinking or to make connections among ideas. Second, the cases extend the earlier work by sharpening the focus on the specific mathematical ideas at stake

in the lesson and by explicitly calling attention to ways in which the instructional actions of the teacher support or inhibit students' opportunities to learn worthwhile mathematics. In particular, the cases in this volume draw attention to key aspects of proportionality.

Now that we have described the contents of this book, in the following section we provide a rationale for selecting proportionality as the content focus.

Why Proportionality?

Proportionality has been called both the capstone of elementary school arithmetic and the cornerstone of higher mathematics (Lesh, Post, & Behr, 1988). Proportionality is associated with many concepts and skills taught in the middle grades, and so it has been suggested as a unifying thread to tie together the middle-grades curriculum (NCTM, 2000). Viewed in this way, proportionality deserves more attention, and a different kind of attention, from teachers, teacher educators, and students than has been the case in the past. Yet proportionality is also closely tied to a long-standing nemesis of teachers of mathematics in the middle grades—the teaching and learning of rational number concepts and skills.

If you asked teachers 50 years ago to identify mathematics topics in the middle grades that were difficult for them to teach and for their students to learn, it is almost certain that rational numbers (fractions and decimals) would have been at or near the top of their list. The same judgment would be likely if teachers were asked today, and the increasing recognition of proportionality as a key idea in the middle grades gives even greater import and urgency to the need to help teachers gain greater proficiency in teaching this cluster of mathematical ideas.

The materials in this volume are intended to do just that. In particular, they help teachers to focus on the flexible use of a variety of representations and strategies in solving problems involving proportional relationships. They also draw attention to some typical student misunderstandings that have been identified in research and shown to impede students' mathematical progress, such as difficulty distinguishing comparisons between quantities that are multiplicative rather than additive.

THIS VOLUME AND ITS COMPANIONS

This is one of three volumes of materials intended to help teachers of mathematics identify and address some key challenges encountered in contemporary mathematics teaching in the middle grades. This volume provides opportunities for teachers to delve into and inquire about the teaching and learning of rational numbers and proportionality. Two companion volumes focus on other familiar and important mathematics topic domains in the middle grades: algebra, and geometry and measurement. We encourage readers of this volume to use the cases provided in the companion volumes to investigate the teaching and learning of mathematics across a broader spectrum of topics in the middle grades.

The materials in this volume and its companions are designed to be used flexibly. As a complete set, the three volumes provide a base on which to build a coherent and cohesive professional development program to enhance middle school teachers' knowledge of mathematics and mathematics pedagogy, and of students as learners of mathematics. These materials, either as individual cases, separate volumes, or the entire set, also can be used as components of other teacher professional development programs. For example, many users of preliminary versions of these materials have included our cases in their mathematics methods and content courses for preservice teachers, in their professional development efforts for practicing teachers, and in their efforts to support implementation of reform-oriented curricula. Our most sincere hope is that they will be used in a wide variety of ways to enhance the quality of mathematics teaching and learning in the middle grades.

Improving Instruction in Rational Numbers and Proportionality

Using Cases to Transform Mathematics Teaching and Learning, Volume 1

PART I

USING CASES TO ENHANCE LEARNING

In the Introduction, we provided a rationale for this volume and an overview of the materials it contains. In Part I of this book (Chapters 1–5), we turn our attention to using cases to enhance learning. Chapter 1 serves as an opening to this section of the book and describes how to use the case materials presented in Chapters 2 through 5. Chapters 2 through 5 provide case materials intended to engage teachers, prospective teachers, or other readers in analyzing and reflecting on important ideas and issues in the teaching and learning of mathematics.

1

Using Cases to Learn

In this chapter, we describe the cases presented in this volume and discuss the opportunities for learning they afford. We then provide suggestions for using the cases and related materials for reflection, analysis, and, when applicable, as springboards for investigation into a teacher's own instructional practices.

THE CASES

Each of the four cases in this book portrays the events that unfold in an urban middle school classroom as a teacher engages her students in solving a challenging mathematical task. For example, in Chapter 3, Marie Hanson (one of the four teachers featured in the cases) and her students explore several problems that involve constructing equivalent ratios of discrete objects and finding the missing value in proportions when one of the quantities is not given. Since students in Ms. Hanson's class have not previously learned a procedure for solving missing-value problems, they must invent their own strategies rather than applying memorized rules that have no meaning to them.

Each case begins with a description of the teacher, students, and the urban middle school, so as to provide a context for understanding and interpreting the portrayed episode. It then goes on to describe the teacher's goals for the lesson and the unfolding of the actual lesson in a fairly detailed way. Each case depicts a classroom in which a culture has been established over time by the implicit and explicit actions and interactions of a teacher and her students. Within this culture a set of norms have been established regarding the ways in which students are expected to work on a task (e.g., being willing to take risks, being respectful toward members of the classroom commu-

nity, being accountable for explaining a solution method).

The cases illustrate authentic practice—what really happens in a mathematics classroom when teachers endeavor to teach mathematics in ways that challenge students to think, reason, and problem-solve. As such they are not intended to be exemplars of best practice to be emulated but rather examples to be analyzed so as to better understand the relationship between teaching and learning and the ways in which student learning can be supported.

The cases in this volume have been created and organized so as to make salient important mathematical ideas related to rational numbers and proportionality and a set of pedagogical ideas that influence how students engage in mathematical activity and what they learn through the process. Each of these ideas is described below.

Important Mathematical Ideas

Proportionality has been described as a unifying theme in middle school mathematics (NCTM, 2000). In this view, proportionality (often called proportional reasoning) involves much more than setting two ratios equal and finding the missing term. It involves "recognizing quantities that are related proportionally and using numbers, tables, graphs, and equations to think about the quantities and their relationships" (NCTM, 2000, p. 217).

Each case features students working on a mathematical task in which they use various strategies (e.g., unit rate, factor-of-change, ratio table) and representational forms (e.g., diagrams, verbal descriptions, numbers and symbols) to make sense of multiplicative relationships. As a collection, the tasks highlight various contexts (e.g., scale drawings, mixture problems) and topics (e.g., fractions, percents, similarity) that require an understanding of proportionality.

The teacher featured in a case usually solicits several different approaches for solving a problem so as to help students develop a flexible set of strategies for solving problems that involve proportions and to see the connections between different ways of representing the ideas. For example, in "The Case of Marie Hanson" (Chapter 3) we see students solving the candy jar problem (i.e., finding the number of Jawbreakers if the ratio of 5 Jolly Ranchers to 13 Jawbreakers is preserved in a new candy jar that contains 100 Jolly Ranchers) by identifying the factor-of-change, by determining the unit rate, and by using an incorrect additive approach. As students share and discuss their solutions publicly, they come to understand the fallacy of using an additive approach and begin to see how the different solution strategies are related.

Pedagogical Moves

Each case begins with a challenging mathematical task that has the potential to engage students in high-level thinking about important mathematical ideas related to rational numbers and proportionality. Throughout the case the teacher endeavors to support students as they work to make sense of the mathematics, without removing the challenging aspects of the task. This support includes uncovering and using student thinking in productive ways, pressing students to explain and justify their thinking and reasoning in both public and private forums, and encouraging students to generate and make connections between different solution paths, ways of representing a mathematics concept, and observations about mathematical phenomena.

As such, each case highlights a set of pedagogical moves that support (or in some cases inhibit) student engagement with important mathematical ideas. For example, in the case involving the Jolly Ranchers and Jawbreakers problem (Chapter 3), Ms. Hanson supported students' engagement by allowing the class to determine that using an additive constant does not work, by pressing students to publicly explain and debate their solutions and ideas, and by scaffolding students' thinking by making conceptual connections between different strategies and representations. By orchestrating the lesson as she did, Ms. Hanson advanced her students' understanding of proportional relationships—the ultimate goal of the lesson.

THE CASES AS LEARNING OPPORTUNITIES

Reading a case is a unique experience. Although it bears some similarities to reading other narratives (e.g., the reader has a story line to follow, may identify with the joys and dilemmas experienced by the protagonist, may end up glad or sad when the story concludes), a case differs from other narrative accounts in an important way. Cases are intended to stimulate reflection, analysis, and investigation into one's own teaching and, in so doing, help teachers continue to develop their knowledge base for teaching.

As they read and discuss a case and solve the related mathematical task, teachers examine their own understanding of the mathematics in the lesson and how the mathematical ideas are encountered by students in the classroom. Through this process teachers can develop new understandings about a particular mathematical idea, make connections that they had not previously considered, and gain confidence in their ability to do mathematics. In addition, teachers may begin to develop an appreciation of mathematical tasks that can be solved in multiple ways and allow entry at various levels. Take, for example, "The Case of Janice Patterson" (Chapter 5). As teachers attempt to make sense of the ways in which Ms. Patterson's students solve algebra problems, they may begin to see for the first time that diagrams can be used by students to make sense of problems before they know how to write and solve equations in a more formal way. With this insight, teachers may see that students can access many problems prior to learning specific rules and procedures for solving them.

Cases also provide the reader with an opportunity to analyze the pedagogical moves made by the teacher in the case. Through this analysis of the case, readers are encouraged to go beyond the superficial features of a classroom to investigate what students are learning about mathematics and how the teaching supports that learning. For example, in Chapter 5 the reader initially might conclude that Janice Patterson had a minimal role in her students' learning since the students seem to move through the lesson with little explicit direction from or involvement by the teacher. A deeper analysis, on the other hand, requires the reader to account for what Janice Patterson did (or might have done in previous classes) to enable students to work productively with limited direct assistance.

Finally, cases provide teachers with an opportunity to focus on the thinking of students as it unfolds during instruction and to offer explanations regarding what students appear to know and understand about the mathematics they are learning. Through this process teachers expand their views of what students can do when given the opportunity, develop their capacity to make sense of representations and explanations that may differ from their own, and become familiar with misconceptions that are common in a particular domain. For example, in reading "The Case of Marie Hanson" (Chapter 3), teachers see that one approach to solving the problem yields an incorrect answer. As readers analyze what Jordan (the student who produced the incorrect answer) did and how Ms. Hanson orchestrated the discussion of his work, they come to realize that Jordan used an additive strategy and in doing so did not maintain the original ratio. Jordan's additive strategy is more than a simple incorrect answer. Rather, it represents confusion about the relationship between the quantities represented in a proportion and is at the heart of many of the difficulties students have in reasoning about situations in which quantities are related proportionally.

Reading and analyzing a case thus can help a teacher develop critical components of the knowledge base for teaching—knowledge of subject matter and pedagogy, and of students as learners—through the close examination of classroom practice. Although this is a critical step in developing knowledge for improved practice, the payoff of learning from cases is what teachers take from their experiences with cases and apply to their own practice. Teachers must learn to recognize specific situations in the cases as instances of something larger and more generalizable. In order for teachers to be able to move from a specific instance of a phenomenon to a more general understanding, they need multiple opportunities to consider an idea, to make comparisons across situations, and ultimately to examine their own practice. For example, in order to help students develop their skills as proportional reasoners, teachers need to understand the difficulties that students often have distinguishing between situations in which the quantities are related multiplicatively versus additively. The cases in this volume invite the reader to explore this misconception in several different ways—through Jordan's incorrect procedure for scaling up a ratio in "The Case of Marie Hanson" (Chapter 3); through Jason's solution to the mixture problem in "The Case of Janice Patterson" (Chapter 5); and in Marcia Green's concern that students may not be seeing multiplicative relationships when comparing similar figures (Chapter 4). By grappling with these three separate but related incidents, teachers can begin to build a robust understanding of

this mathematical difficulty experienced by middle school students, which ultimately will enable them to identify the same difficulty in their own students.

USING THE CASES

It is important to note that learning from cases is not self-enacting. Reading a case does not ensure that the reader automatically will engage with all the embedded ideas or spontaneously will make connections to their own practice. Through our work with cases, we have found that the readers of a case need to engage in specific activities related to the case in order to maximize the opportunities for learning. Specifically, readers appear to benefit from having a lens through which to view the events that unfold during a lesson and that signals where they profitably might direct their attention. For that reason we have created a set of professional learning tasks that provide a focus for reading and analyzing each case.

In the remainder of this chapter we provide suggestions for using the cases and related materials that are found in Chapters 2 through 5. These suggestions are based on our experiences in a range of teacher education settings over several years. For each case, we describe three types of professional learning tasks: solving the mathematical task on which the case is based; analyzing the case; and generalizing beyond the case (i.e., making connections to your own teaching practice and to the ideas of others).

Although it is possible to read through the cases and complete the accompanying professional learning tasks on your own, we recommend that you find a partner or, better yet, a group of peers who are likewise inclined to think about and improve their practice. In this way, you will not only feel supported, but also develop a shared language for discussing your practice with colleagues.

Solving the Mathematical Task

Each case begins with an Opening Activity that consists of the same (or similar) mathematical task that is featured in the case. It is important that you spend sufficient time solving the task, ideally working through it in more than one way. This is a place in which working with colleagues is particularly advantageous. Others may solve the task in ways different than you; seeing their approaches will help to elaborate your own understanding of the task and enrich your repertoire of applicable strategies.

We have found that it is important for teachers to first engage with the mathematical task for two reasons. First, teachers go on to read the case with much more interest and confidence if they first engaged with the mathematical ideas themselves, whether individually or with the help of colleagues. Second, teachers are "primed for" and able to recognize many of the solution strategies put forth by students in the case. This way, teachers' understanding of the multiple pathways to solving the problems becomes strengthened and their perception of student thinking becomes sharper.

For each of the cases in Chapters 2 through 5 there is a corresponding appendix (A through D, respectively) that provides a set of solutions to the Opening Activity. These solutions were produced previously by teachers with whom we have worked. We encourage readers to review these solutions after they have completed the task, and to try to make sense of and relate the different approaches.

Analyzing the Case

We have found it helpful to focus teachers' reading of the case by providing a professional learning task to frame the initial analysis. The professional learning tasks, found in the "Reading the Case" section of Chapters 2 through 5, focus readers' attention on specific or general pedagogical moves made by the teacher during the lesson. The analysis continues as the reader is asked to explore the pedagogy in a deeper way, focusing on specific events that occurred in the classroom and the impact of these events on students' learning. A professional learning task intended to stimulate this deeper analysis is provided in the "Analyzing the Case" section of each case chapter. To facilitate analysis and discussion of key issues in relation to specific events in a case, the paragraphs of the text in each case are numbered consecutively for easy reference.

For example, as teachers begin to read the case in Chapter 2, they are asked to identify key pedagogical moves made by Randy Harris during the lesson. After completing their reading, teachers begin a deeper analysis of the case by reviewing the list of pedagogical moves identified, determining whether each move supported or inhibited students' learning of mathematics, and identifying specific paragraph numbers from the case to support claims that are made.

For each case, we have identified a specific focus of analysis. This focus is intended to highlight what each

case can best contribute to the reader's investigation of teaching and learning. For example, in "The Case of Janice Patterson" (Chapter 5) readers are asked to consider Janice Patterson's role in the lesson and whether or not she actually teaches. Although this question could be explored in any case, we feel that Janice's efforts to facilitate rather than direct learning make it particularly appropriate for her case. Janice's teaching provides a contrast with the role of the teacher in more traditional classroom settings and hence calls into question many assumptions about the roles and responsibilities of the teacher.

Additional questions that extend the analysis are provided in the "Extending Your Analysis of the Case" section. These questions focus the reader's attention on a specific event depicted in the case and invite the reader to critique or explain what occurred. Teachers may want to review the questions and identify one that resonates with their experiences or interests. These questions vary greatly from case to case and represent our best effort to bring to the fore a wider set of issues that might be explored within the context of a case.

The true value of the case analysis comes from the group discussion. It is through these discussions that teachers begin to develop a critical stance toward teaching and learning. If teachers do not have colleagues within their buildings with whom they can discuss the case face-to-face, new technologies may make it reasonable to conduct a discussion about a case via email or a web-based discussion group.

Generalizing Beyond the Case

Following the analysis of each case, readers are invited to engage in one or more activities in which the mathematical and pedagogical ideas discussed in the case are connected to their own practice or to other related ideas and issues regarding mathematics teaching and learning. In the section entitled "Connecting to Your Own Practice," teachers move beyond the specifics of a case and task and begin to examine their own practice in light of new understandings about mathematics, instruction, and student learning. This process is critical to the transformation of a teacher's practice.

While the specific activities vary from case to case, there are three general types of connections to practice that we recommend: enacting high-level tasks in your classroom, analyzing your own teaching, and working on specific issues that were raised for you during the case reading and analysis. These activities are intended to invite exploration of and critical reflection on a teacher's own practices. As we indicated earlier in the chapter, the activities in this section are intended to build upon the thinking the reader has done in the initial reading of the case and in the case analysis. For example, following the analysis of Janice Patterson's role in the lesson in Chapter 5, readers are asked to record a lesson in their own classroom and to reflect on their role during the lesson and to note ways in which they are similar to and different from Janice Patterson. In doing so, teachers can become more aware of their own actions in the classroom and how what they do influences students' opportunities to learn mathematics.

Teachers have additional opportunities to explore their own practice in the section entitled "Exploring Curricular Materials." In this section, teachers are invited to investigate their own curriculum so as to determine the way in which mathematical ideas related to rational numbers and proportionality are developed and the opportunities it provides for thinking and reasoning about mathematics. In addition, in this section teachers are encouraged to explore mathematical tasks from other curricula that make salient the mathematical ideas featured in the case.

In the last section of each chapter, "Connecting to Other Ideas and Issues," we identify a set of readings from teacher-oriented publications (e.g., *Mathematics Teaching in the Middle School*) and other resources that elaborate, extend, or complement the mathematical and pedagogical content in the case in some way. The readings provide new models for developing conceptual understanding related to rational numbers and proportionality (e.g., the Parker article referenced in Chapter 3); report findings from research on student learning (e.g., the Miller and Fey article referenced in Chapter 4); or present actual activities that could be used in your classroom in a unit on rational numbers and proportionality (e.g., the Sweeney and Quinn article referenced in Chapter 2). In each case chapter a specific set of suggestions are given regarding how to use the cited material to support the reader's understanding of the case or the ideas and issues that arise from the case.

Connecting Fractions, Decimals, and Percents

The Case of Randy Harris

This chapter provides the materials to engage you in reading and analyzing the teaching and learning that occur in the classroom of Randy Harris as he and his 7th-grade students explore ways of using rectangular grids to represent quantities expressed as fractions, decimals, and percents.

Prior to reading the case, we suggest that you complete the Opening Activity. The primary purpose of the Opening Activity is to engage you with the mathematical ideas that you will encounter when you read the case. The three problems that are found in the Opening Activity for "The Case of Randy Harris" are identical to those found in Problem Set B in the case—problems in which Randy engages his students during the second day of class. In solving the three problems, you are encouraged to utilize the diagrams provided and not to rely solely on arithmetic procedures for equating fractions, decimals, and percents.

Once you have completed the Opening Activity, you may want to refer to Appendix A, which contains some solutions generated by teachers who completed the Opening Activity as part of a professional development experience that focused on "The Case of Randy Harris." You are encouraged to examine the different solutions provided and to consider the relationship between your solution and those produced by others.

OPENING ACTIVITY

The Opening Activity for "The Case of Randy Harris" is presented in Figure 2.1. Please engage in the three problems and respond to the "Consider" question before reading the case.

READING THE CASE

As you read the case, we encourage you to make note of what appear to be key pedagogical moves made by the teacher during the lesson. (You may want to use a highlighter or Post-it notes to keep track of these as you read the case.) You may identify something that Randy Harris does during the lesson that you don't fully understand (e.g., placing an emphasis on the use of diagrams rather than procedures), that you don't agree with (e.g., beginning class on Day 2 without providing an example of how to solve the problems in Set B), that is intriguing to you (e.g., having students present solutions at the overhead), or that you have never considered but might like to pursue (e.g., placing the burden of explaining something in the hands of a student, as Randy did with Denise).

We encourage you to write down the "moves" that you identify. These can serve as topics for discussion with a colleague who also has read the case, as topics to investigate as you read additional cases, or as starting points for exploration in your own classroom. For example, you may begin to consider whether and how diagrams could help your students develop a deeper understanding of the meaning of fractions, decimals, and percents, and of the connections among them. As a consequence, you might decide to modify your lessons to include the use of grids of different sizes. We will discuss additional connections to your own practice at the end of the chapter.

FIGURE 2.1. The Opening Activity for "The Case of Randy Harris"

Solve

Try to solve each of the three problems listed below using the rectangular grid. Explain how you solved each problem.

1. Shade the portion of the area of the rectangle that represents .725.

    What fractional part of the area is shaded?

    What percentage of the area is shaded?

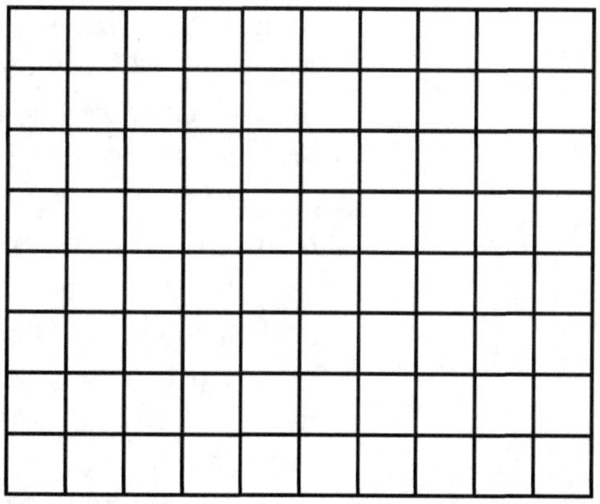

2. Shade ⅜ of the area of the rectangle.

    What percentage of the area is shaded?

    What decimal number is represented by the shaded portion of the rectangle?

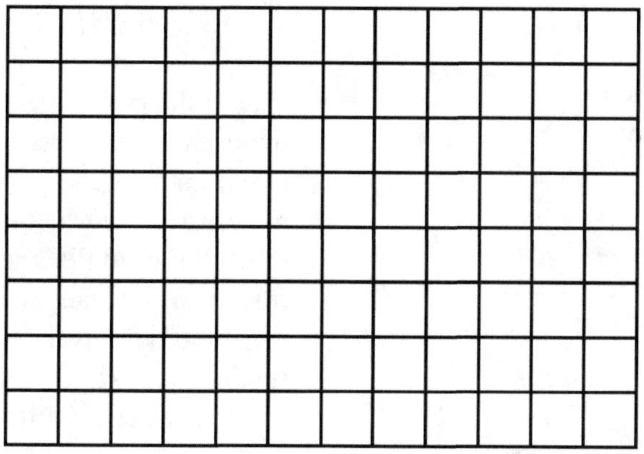

3. Shade 87½% of the area of the rectangle.

    What fractional part of the area is shaded?

    What decimal number is represented by the shaded portion of the rectangle?

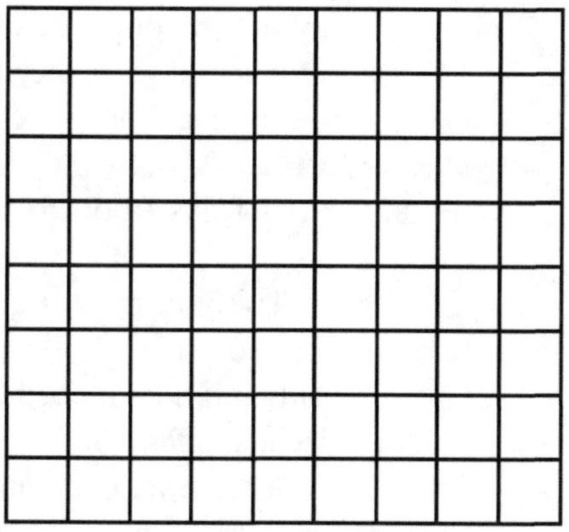

Consider

In what ways did the diagram help you make sense of the equivalence among fractions, decimals, and percents?

THE CASE OF RANDY HARRIS

1.   Randy Harris has been teaching mathematics at Stevenson Middle School for the past 10 years. Stevenson is a school characterized by diversity. Approximately 65% of the students are Caucasian, 25% are African American, and the remaining 10% are Hispanic or Native American. While some students come from a middle-class community that is located near a university, the majority of students live in a large, low-income housing project just a block from the school. Although some of the students have a history of academic success, many have been relatively unsuccessful in school.

2.   Randy has some students in his classes who are not computationally proficient, but he believes that all students should have access to mathematics that is challenging and makes them think. Although he recognizes the power and importance of having his students learn rules and procedures, Randy tries to ensure that his students understand the mathematics they are learning and that they are challenged to think on a regular basis. He makes an effort to select problems that can be approached in a variety of ways so that students with different experiences and ways of thinking will be able to successfully engage with the problems.

3.   For the past 2 years Randy's job has been made easier by the availability of curricular materials that focus on developing a conceptual understanding of mathematics. From Randy's perspective, one of the strengths of the materials is the way they make explicit connections among mathematical ideas. For example, the materials make salient the relationship among fractions, decimals, and percents, and treat percents as a special kind of ratio. Randy feels that too often students learn things in isolation and are unable to make connections between related situations and ideas.

4.   Randy believes that developing conceptual understanding of mathematics is facilitated by the use of visual diagrams. As he sees it, diagrams provide students with a tool for making sense of situations. Although he doesn't discount the power of procedures, he wants his students to understand what they are doing and why they are doing it. He sees the use of diagrams as a central component in building understanding.

Randy Harris Talks About His Class

5.   This year my 7th-grade students have spent quite a bit of time learning about decimals. We started by relating fractions to decimals using 10×10 grids and then moved on to using base-10 pieces to develop meaning for decimal operations. Through work with the various models, I tried to help students develop an understanding of what decimals were, how they could be represented, and how they could be used to solve problems. Last week we started a unit on percents. So far we have used rectangular grids of different dimensions (starting with a 10×10) to develop a basic understanding of what percent means and how different percents (e.g., 75%, 37½%, 147%, 0.23%) could be represented.

6.   Now I want to link fractions, decimals, and percents so that my students will see that they are different ways of expressing essentially the same thing. Although we spent some time earlier in the year talking

about the relationship between fractions and decimals, I now want to expand the conversation to include percents. Basically, I want my students to be comfortable moving back and forth among these different ways of representing fractional parts so that they can use these to express a quantity interchangeably and use the one that is most appropriate for solving a problem.

7.   The work we are doing today, and all the work that has preceded it, will contribute to the development of students' ability to reason proportionally. Proportional reasoning is not just about being able to set two ratios equal to one another and solve for the missing term. It involves seeing a multiplicative relationship between quantities. Two ideas that are likely to come out during this set of lessons—generating equivalent fractions and determining unit rates—highlight multiplicative relationships. This work eventually will be extended to more formal discussions of ratios and proportions, similarity, scaling, and linear equations.

8.   Over the next 2 days students will be working with two different types of problems. In the first type (Set A—see Figure 2.2), students will be presented with a rectangular grid, in which some subsection has been shaded. The shaded subsections are not limited to complete rows or columns, and the grids vary in dimension. For each problem, the students will need to represent the shaded area as a fraction, a decimal, and a percent. In the second type of problem (Set B—see Figure 2.7), the students will be given a rectangular grid and asked to shade in a specific amount (given as either a fraction, decimal, or percent). Then they are asked to represent the shaded area as a fraction, decimal, or percent, depending on what originally was given.

9.   Students should be able to do the first set without too much trouble since they can find the fraction by counting the shaded squares and comparing this to the total number of squares in the grid. However, I do not want them to rely on algorithmic approaches for converting fractions to decimals and percents. I want them to really understand the relationships and to be able to make sense of the situations, and I think this is more likely to occur if they use the visual diagram. So I will push them to move beyond the algorithmic approaches that they are comfortable with in order to help them develop a deeper understanding of the relationships involved.

10.   The second set of problems may be more difficult for students for two reasons—because they will be asked to shade an amount that is *not* represented by a whole number and because the grid is not a 10 × 10. I think it is important to deal with problems like this, that are more difficult, because the real test of their knowledge is to see if they can apply what they have learned in one situation to a new one.

The Class—Day 1

11.   *Getting started on Set A.* I placed a transparency for Problem Set A (shown in Figure 2.2) on the overhead and distributed a copy of the problems to each student. I told the class that today we would be representing area using fractions, decimals, and percents. I called their attention to the first problem on the sheet. I asked how we could represent the shaded area as a fraction. Several hands shot up and I asked

FIGURE 2.2. Set A

For each of the rectangular grids shown below, express the shaded region as a fraction, decimal, and percent.

1.

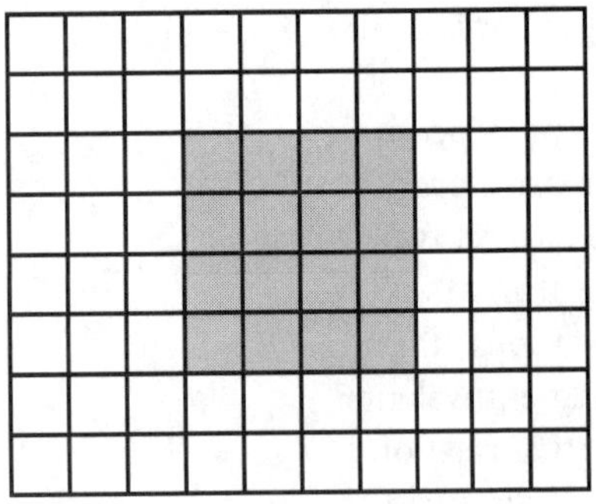

2.

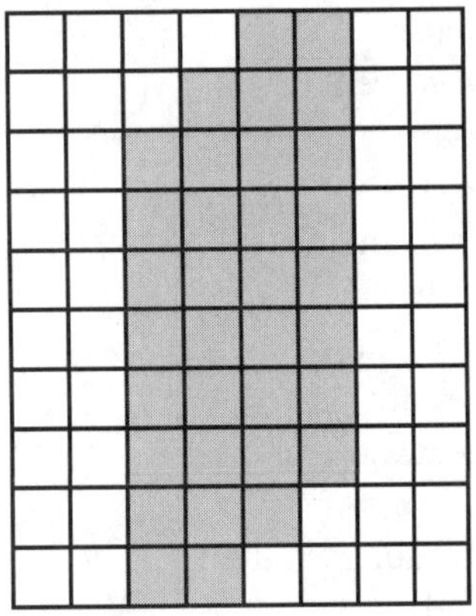

3.

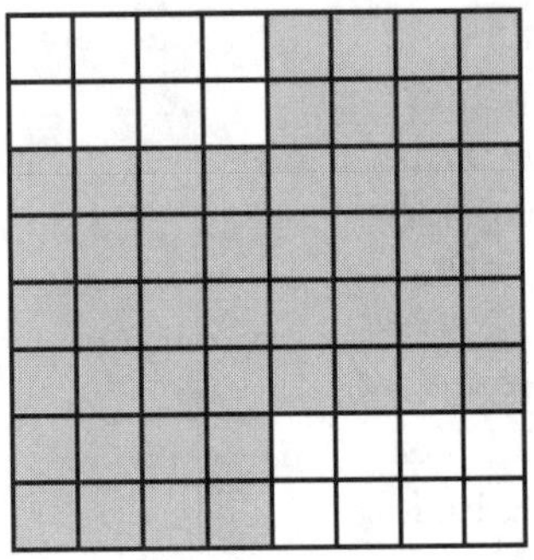

4.

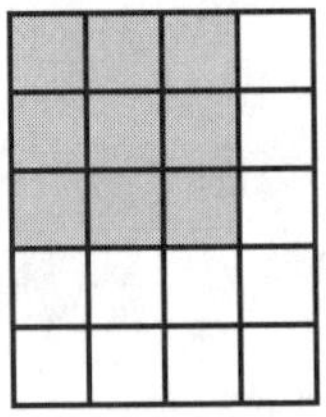

5.

6.

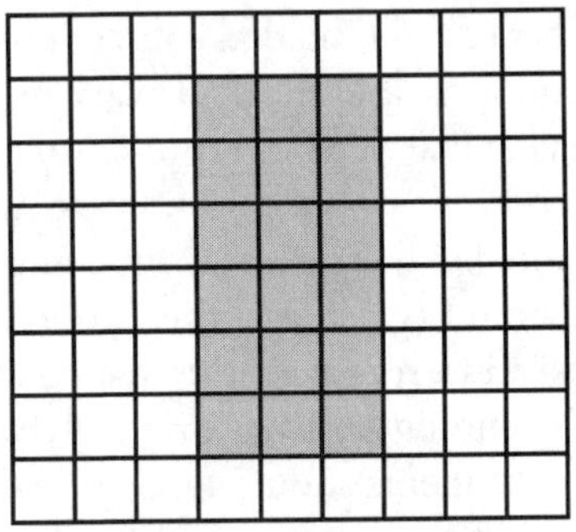

7.

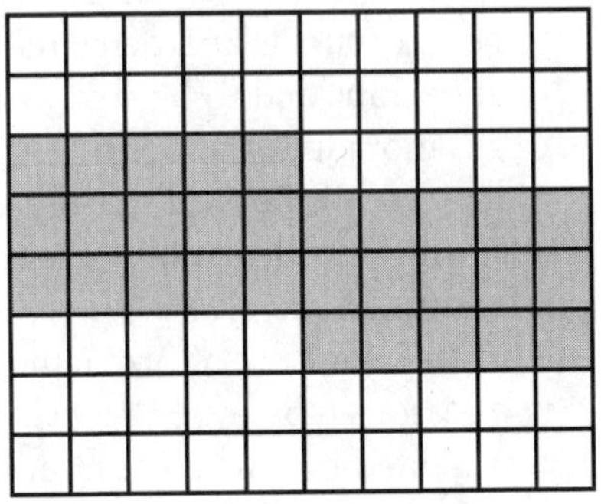

8.

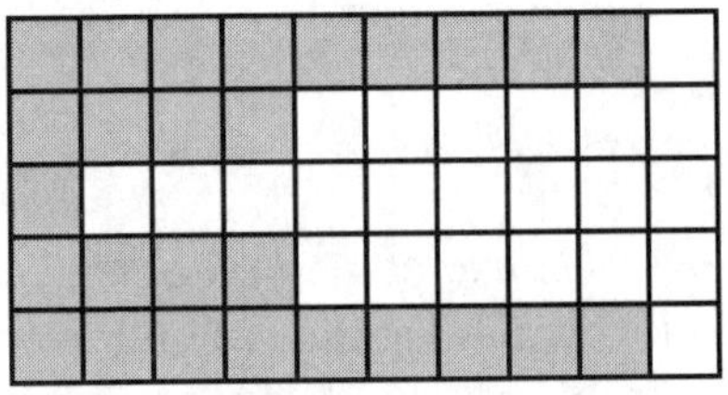

Danielle what she thought. She said "a 4 by 4 is shaded so that would be 16 and the whole rectangle is an 8 by 10 so that would be 80. It would be $16/80$." Sheryl added that it could be reduced to $1/5$.

12.   I then asked how we could represent $1/5$ as a percent. David volunteered that $1/5$ was equal to 20% or 0.20. I asked him how he knew this. He explained, "That was one of the ones we kept running into so I just remembered it." I was pleased that he remembered and commented to the class that remembering the fraction, decimal, and percent equivalents for unit fractions would be very helpful to them in life and in math classes. Although I was hoping for an explanation that relied less on memory or procedure, I decided that rather than ask for other ways to do the first problem, I would just have students begin to work on the problem set. We could deal with this issue when we began discussing the remaining problems.

13.   I explained that they would have about 15 minutes to begin work on the problems with their partners and we would then discuss the problems. I stressed that I wanted them to explain their thinking and to come up with different ways of doing the problems. As students worked on the problem set, I walked around the room reviewing and collecting homework from the previous evening. Although I often go over homework in class, today I did not want to spend class time going over the work, but I did want to take a quick look at it just to make sure that students were on track. The assignment had been to finish some problems that we had been working on that related percent to length. So far the papers I saw looked pretty good. Of course, I ran into the usual excuses from some students about leaving the paper in their locker or forgetting it at home. This does continue to be a problem for which I have little patience. I just keep trying to encourage my students to do the work, and to encourage their parents to check up on them.

14.   *Sharing solutions.* By the time I finished checking the homework, it was time to see how students were doing with the problem set. I called the class together and said that I wanted to start going over a few of the problems. I asked for a volunteer to go to the overhead to share his or her solution to the second problem (Problem 2 in Figure 2.2). Natalie said that she would do it and proceeded to the front of the room. She gave the solution as $34/80$, explaining that there were 80 squares in the 8 by 10 grid and that 34 of them were shaded. She went on to explain that this was equal to 0.425 and 42.5%. I asked her to explain how she got her answer and she said that she had "divided the bottom into the top" using a calculator, got a decimal, and moved the decimal point over two places to obtain the percent. Charles questioned how she had gotten 0.425. Natalie used the overhead calculator to demonstrate the procedure of dividing 34 by 80. (The calculator resides on the overhead cart and students routinely use it as needed while working at the overhead. I don't want a student's lack of computational proficiency to be an impediment to his or her opportunities to solve challenging, conceptually rich problems.)

15.   Natalie's calculation seemed to satisfy Charles, but it did not satisfy me. I wanted students to make sense out of the decimal and percent values, not just use a procedure that had no connection to the diagram and, more important, no meaning to them. I decided to ask if anyone had looked at the problem another way. Deanna suggested that $34/80$ was

the same as $^{340}/_{800}$, and dividing the numerator and denominator by 8 would give you $^{42.5}/_{100}$. I was curious about this approach and asked Deanna why she had done it that way. She explained, "I made the 80 into 800 by multiplying by 10. So I made 34 into 340 by multiplying by 10. It makes it easier to find the percent if you can make it per hundred. Now I can divide by 8 to get 100 on the bottom and 42.5 on top. So it must be 42.5 percent."

16.   Deanna's solution provided another way to think about the problem, but the solution still did not make any connection with the diagram. I wanted students to be able to determine the percent represented by each square relative to the size of the grid, and I thought that focusing on the diagram could help them think about this. It was one thing to recognize that each square is 1% when there were 100 squares. It was another thing to determine what percent each square is when there are more or less than 100 squares.

17.   I asked if each of the 80 squares in the grid would be more than, less than, or equal to 1%. There was a chorus of "more." I asked for a volunteer to explain. Rashid explained, "We've got 100 percent and only 80 squares. So each square takes 1 percent but there is still 20 percent left over to distribute." So I then asked what we could do with the 20% that was left over. Beverly said that we could distribute that to the squares too. "How much do they get?" I asked. She said that each would get ¼ more. I asked why. "Because, Mr. Harris, 20 divided by 80 is ¼!"

18.   "So," I asked, "how much would each of the 80 squares get?" Beverly said that they would each get 1¼%. "So, how could we use this information to find out what percent of the grid was shaded?" Joe explained that you needed to multiply them together. So at this point I suggested that we all do that. I went to the overhead and entered 1¼ × 34 into the calculator while students did the problem at their seats. There was a chorus of "42 point 5." They seemed excited to find that they got the same answer with this approach.

19.   Before moving on to another problem, I thought it might be helpful to review the three different approaches that we used to find the percent in this problem. This way, as we did additional problems, we could refer to the methods that had already been discussed. I went to the blackboard and wrote a brief description of each method (as shown in Figure 2.3) while verbally stating them.

20.   I decided that it was time to move on to another problem. Michael volunteered to do the third problem (Problem 3 in Figure 2.2). He began by indicating the grid was 8 × 8 so there were 64 squares altogether. Since there weren't too many squares that were unshaded, he decided to subtract the 16 unshaded squares from the 64 squares to get 48 shaded squares. He proceeded to explain that $^{48}/_{64}$ was equal to $^{6}/_{8}$, which could still be reduced to ¾. He then went on to say, "Then you multiply both 3 and 4 by 25 so that you get 100 on the bottom and 75 on the top. That would be 75 percent." I indicated that Michael was using Method 2 and that it seemed to work pretty well on this problem.

21.   Peter noted that if you divided the shaded area "just right," you could "see" the 75% on the diagram. Using the diagram (as shown in Figure 2.4), Peter explained, "If you take this part here (referring to the 2 × 4 in the top right corner of the figure) and put it with this one here (referring

FIGURE 2.3. Descriptions of Each of the Methods Used to Solve the Problems in Set A

Finding the Percent

Method 1—divide numerator by denominator and move the decimal point two places to the right

Method 2—make an equivalent fraction with a denominator of 100

Method 3—assume that the entire grid is 100%, determine what percent each square is worth, and then multiply by the number of shaded squares

---

to the 2 × 4 in the bottom left corner of the figure), you get a 4 by 4 square. Then you have two other 4 by 4 squares that are shaded. Then the unshaded squares make another 4 by 4 square. So 75 percent or ¾ of the grid is shaded." I commented that both of the methods used by Michael and Peter were good. I was pleased to see less reliance on the procedure and more effort to use alternative strategies that made sense to them.

22.   Denise volunteered to do the fourth problem (Problem 4 in Figure 2.2). She explained that the rectangle was 4 × 5 and had 20 squares and that a 3 × 3 or 9 squares were shaded, so it would be ⁹/₂₀.

23.   She went on to say that if you multiplied the numerator and the denominator by 5, it would be 45 over 100 or 45%. She then added that the decimal would be 0.45 "since the decimal and the percent are the same, it's just moved over." At this point Ramon had a puzzled look on his face. I asked him if he had a question for Denise. He asked, "Wouldn't 0.45 just be a little piece?" Denise repeated that .45 was the decimal and 45 was the percent and that they were the same amount. This did not seem to help Ramon. I suggested that Denise use a 10 × 10 grid to explain. (Since we had been doing lots of work with grids, I had a transparency of a 10 × 10 grid on the overhead cart for just such an occasion.)

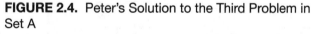

FIGURE 2.4. Peter's Solution to the Third Problem in Set A

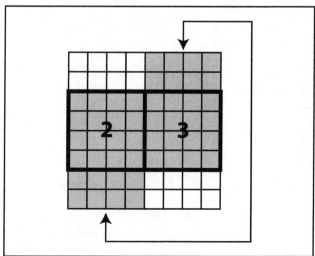

24.   Denise put the 10 × 10 grid on the overhead. I asked her if she could show us what 45% would be. Using the diagram shown in Figure 2.5, she explained, "Each square is worth 1 percent because there are 100 of them so each column is worth 10 percent. So you need to shade in four columns which would be 40 percent plus a half of a column which would be 5 percent." I asked her if she could explain why this was equal to 0.45. She continued, "Each column is one-tenth of the square so that is 0.10. So if I have four columns shaded, this would be 0.40. Then there are five more shaded out of 100 so it would be 0.05. If you add them up you get 0.45. So 0.45 and 45 percent mean the same thing."

25.   Ramon repeated that he had thought that the decimal point would make 0.45 "just a little piece of a little square." I realized that he might have been thinking about 0.45% or that the unit whole was only one small square. Since Denise was still at the overhead, I asked her to remind us what the unit whole was and then draw .45% of the whole for us. She explained, "The entire grid is the whole and if each square is worth 1 percent then 0.45 percent would be a piece that was less than half of one square. So it is really tiny." She continued her explanation as she began to draw a miniature version of the square that represented 0.45 (shown in Figure 2.6): "See, we can take one of these little squares and it would have 100 teeny squares in it and 45 of them would be shaded." I thanked Denise for her explanation. Ramon's question provided an opportunity to examine the difference between 0.45 and 0.45%. I was happy to have an opportunity to revisit this distinction since this is often confusing to students.

26.   I glanced at the clock and noted that the bell was going to ring any second. I told students that for homework they were to complete the

FIGURE 2.5. Denise's Diagram to Show That 0.45 Is the Same as 45%

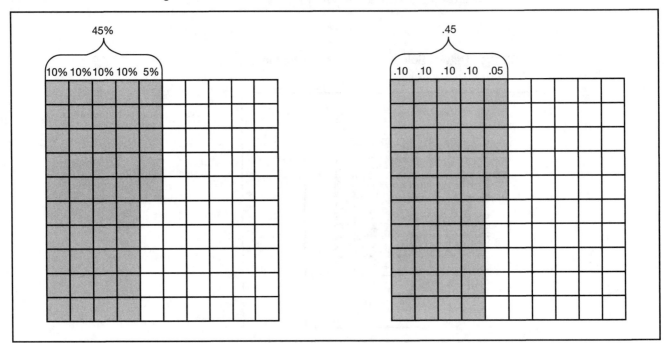

FIGURE 2.6. Denise's Explanation of 0.45%

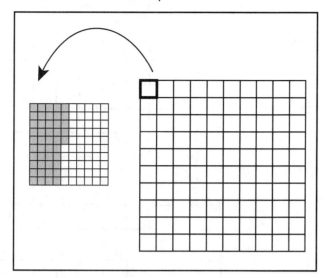

remaining problems in Set A *without* using Method 1. For each problem, I reminded them that they needed to explain their solution in writing.

The Class—Day 2

27.   Since we had done several problems in class yesterday, I did not see the need to go over the remaining problems in Set A in class. I did, however, want to see how students had gone about solving the problems. I told the students to make sure that they put their homework from Set A in their work folders so that I could check them. My plan was to go through them quickly before I left for the day just to be sure that there were no big problems. Also, it was time to make a few phone calls to parents if there were students who had not done the assignment at all.

28.   *Moving on to Set B.* I quickly distributed Set B (shown in Figure 2.7) and indicated that students could work on these problems in their groups. Students were seated at tables of four. With this arrangement students would sometimes work with their partner—the person sitting on the same side of the table—and at other times with the foursome. Sometimes I believe two heads are better than one, and at times four heads are better than two!

29.   I decided not to begin by doing an example with the whole class. Although I knew the problems were going to be hard for students, I wanted to see what they could do without my guidance and what problems might arise. Also, since each problem is a little different, I didn't want to send the message that if we did the first one together, the others could be solved in a similar way. I have found that while examples can be very powerful, they also can funnel students' thinking toward a particular solution path. So I decided to keep my eye on what the groups were doing and intervene as needed to keep students productively engaged.

30.   As students began to work, I started visiting the groups. My first reaction was that what I had anticipated was correct; this was difficult for the students. I saw many students shading in 72.5 squares on the grid. I

FIGURE 2.7. Set B

1. Shade the portion of the area of the rectangle that represents .725.

   What fractional part of the area is shaded?

   What percentage of the area is shaded?

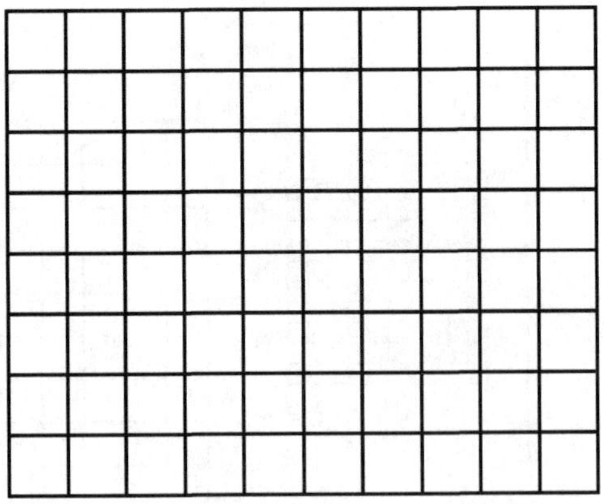

2. Shade ⅜ of the area of the rectangle.

   What percentage of the area is shaded?

   What decimal number is represented by the shaded portion of the rectangle?

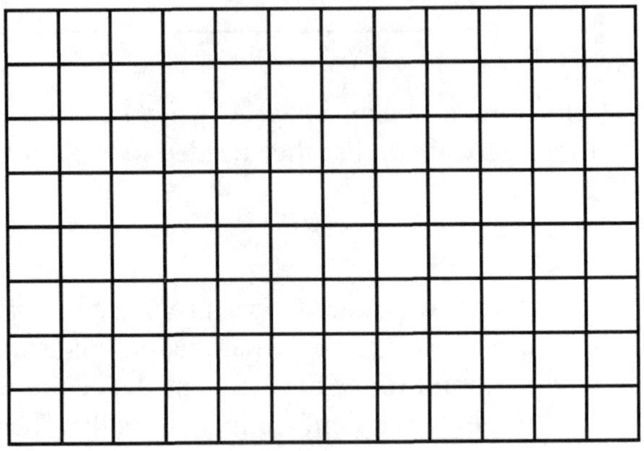

3. Shade 87½% of the area of the rectangle.

   What fractional part of the area is shaded?

   What decimal number is represented by the shaded portion of the rectangle?

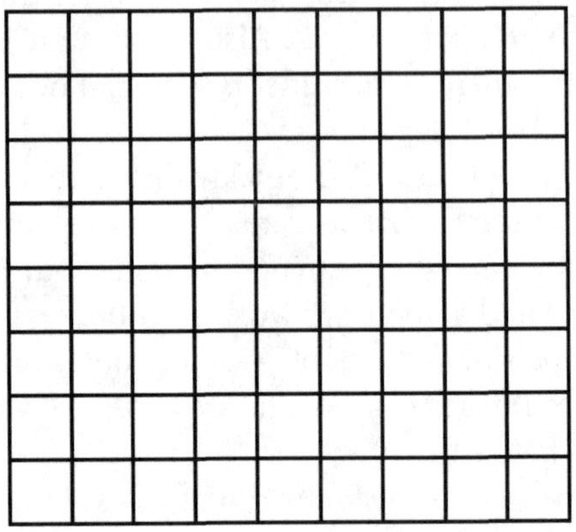

started asking questions such as, "How many squares are there all together?" and "How much would each square be worth?" trying to get them to make sense of the situation. Although a few saw that they had shaded in too many squares, they were not sure how to figure out how many to shade. After about 10 minutes, I decided that it might be helpful to pull the class together and try to deal with the misconceptions that were surfacing.

31.   I asked if anyone would like to get us started on the first one. Marilyn volunteered and made her way to the overhead. She quickly began to shade in squares on the grid, as shown in Figure 2.8a. When she appeared to be done, I asked her if she could explain her thinking. She hesitantly said she wasn't sure, but that she had shaded in 72½ of the squares on the grid.

32.   At this point we began an interchange that was intended to help Marilyn (as well as the other students who made this mistake) figure out how to make sense of the problem. This is always a tricky point—how do I ask questions that will help students figure out how to solve the problem without telling them exactly how to do it? I proceeded as follows:

33.   ME: What's the problem asking you to do?
           MARILYN: Shade point seven two five.
           ME: Okay, look at that number, 0.725. Is there some other way of
                saying that, that might be helpful?
           DANIELLE: 72 point 5 percent.
           ME: How many squares are there all together then?
           CLASS: 80.
           ME: If there are 80 squares, how can we use that information to get
                some more facts on that?
           MARILYN: Umm. I'm not sure.
           ME: Would any of the methods we used yesterday help us with this?
           MARILYN: Method 3?
           ME: What did we do in Method 3?

FIGURE 2.8. (a) Marilyn's Initial Solution to the First Problem in Set B; (b) Marilyn's Revised Solution

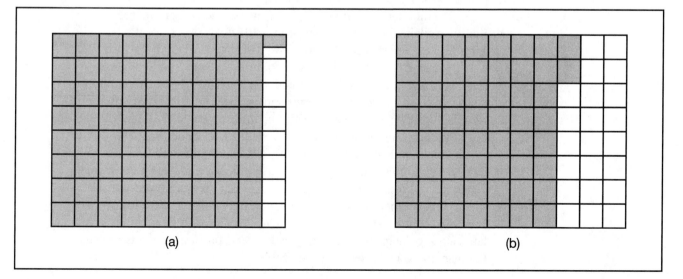

(a)   (b)

MARILYN: We figured out what percent each square is.

ME: In this case, would each square be more or less than 1 percent?

CLASS: MORE!

ME: More. If we have 80 squares and 100 percent, we know that it's at least going to be 1, right? If we put 1 percent in each square, what would be the total percent used?

MARILYN: 80. That would leave us 20 percent to distribute to the 80 squares. So it would be 1¼.

DAVID: I know how to do it. Get 1¼ times 72 point 5.

CLASS: No, no, no. That's not right!

ME: (Choosing to ignore David's suggestion.) So if each square is 1¼ percent, how much would one column be?

MARILYN: Umm . . . it would be eight 1-and-¼s. So that would be four 2-and-½s or two fives. So it would be 10 percent. Oh, I get it. Then you go over 'til you get 70 percent of them. Then you need 2½ percent more which would be two more squares. (At this point Marilyn began to alter her original drawing to show the correct number of squares shaded, as shown in Figure 2.8b.)

ME: So how many squares have you colored in then?

MARILYN: 7 times 8 plus 2, which would be 58. So the fraction would be $58/80$.

ME: So how does this answer differ from your first answer?

MARILYN: The first time I had 72.5 *squares* shaded, NOT 72.5 *percent* of the squares.

ME: What percent of the squares did you shade the first time? Can you figure it out?

MARILYN: If each column is 10 percent then I had 90 percent plus a little more.

34.   At this point I was interested in seeing if there were any other ways to think about the problem. James indicated that he had just multiplied .725 × 80 and got 58. Then he shaded in 58 squares, as Marilyn had just done. He went on to say, "Which equaled $29/40$ and that can't be reduced any more so that was my fraction. And when you have the decimal ones like that all you have to do to get the percent is move the decimal point 2 places to the right and you get your answer."

35.   I was still interested in seeing if anyone had done it another way. Kendra explained, "I just divided it into 10 equal parts since it's 10 across. So each part was 0.10. So then I just shaded in 7 parts which would give me 0.7. Then I just did two more squares." I asked Kendra how she knew to color in 2 at the end. She continued, "If one column of 8 squares was 10 percent, then four squares would be 5 percent and two squares would be 2½ percent." She concluded by saying that she then found the fraction by counting up the number of shaded squares.

36.   At this point I thought it might be helpful to quickly review the different strategies. I recapped that we found that each square was worth 1¼%, we looked at one whole column that was 10%, and we multiplied the decimal by the total number of squares. At this point, I told the groups to continue work on the last two problems. Once again, I circulated among the groups, asking questions and pushing students to use the diagram to make sense of the problem.

37.   Once I noticed that most groups had completed Problem 2, I asked
for a volunteer to share his or her solution and method with the class.
Devon, who had been pretty quiet throughout the class, had an interesting solution to the problem. (I had noticed this when I was walking
around the room.) I was pleased to see him volunteer to share his
solution and invited him to the overhead. As he constructed the diagram
shown in Figure 2.9a, Devon explained: "First I broke the rectangle into
four parts. There would be six columns in each half and then three
columns in each quarter."

38.   "Once I had four parts," he continued, "I had to split the fourths in
half to get eighths (as shown in Figure 2.9b). So 1½ columns would
make an eighth." Devon concluded, "Then I shaded in three of the
eighths" (as shown in Figure 2.9c).

39.   I then asked Devon what percent of the grid was shaded. He said that
he wasn't sure. I asked him to think about what he already knew. I asked
him what percent one half of the rectangle would be. He responded, "50

FIGURE 2.9. (a) Devon's First Step in Solving the Second Problem in Set B—Dividing the Grid into Fourths;
(b) Devon's Second Step—Dividing the Fourths into Eighths; (c) Devon's Final Step—Shading Three of
the Eighths

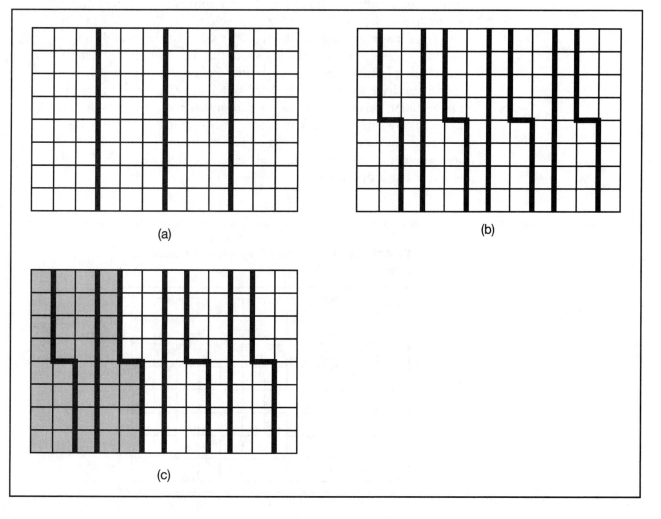

percent." I then asked what percent one-fourth of the rectangle would be. He responded, "25 percent." I then asked how this information could help solve the problem. Devon appeared to think about the question for a minute and responded, "Each of the shaded sections was ¹/₈ which was half of one fourth. So the percent must be half of 25 percent. So it is 12½ percent." I asked if that was the answer. Devon said that he had three pieces that were each ¹/₈ or 12½% which would be 12½ + 12½ + 12½ or 37½%. I then asked the class how we could write this as a decimal. A small chorus of voices responded with, "Point three seven five."

40.   At this point I wanted to get at least one more solution to the problem. I did not see any eager volunteers but I had noticed that Darlene had done the problem yet another way and asked her if she would share her solution. She tends to be a bit shy, but usually responds well when I call on her. She explained, "I looked at it the other way. Since there were eight rows, each row was one-eighth of the rectangle so I just shaded in three rows" (as shown in Figure 2.10). I asked her how she found the percent. She said that she didn't do it before because she wasn't sure. I asked if she could do it now. She said that each eighth was equal to 12½% so that it would be 37½%, "like Devon just did."

41.   At this point we were about out of time. I thanked all the students for their contributions. I told them that for homework I wanted them to complete the last problem in Set B (Problem 3 in Figure 2.7) and to try to solve it as many ways as they could. I said that this would count as a quiz. There was some groaning about this, but that did not deter me. I think it is important, especially after extended group- or pairwork, to have some individual accountability. Gathering this type of information periodically helps me plan instruction as well as determine what my students know and can do mathematically. I wanted to make sure that they had a pretty good understanding of the relationships among fractions, decimals, and percents before we began discussing ratios and proportions.

FIGURE 2.10. Darlene's Solution to the Second Problem in Set B

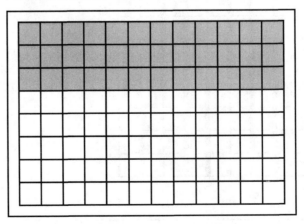

ANALYZING THE CASE

Now that you have had an opportunity to "visit" Randy Harris's classroom and note the pedagogical moves he made during the lesson, we invite you to consider how these moves supported or inhibited his students' learning of mathematics. Focusing your analysis in this way is not a straightforward or simple task. Features of the lesson that initially stood out or seemed intriguing may not have had a significant influence on what students learned or how they learned it. Here are a few suggestions about how to proceed.

- Review the list of pedagogical moves that you created as you read the case. For each move that you identified, decide whether the move appeared to have supported or inhibited students' learning of mathematics during the lesson. Be sure to cite specific evidence (i.e., paragraph numbers) from the case to support your claims.
- If you have colleagues who also are reading this case, compare and contrast the ideas in your individual lists and possibly generate a master list. Note points of disagreement since these are likely to be fruitful topics for further discussion and debate. If you are working on this activity alone, we encourage you to refer to Appendix A, which includes a similar two-column chart that was produced by teachers who participated in a professional development experience that focused on "The Case of Randy Harris." You may want to note points of agreement and disagreement and identify issues that you wish to investigate.

You may wish to extend your analysis of the case by considering the questions in the next section. Alternatively, you can skip the next section and proceed directly to the "Connecting to Your Own Practice" section, in which you are encouraged to relate the analysis of the ideas and issues raised in the case to your own teaching practice.

EXTENDING YOUR ANALYSIS OF THE CASE

The questions listed in this section are intended to help you focus on particular aspects of the case related to teacher decision-making and student thinking. If you are working in collaboration with one or more colleagues, the questions can serve as a stimulus for further discussion.

1. Mr. Harris comments that Set B is mathematically more difficult than Set A (para. 10). In what ways is Set B more difficult than Set A?
2. Mr. Harris has a goal for the students to make connections among fractions, decimals, and percents. In Mr. Harris's classroom, what counts as "making a connection" among representations? Can you find specific examples in the case where Mr. Harris or his students explicitly make connections among fractions, decimals, and percents?
3. In paragraph 19, Mr. Harris reviews and records three methods used for finding percents, only one of which explicitly connects to the use of a diagram. Can you develop other methods for solving the problems in Set A that involve the use of a diagram? Also, Mr. Harris believes the experience from Set A will assist students in solving the problems in Set B. Which of the methods (either the three methods recorded by Mr. Harris or others you have developed) would help students tackle the problems in Set B? Which methods would not be helpful? Be prepared to explain why some methods may be helpful and others may not be helpful.
4. Ramon's difficulty distinguishing between 0.45 and .45% (para. 23) is a common difficulty among students. Why might making this distinction be so difficult for students? What early mathematical experiences might help students gain a firm understanding of this distinction?
5. The methods that Mr. Harris records in writing (para. 19) and summarizes orally (para. 36) do not include all of the strategies used by the students in the class. Find all of the strategies used by the students in the case and compare your findings with Mr. Harris's lists. Why do you think Mr. Harris leaves out some strategies? What benefits, in terms of supporting student thinking, might be gained or lost by only selectively recording or calling attention to student ideas and strategies?
6. Mr. Harris believes it is important for students to be able to move from working with 10 × 10 grids to grids that are not 10 × 10 (para. 10). Why might Mr. Harris think this is an important transition for students? Do you agree with him? Why or why not? What are the advantages and disadvantages of beginning with 10 × 10 grids?
7. Mr. Harris encourages his students to communicate their thinking in many ways. To what extent do you think Mr. Harris holds his students accountable for providing good mathematical

explanations? Find specific examples in the case to support your judgment.

8. Mr. Harris decided not to pursue David's suggestion (para. 33). What are the advantages and disadvantages of not dealing with David's comment immediately?

9. To what extent does Mr. Harris hold his students accountable for using strategies that make use of visual diagrams rather than rely on algorithms? Find specific examples in the case to support your claim.

10. At the beginning of Day 2 (para. 29) Mr. Harris mentions a concern about doing examples with students because this can funnel students' thinking. How did the examples modeled during the work on Set A support or inhibit student thinking as students worked on the remainder of the task? What are the advantages and disadvantages of working through examples with students?

11. Identify Mr. Harris's goals for his students' learning. To what extent do you think Mr. Harris's goals were met during the lesson? Cite specific evidence from the case to support your claim.

CONNECTING TO YOUR OWN PRACTICE

The activities described in this section are designed to help you consider the ways in which the issues identified in Mr. Harris's classroom have implications for your own teaching of mathematics. Reflecting on one's teaching is a valuable, yet often neglected, activity. It is through reflection that "teachers can gain insight into how their actions and interactions in the classroom influence students' opportunities to learn mathematics" (Smith, 2001a, p. 11). Here are a few activities that will help you move from consideration of Randy Harris's teaching to a focus on your classroom practices.

• In the "Analyzing the Case" section, you considered ways in which the pedagogical moves Randy Harris made supported or inhibited student learning during the lesson. Teach a lesson (using the task from "The Case of Randy Harris" or another task that has the potential to foster students' thinking and reasoning) and record the lesson using videotape or audiotape, or have a colleague observe and take notes. As you reflect on the lesson, consider the following questions: What

did you do that appeared to support or inhibit your students' learning of mathematics? How do your supporting and inhibiting moves compare with those you identified for Randy Harris? What might you do differently the next time you teach the lesson to further enhance students' learning?

• Review the list of pedagogical moves that you constructed during your reading of the case and select one that you feel has implications for your own teaching. Plan and teach a lesson in which you purposefully address the identified pedagogy. For example, you may be curious about the ways in which diagrams can help students develop meaning and understanding of concepts and procedures. You might then identify one of your own lessons in which diagrams may be useful in helping students develop meaning and understanding for a procedure (e.g., multiplication of fractions) and seek out resources that will help you to plan and implement the lesson. If possible, record the lesson on audiotape or videotape, or have a colleague observe and take notes. As you go back over the lesson, reflect on the changes you made and the impact these changes appeared to have had on students' learning. Also indicate what you still need to work on with respect to this pedagogy.

EXPLORING CURRICULAR MATERIALS

You may want to explore your curriculum for ideas related to connecting fractions, decimals, and percents by considering the following questions: Are there tasks in your curriculum that promote students' understanding of the relationships among fractions, decimals, and percents? If not, could the curriculum be modified (i.e., adapting existing tasks or inserting new tasks) so as to provide students with such experiences? What role do (or could) visual models play in helping students understand the equivalence of these three representational forms?

You also may want to explore the mathematical ideas made salient in the case, by investigating mathematical tasks drawn from other curricular materials. The following list identifies curricula that contain problems that are considered to be "mathematically similar" to the task used in Randy Harris's class.

Billstein, R., & Williamson, J. (1999). *Middle grades math thematics: Book 1*. Evanston, IL: McDougal Littell.

Of particular interest is an exploration activity (pp. 174–175) in which students use 10×10 grids to relate fractions, decimals, and percents.

Education Development Center, Inc. (1998b). *MathScape: From zero to one and beyond: Fractions, decimals, and percents* (*Student guide*). Mountain View, CA: Creative Publications.

Of particular interest is Lesson 7 (An Important Point) (pp. 22–23), in which students use 10×10 grids to relate fractions, decimals, and percents.

Foreman, L. C., & Bennett, A. B., Jr. (1996b). *Visual mathematics: Course II, lessons 21–30.* Salem, OR: The Math Learning Center.

Of particular interest in Lesson 22 (Picturing Percentage Problems) are Actions 1–5 in the Connector Teacher Activity (pp. 339–343). Students are asked to express the shaded regions of grids of various shapes and sizes as fractions, decimals, and percents. A subset of the problems found in this lesson is identical to the problems that appear in "The Case of Randy Harris."

Lappan, G., Fey, J. T., Fitzgerald, W. M., Friel, S. N., & Phillips, E. D. (1998). *Bits and pieces I: Understanding rational numbers.* Menlo Park, CA: Dale Seymour.

Of particular interest is Problem 6.3 (p. 75), in which students use a 10×10 grid to convert among fractions, decimals, and percents.

The Mathematics in Context Development Team. (1997). *Mathematics in context: Per sense* (Student guide). In National Center for Research in Mathematical Sciences Education & Freudenthal Institute (Eds.), *Mathematics in Context*. Chicago: Encyclopaedia Britannica.

Of particular interest are Problems 11–12 (pp. 5–6), in which students use rectangular diagrams to represent fractions and percents.

CONNECTING TO OTHER IDEAS AND ISSUES

If you have additional time, you may want to explore some aspect of the case in more depth. The resources identified below provide some possibilities for exploring the mathematical and pedagogical issues raised in the case. For example, you might: (1) consider how the strategy for solving percent problems presented in Bennett and Nelson (1994) is similar to or different from the strategies used by students in Randy Harris's class; (2) consider how the activity pro-

posed in Sweeney and Quinn (2000) also could help students make connections among fractions, decimals, and percents, and whether the activity would have been helpful to Randy Harris's students; or (3) use the Lamon (1999) chapter as a basis for considering how conceptual work related to fractions, decimals, and percents provides the underpinnings for developing proportional reasoning.

Bennett, A. B., & Nelson, L. T. (1994). A conceptual model for solving percent problems. *Mathematics Teaching in the Middle School, 1,* 20–25.

The authors describe how 10×10 grids can be used to help students conceptualize percent. Specifically, their proposed strategy focuses on the basic concept of percent as "parts per hundred" and requires students to recognize 100% as represented by a unit square (i.e., a 10×10 grid) and 1% as represented by one small square that is one-hundredth of the unit square. Several examples of percent problems that can be solved using a 10×10 grid are provided.

Lamon, S. (1999). *Teaching fractions and ratios for understanding: Essential content knowledge and instructional strategies for teachers.* Mahwah, NJ: Erlbaum.

In Chapter 15 (pp. 239–245), the author defines percent as a "special kind of ratio in which the second quantity is always 100." In the same chapter, the author illustrates how procedural percent problems (e.g., 31.5 is what percent of 70?) can be solved using grids of different sizes. Of particular interest are several percent problems at the end of the chapter (Problems 12–17; pp. 253–254) that ask the reader to use drawings, grids, or mental computation rather than computational strategies.

Sweeney, E. S., & Quinn, R. J. (2000). Concentration: Connecting fractions, decimals, & percents. *Mathematics Teaching in the Middle School, 5,* 324–328.

The authors describe a multiday lesson aimed at developing students' fluency with fractions, decimals, and percents. In these lessons students engage in a whole-group discussion of what they already know about fractions, decimals, and percents; a small-group activity in which they create cards that contain different representations of the same number (i.e., fraction, decimal, percent, circle graph); and a "Concentration" game using the cards they created.

Introducing Ratios and Proportions

The Case of Marie Hanson

This chapter provides the materials to engage you in reading and analyzing the teaching and learning that occur in the classroom of Marie Hanson as she and her 6th-grade students solve a set of ratio problems using strategies that make sense.

Prior to reading the case, we suggest that you complete the Opening Activity. The primary purpose of the Opening Activity is to engage you with the mathematical ideas that you will encounter when you read the case. The problems posed in the Opening Activity are a subset of those encountered by Marie Hanson's students. After solving the problems, you are encouraged to engage in the "Consider" portion of the activity, in which you are challenged to solve each problem in a different way and to identify relationships between the different strategies that you have used.

Once you have completed the activity, you may want to refer to Appendix B, which contains a set of solutions generated by teachers who completed the Opening Activity as part of a professional development experience that focused on "The Case of Marie Hanson." You are encouraged to make sense of the different solutions provided and to consider the relationship between your solution and those produced by others.

OPENING ACTIVITY

The candy jar shown in Figure 3.1 contains Jolly Ranchers (the rectangles) and Jawbreakers (the circles). Please use this candy jar to solve Problems 1–3 and respond to the "Consider" question before reading the case.

Solve

1. Suppose you have a larger candy jar with the same ratio of Jolly Ranchers to Jawbreakers as shown in the candy jar in Figure 3.1. If the jar contains 100 Jolly Ranchers, how many Jawbreakers are in the jar?
2. Suppose you have an even larger candy jar with the same ratio of Jolly Ranchers to Jawbreakers as shown in the candy jar in Figure 3.1. If the jar contains 720 candies, how many of each kind of candy are in the jar?
3. Suppose you are making treats to hand out to trick-or-treaters on Halloween. Each treat is a small bag that contains 5 Jolly Ranchers and 13 Jawbreakers. If you have 50 Jolly Ranchers and 125 Jawbreakers, how many complete small bags could you make?

Consider

After you have solved Problems 1–3, try solving each problem using a different approach. What is the rela-

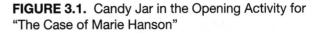

FIGURE 3.1. Candy Jar in the Opening Activity for "The Case of Marie Hanson"

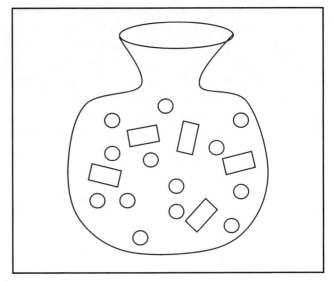

tionship between the two different approaches you used to solve each problem?

READING THE CASE

As you read the case, we encourage you to make note of the aspects of Marie Hanson's pedagogy that appear to support her students' learning throughout the lesson. (You may want to use a highlighter or Post-it notes to keep track of these as you read the case.) You may identify something specific that Marie Hanson does during the lesson (e.g., eliciting the incorrect additive solution first; returning to Jerlyn and Kamiko's ratio table later in the lesson to show multiplicative relation-

ships), or something more general (e.g., weaving ratio and proportion ideas throughout the curriculum) that seems to benefit students' learning.

We encourage you to make a list of the aspects of Marie Hanson's pedagogy that you identify. These can serve as topics for discussion with a colleague who also has read the case, as issues to investigate as you read additional cases, or as starting points for exploration in your own classroom. For example, you might wonder what intuitive proportional reasoning strategies your students might use to solve the candy jar problems and how you might foster a discussion about multiplicative versus additive reasoning in your classroom. We will discuss additional connections to your own practice at the end of the chapter.

THE CASE OF MARIE HANSON

1.   Until recently, Marie Hanson had a very limited understanding of ratio
and proportion. Looking back on her middle school education, she now
realizes that she was taught little beyond how to carry out procedures
such as cross-multiplication. In fact, she still remembers dreading the
word problems that came at the end of the unit—the ones that required
students to "set up" proportions in order to solve them. She was never
quite sure where to put which numbers. It should come as no surprise,
then, that Marie usually accomplished little beyond getting her 6th-
graders to learn the formal notation for expressing ratios and how to
solve simple problems involving equivalent ratios.

2.   All this has changed over the past few years. Shortly after joining
the faculty at Freemont Middle School, Marie and her colleagues
embarked on an ambitious effort to redo their mathematics program.
In weekly after-school sessions, they learned about the many different
ways in which ratios and proportions show up throughout the middle
school curriculum. For example, after working through problems
involving fractions, percents, rates, and scale factors, they were invited
to reflect on the ratio and proportion ideas embedded in the problems.
Based on the thinking that was demanded of her in these professional
development sessions, Marie's understanding of proportional reasoning has been greatly enriched. She now appreciates the importance of
exposing her students to a variety of different strategies for solving
proportional reasoning problems, such as making a table, finding a
unit rate, or looking at the relationships between the numbers in a
ratio table both horizontally and vertically. Marie believes that having a
variety of available strategies will give her students flexibility in working with the different contexts and numbers involved in proportional
situations.

3.   Marie is now trying to weave ratio and proportion ideas and ways of
thinking throughout her 6th-grade curriculum. As agreed upon by
Marie and her colleagues, the 6th-grade teachers would begin the year by
inviting their students to make sense of problems that demand thinking
about relative change and multiplicative relationships. As the year
progressed, they would continue to provide a variety of opportunities
for their students to think informally, but systematically, about simple
quantities and their interrelationships. The 7th- and 8th-grade teachers
would pick up from there, gradually introducing more difficult problems and more abstract solution strategies.

Marie Hanson Talks About Her Class

4.   I have great plans for my 6th-graders! Although I've been infusing
ratio and proportion problems throughout the 6th-grade curriculum for
a couple of years now, I feel especially ready and confident this year. Not
only has my own knowledge of ratio and proportion grown, but I've also
become more attuned to how students learn to think and reason in this
area.

5.   Yesterday, I introduced the term *ratio* in a very general way—as a comparison between two sets of things. We then worked on some simple problems that I hoped would get students thinking about different ways of making comparisons. I gave students two pictures, one that showed two Twinkies boxes and six Twinkies and another that showed 12 lollipops and four stick figures. The instructions asked them to (a) look at each picture and write the ratio it suggested; and (b) write as many ratios as they could that were equivalent to that ratio.

6.   Because I had not introduced the formal way of writing ratios, students were asked to portray the comparisons in whatever way made sense to them. Some students, for the second problem, spontaneously circled combinations of one stick figure and three lollipops, as a way of thinking about the relationship between the two quantities (as shown in Figure 3.2). I encouraged those who were having difficulty to use this method as well.

7.   Using different combinations of pictures, numerals, words, and labels (e.g., 3T to 1B for 3 Twinkies to 1 Box), the majority of my kids were able to write the ratio for each of the pictures. Most students also were able to come up with equivalent ratios. Some even drew additional pictures and circled the appropriate groupings to represent the larger equivalent ratios. We were ready for something harder.

Thursday's Class

8.   As my students filed into the classroom on Thursday, they found the first candy jar problem on the overhead (shown in Figure 3.3).

9.   In response to Question a, some students tried to draw a circle around various combinations of Jolly Ranchers and Jawbreakers, but found it impossible to create equivalent groups as they had been able to do yesterday with the lollipop and Twinkies problems. Most students, however, had no difficulty expressing the ratio of Jolly Ranchers to Jawbreakers as "five Jolly Ranchers to 13 Jawbreakers." As they turned to Question b, however, many students did run into difficulty.

FIGURE 3.2. Student's Diagram for the Lollipop Problem

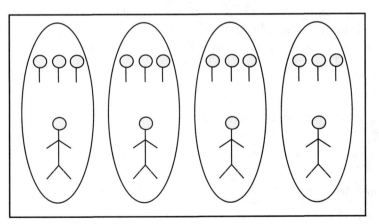

FIGURE 3.3. The First Candy Jar Problem

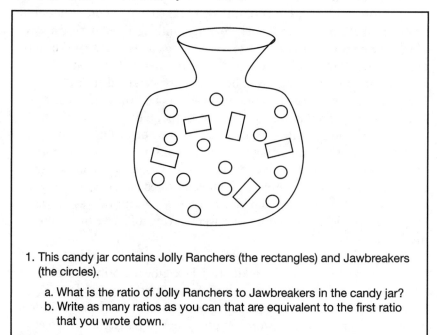

1. This candy jar contains Jolly Ranchers (the rectangles) and Jawbreakers (the circles).

    a. What is the ratio of Jolly Ranchers to Jawbreakers in the candy jar?

    b. Write as many ratios as you can that are equivalent to the first ratio that you wrote down.

As I stopped at individual students' desks, I urged them to think about adding more candies but keeping the ratio of Jolly Ranchers to Jawbreakers the same.

10.   After a few minutes, I asked Jerlyn and Kamiko to show their work to the class. They had created a table (shown in Table 3.1), something that we had not done in previous classes.

11.   I asked the girls to explain what they had done. Kamiko said, "We added five more Jolly Ranchers and 13 more Jawbreakers each time." When I asked how they knew to do this, Jerlyn responded, "You have to add the same amount each time so the ratio stays even."

12.   No one had any questions and I couldn't quite tell if their explanation made sense to the rest of the class. I turned to the class and asked, "What makes this more difficult than the lollipop problem?" James replied, "You couldn't divide them evenly." Another student, Jerry, chimed in, "You can't get back to one, like we were able to do with the lollipops and the Twinkies. Remember how we circled three lollipops for each ONE of the children?" Then he paused for a moment as if a light

TABLE 3.1. Jerlyn and Kamiko's Ratio Table

5 Jolly Ranchers	13 Jawbreakers
10 Jolly Ranchers	26 Jawbreakers
15 Jolly Ranchers	39 Jawbreakers
20 Jolly Ranchers	52 Jawbreakers

FIGURE 3.4. Diagram Created by April to Determine the Number of Jawbreakers for Every 1 Jolly Rancher

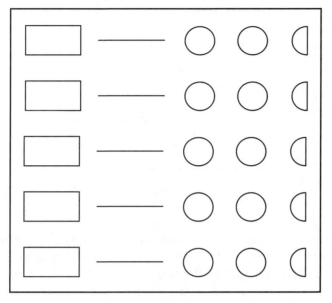

bulb had just gone off in his head. "Well, I guess you could, but then you'd have little teeny pieces of candy."

13.   At this point, April practically jumped out of her seat, saying this was possible—and that she had done it. With a little coaxing, she came to the front of the room and drew the diagram shown in Figure 3.4.

14.   She explained, "Since the ratio is five Jolly Ranchers for every 13 Jawbreakers, for each Jolly Rancher you would have two Jawbreakers; that would use up 10 Jawbreakers. So, you have three Jawbreakers left over. If you divide those evenly with the Jolly Ranchers, that would mean each Jolly Rancher candy gets one-half of a Jawbreaker. So that used up two and one-half Jawbreakers out of the three. But then you still have that last one-half Jawbreaker . . ."

15.   As her voice trailed off, I asked if anyone could come to the front of the room to help April put the finishing touches on what was the start of a well-thought-out solution strategy. Jerry offered and came up to the overhead projector and began drawing a half circle in the lower right-hand corner of April's drawing. With April looking on, he then divided the half-circle into fifths saying: "You'd have to take the half-piece of candy that is left over and divide it up among the five Jolly Ranchers. That means each Jolly Rancher would get a fifth." As he said this, he divided the half-circle into five pie-shaped pieces, as shown in Figure 3.5.

16.   At this point, he did not seem sure what to do next—how to connect what he'd done to April's work. I asked the class if anyone had any questions about Jerry's work so far. Sharee, one of my quiet but very thoughtful students, crinkled her brow and asked Jerry why he decided that the small pieces he had drawn were fifths. Before Jerry could answer, she continued, "If you think about the whole candy, then those small pieces wouldn't be fifths, they'd be tenths." Now it was Jerry's turn

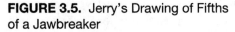

FIGURE 3.5. Jerry's Drawing of Fifths
of a Jawbreaker

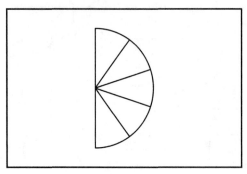

to crinkle his brow. Sharee saw his confusion and asked to go to the
overhead projector to show him what she meant. She then added the
other half of the candy to the half-candy that Jerry had drawn, as shown
in Figure 3.6. "See how the pieces are really tenths?" she asked. Jerry
nodded. He "got it" now.

17.   So did April. At this point, she eagerly jumped back in and picked up
the explanation of her solution strategy: "So," she said, "you'd have two
and six-tenths Jawbreakers for every Jolly Rancher candy. It would be
six-tenths," she added, "because you already had half a Jawbreaker
which is five-tenths and now you are adding one more tenth." I thanked
April, Jerry, and Sharee, and said that I wanted to return to Jerlyn and
Kamiko's table to see how our new ratio fit into it.

18.   I put the table back up on the overhead and asked where the ratio of
1 Jolly Rancher to 2.6 Jawbreakers would go. The students said that it
would go in the first row because the numbers were the smallest. I
placed the numbers in the table (as shown in Table 3.2) and immediately
noticed a frown on Kamiko's face.

19.   She raised her hand and said that the new ratio couldn't be right
because it didn't fit the pattern of the table. "If you add five to one,
you'd get six, so it can't be right," she said. I asked the other students if
they thought our new ratio was correct and, if so, could they explain why

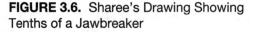

FIGURE 3.6. Sharee's Drawing Showing
Tenths of a Jawbreaker

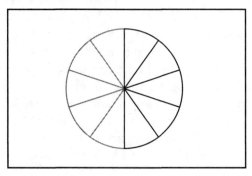

TABLE 3.2. Jerlyn and Kamiko's Table, Including the Ratio of 1 Jolly Rancher to 2.6 Jawbreakers

1 Jolly Rancher	2.6 Jawbreakers
5 Jolly Ranchers	13 Jawbreakers
10 Jolly Ranchers	26 Jawbreakers
15 Jolly Ranchers	39 Jawbreakers
20 Jolly Ranchers	52 Jawbreakers

it didn't fit the pattern. As I expected, I saw a lot of puzzled faces and had no "takers." I said that we would put this dilemma on hold for the time being and return to it later.

20.   Checking my watch, I noticed that we were now more than halfway through the period and I quickly moved on to the second candy jar problem, as shown in Figure 3.7.

21.   I thought this would be hard for the students so I was planning on having them work in groups. As soon as I looked up from writing the problem on the overhead, however, I noticed that all of them were working on their own at their seats. I decided to let them continue and began walking around the room.

22.   I was amazed at the variety of ways in which students were attacking the problem. Some of the students continued to build on the table that Jerlyn and Kamiko had started; others were trying to work with the 1 to 2.6 ratio that April, Jerry, and Sharee had established. Most were playing around with different ways of multiplying the numbers. A few, however, were using addition when they really needed to be using multiplication.

23.   As the time to share solution strategies approached, I struggled with the decision of which strategies to get out publicly and in what order. I decided to ask Jordan to share his strategy—which was erroneously based on additive reasoning—first. I wanted to expose the fallacy of this approach as soon as possible and move on to the others. Although I spotted several students incorrectly using an additive strategy, I suspected that others would be ready to challenge Jordan and that it wouldn't bother him.

24.   Jordan walked up to the overhead projector muttering, "Easy, peasy," under his breath. He recorded his solution to the problem on the transparency, as shown in Figure 3.8a.

25.   When he finished, he looked up and said, "Since I had to add 95 to get to 100 Jolly Ranchers, I did the same thing to the Jawbreakers—I

FIGURE 3.7. The Second Candy Jar Problem

2. Suppose you had a new candy jar with the same ratio of Jolly Ranchers to Jawbreakers (5 to 13), but it contained 100 Jolly Ranchers? How many Jawbreakers would you have?

FIGURE 3.8. (a) Jordan's Solution to the Second Candy Jar Problem; (b) Jerry's Solution to the Second Candy Jar Problem; (c) Jerlyn's Explanation of Why Jerry's New Jar Has the Same Ratio as the First Jar; (d) Owen's Solution to the Second Candy Jar Problem

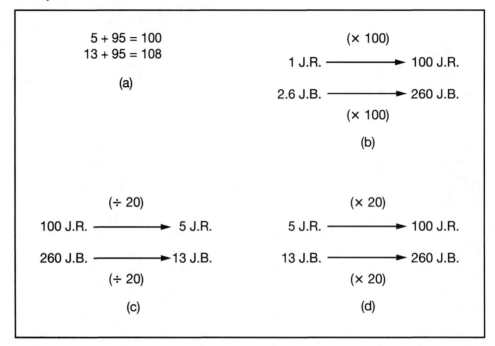

added 95, so the answer is 108." I asked if anyone had any questions for Jordan and I called on one of my quieter students who hadn't raised her hand but clearly looked puzzled. "Sarah, it seems like something isn't sitting right with you. Do you have a question to ask Jordan?" In a shy, soft voice, Sarah asked Jordan why the Jawbreakers and Jolly Ranchers would be almost even in the new jar when there had been a lot more Jawbreakers in the first jar. "Something isn't right," she said. Jordan appeared unfazed, replying, "You have to do the same thing to both numbers so 108 has to be the answer."

26.   "Does everyone agree with Jordan?" I asked. Jerry volunteered that he did not because "the problem specifically said that the new candy jar had the same ratio of Jolly Ranchers to Jawbreakers and that in Jordan's new jar the ratio was almost one to one." He went on to say he didn't know why Jordan's way was wrong, but he was sure that it was. Still unfazed, Jordan asked Jerry how he did the problem. Jerry came up to the overhead and said that he went back to his old strategy of 1 Jolly Rancher to 2.6 Jawbreakers. He wrote his solution (shown in Figure 3.8b) while he explained: "If one Jolly Rancher turns into 100 Jolly Ranchers, it must have been multiplied by 100. And so, the 2.6 Jawbreakers also have to be multiplied by 100." He put the pen down and appeared to reflect for a moment. "I guess I did the same thing to both numbers, too. But I multiplied. You added," he concluded.

27.   At this point, I invited the class as a whole to reflect on Jerry's new jar versus Jordan's new jar. "Which jar has the same ratio of Jolly Ranchers to Jawbreakers as our first jar?" I asked. After a few seconds

of silence, Jerlyn raised her hand and said, "Jerry's jar has exactly the same ratio as the first." "How can you tell?" I asked. Jerlyn replied, "You can divide Jerry's 260 Jawbreakers and 100 Jolly Ranchers each by 20 and you get 13 Jawbreakers and five Jolly Ranchers—that's what we started out with." I recorded Jerlyn's explanation on the overhead (shown in Figure 3.8c) and asked her if I had gotten it right. After Jerlyn agreed, I called on another student, Owen, who had been listening intently. He said, "I sort of did what Jerlyn did, but in the opposite direction." Pleased that Owen was staying with the conversation (he often has a tendency to drift), I asked him to explain what he had done. He said, "I knew it was 260 Jawbreakers because you had to multiply the five Jolly Ranchers by 20 to get 100, so you'd also have to multiply the 13 Jawbreakers by 20 to get 260—kinda like what Jerry did, but I started with 5 and 13, not 1 and 2.6." I recorded Owen's explanation on the overhead (shown in Figure 3.8d).

28.   "So, is this what you did, Owen?" I asked. When he agreed, I decided to try to bring the discussion surrounding this problem to a close by circling back to Jordan's strategy and trying to form a classroom-wide consensus that using a multiplicative constant was the way to go. "You know," I began, "Jordan was right to point out that what we do to the Jolly Ranchers we also have to do to the Jawbreakers. However, if we want to keep the same ratio, Jordan's answer shows us that adding the same amount doesn't work." At this point, I made eye contact with Jordan to see if he was with me. He nodded and said, "Yeah, when I added the same amount, the Jawbreakers and Jolly Ranchers didn't get bigger at the same rate. The Jolly Ranchers sort of caught up with the Jawbreakers."

29.   "That is a good way to think about it," I replied, glad that Jordan was now on board. "As Jordan said, we need to keep increasing the Jawbreakers and the Jolly Ranchers at the same rate and that means that adding the same amount to each of them won't work.

30.   "Now," I said as I put Jerlyn and Kamiko's table back on the overhead (shown in Table 3.2), "I want to return to Jerlyn and Kamiko's table. These girls said that every time they added 13 to the Jawbreaker side, they added five to the Jolly Rancher side. So it is important to realize that although they were adding, they were NOT adding the same amount to both sides."

31.   We still had to deal with Kamiko's comment from earlier in the class, however, that the first row doesn't fit the addition pattern of adding five each time to the Jolly Rancher side and 13 each time to the Jawbreaker side.

32.   "So," I continued, "if adding doesn't work, what does?" Sarah—without raising her hand—shouted, "Multiplying by five will work!" I asked her to explain. She said that you could get from the first row in the table to the second row by multiplying by five. After a multiplication check—with some students pulling out their calculators and others doing a quick calculation—we agreed that Sarah was right. Then Jerry noted that "times two" also worked: "You can get from the third to the fifth row," he said, "by multiplying by two. Two times 10 equals 20 and two times 26 equals 52." "That's right," I said. "Now, who can tell me how you would get from the third to the fourth row?" This

took a while, but eventually the students arrived at multiplying by a factor of 1.5.

33.   "Let's step back from this a moment," I said. "What can we say about the ways in which we've been playing around with the numbers in this table—what is consistent about what we're doing?" Several students replied, "You are always multiplying the two different sides of the table by the same amount." "That's right," I said. "Just like we had to multiply the Jolly Ranchers by 20 because we multiplied the Jawbreakers by 20 in the second problem. That is how we grow things at the same rate."

34.   Many students appeared to be quite content with this summing up of the day's work and were ready for something harder. Other students, however, looked less sure. I faced a decision: Should I give them another "missing-value" problem like this one (probably with a different story setting) for homework or should I stay with the candy jar and give them yet a different type of ratio and proportion problem? As I thumbed through the various problems that I had prepared for homework, I gravitated toward one that was very different in structure from the one we had just done and that would not lend itself well to an incorrect additive approach. It would be hard for students to follow Jordan's initial strategy with this problem, I reasoned, and—for homework— maybe that was good. I wrote what would be the third candy jar problem on the overhead, as shown in Figure 3.9.

35.   The students moaned at the large number. I told them to make sure that they read the problem carefully before beginning their work and that we would talk about it first thing next class period.

FIGURE 3.9. The Third Candy Jar Problem Assigned for Homework

3. Suppose you had a candy jar with the same ratio of Jolly Ranchers to Jawbreakers (5 to 13), but it contained 720 candies. How many of each kind of candy would you have?

Friday's Class

36.   The students arrived the next morning with lots of different ways of attacking the problem. A few students had extended Kamiko and Jerlyn's table, adding five each time to the left column and 13 each time to the right column. Many of these students also found it necessary to add a third column to keep track of the total number of candies. Needless to say, these tables got to be quite long! A few students had played around with the 1 Jolly Rancher to 2.6 Jawbreaker ratio, mostly using a guess-and-check strategy. Although these methods were inefficient, it didn't bother me because they appeared to make sense to the students who were using them. The students could work on efficiency later.

37.   About half of the students had figured that the 720-candy jar contained 40 times as many candies as the initial jar and so they would need to multiply the five Jolly Ranchers and 13 Jawbreakers by 40. I called one of these students to the front of the room to explain her reasoning. Danielle began by saying that the important thing to figure out was how many 18-candy jars it would take to make the 720-candy jar. She explained that when she divided 720 by 18 and got 40 (a whole number), she knew she was on the right track. After that, she said it was easy: "If the whole jar has 40 times as many candies, there also has to be 40 times as many Jolly Ranchers and 40 times as many Jawbreakers." On the overhead screen, she quickly multiplied 5×40 and 13×40 to get 200 and 520, respectively.

38.   Nobody had any questions, but I was not sure that everyone had followed her explanation completely. I thought that seeing another approach might reach some of the students whom I wasn't quite sure about. As I walked by Joshua's desk, I noticed that he had used an interesting method so I asked him to come to the overhead projector to present and explain his solution. He said that he started by using the table, but that once he got to 50 Jolly Ranchers for 130 Jawbreakers, he realized that there might be a quicker way to do it. He saw that "this" candy jar (pointing to the one with 50 Jolly Ranchers and 130 Jawbreakers) would have 180 candies in it and wondered how many 180-candy jars it might take to create a 720-candy jar. He figured out that four 180-candy jars would be needed. The 720-candy jar then would need to have 4×50 Jolly Ranchers and 4×130 Jawbreakers or 200 Jolly Ranchers and 520 Jawbreakers.

39.   Joshua actually had stumbled upon another useful strategy for ratio and proportion problems. I took a moment to rephrase Joshua's method and then asked if anyone had solved the problem in yet a different way. No one volunteered; I was just about to move on to the next problem when Angelica raised her hand and said, "To me, Joshua's strategy was harder than it had to be." She went on to say that her dad had showed her a MUCH easier way to do the problem. I hadn't made it to Angelica's desk so I wasn't sure what she had done, but I asked her come to the front of the room anyway and share her easy strategy with the rest of the class. She proceeded to record her solution, as shown in Figure 3.10a.

FIGURE 3.10. (a) Angelica's Solution to the Third Candy Jar Problem; (b) Ms. Hanson's Explanation of Angelica's Solution to the Problem

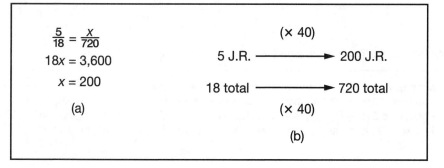

40.   When she finished writing, she looked up from her work with a smile on her face. "See," she exclaimed, "I got the same answer as Joshua!" I was worried that Angelica wasn't quite sure what she had done or why. I turned to the class and asked if anyone had any questions of Angelica. Danielle noted that the problem asked for two answers and that Angelica only gave one. "Which one is it?" she asked, "the Jolly Ranchers or the Jawbreakers?"

41.   When Angelica couldn't answer, I thought it was time to step in. I explained that Angelica had set up the problem in a way that asked, "If there were five Jolly Ranchers in every 18 candies, how many Jolly Ranchers would there be if you had 720 candies?" I continued, "So, her answer showed us that there would be 200 Jolly Ranchers. If the rest of the candies were Jawbreakers, there would be 520 Jawbreakers in the 720-candy jar."

42.   Although Danielle (and the other students) were listening carefully, I wasn't sure if they were really with me. "You know," I said, "Angelica's solution can be related to what Danielle showed us a few minutes ago. Remember how Danielle said that it would take 40 times as much candy to fill the 720-candy jar? She knew this because multiplying 18 times 40 gives us 720. If there were 40 times as many candies altogether, there would also have to be 40 times the number of Jolly Ranchers." As I was talking, I also was writing on the overhead (see Figure 3.10b).

43.   "Doesn't this look familiar?" I asked as I set it side-by-side with Angelica's solution. "I think it was the second step of Angelica's solution that confused folks. That is called cross-multiplication and it is something you'll understand as you learn more algebra. However, you don't need to use cross-multiplication to solve the problem as Angelica set it up. You can see how multiplying 18 by 40 will give you 720 and, as we know, you have to do the same thing to the 5, therefore giving us an answer of 200 Jolly Ranchers."

44.   Some of the students clearly were getting it. I closed this section by noting that, for now, we'd work with strategies that we can make sense of every step of the way. "The strategies we've been using—like what Danielle and Joshua showed us—will work just fine," I said.

45.   It was now time to present the final candy jar problem, which had yet a different structure (shown in Figure 3.11).

46.   I figured that this final problem would be a good test of whether the students were grasping the idea of equivalent ratios. Regardless of how they would try to solve it, thinking through the problem would provide an opportunity to think in terms of a multiplicative constant

FIGURE 3.11. The Fourth and Final Candy Jar Problem

4. Mom gave me 50 Jolly Ranchers and 125 Jawbreakers and asked me to make as many small treat bags of candies as were possible with each bag containing 5 Jolly Ranchers and 13 Jawbreakers. How many treat bags could I make up? How many Jawbreakers and how many Jolly Ranchers would be left over?

(represented by the number of jars that can be made). If they used a table, they'd have to realize that the entry at which they had to stop (45 Jolly Ranchers and 117 Jawbreakers) represented the ninth jar. If they chose to divide, they'd have to realize that the two division problems ($50/5 = 10$ and $125/13 \approx 9$) gave them two different scale factors and that nine (the smaller one) represented the greatest number of jars they could create with the candies that they'd been given. It would be fun to observe how students thought about this one!

ANALYZING THE CASE

Now that you have had an opportunity to "visit" Marie Hanson's classroom and identify ways in which Marie Hanson's pedagogy supported her students' learning of mathematics, we encourage you think deeply about *how* the items on your list served to support students' learning. Here are a few suggestions on how to proceed.

- Using the list you created when you read the case, cite specific evidence from the case (i.e., paragraph numbers) to support the ideas in your list. For each item you have listed, provide a rationale for *how* it served to support students' learning.

- If you have colleagues who also are reading this case, compare and contrast the ideas in your individual lists and possibly generate a master list. Note points of disagreement since these are likely to be fruitful topics for further discussion and debate. If you are working on this activity alone, we encourage you to refer to Appendix B, which includes a list of pedagogical moves that were produced by teachers who participated in a professional development experience that focused on "The Case of Marie Hanson." You may want to note points of agreement and disagreement and flag issues that you wish to pursue.

You may wish to continue your analysis of the case by considering the questions in the next section. Alternatively, you can skip the next section and proceed directly to the "Connecting to Your Own Practice" section, in which you are encouraged to relate the analysis of the ideas and issues raised in the case to your own teaching practice.

EXTENDING YOUR ANALYSIS OF THE CASE

The questions listed in this section are intended to help you focus on particular aspects of the case related to teacher decision-making and student thinking. If you are working in collaboration with one or more colleagues, the questions can serve as a stimulus for further discussion.

1. What were Ms. Hanson's goals for student learning for this lesson? To what extent do you think these goals were met? How did Ms. Hanson support students in achieving these goals? Cite specific evidence from the case to support your claim.

2. How were students thinking about equivalent ratios prior to the lesson in the case? How is their thinking different now? Why did these problems require students to develop new strategies or to be explicit about their thinking? Cite specific evidence from the case to support your ideas.

3. Why does Ms. Hanson choose the initial Jolly Ranchers and Jawbreakers problem? Why does she specifically select the other questions from the many that she has prepared? In what ways does the sequence of the problems serve to support students' learning? In what ways does the final problem serve to summarize the 2-day lesson?

4. What is Ms. Hanson's role during the lesson? What is the role of her students during the lesson? How might Ms. Hanson have established these norms in her classroom?

5. In what ways does Ms. Hanson monitor student understanding during the lesson? In what ways does she try to promote understanding among all students in her classroom?

6. What purpose does presenting multiple strategies serve in the lesson? In what ways does Ms. Hanson use students' ideas to foster learning and understanding?

7. When students discuss multiplicative relationships in the ratio table, the relationship across the table (i.e., between the columns) is not recognized. What is this relationship, and why is it important? What would have made this relationship easier to see? Can this relationship be used to determine the number of Jawbreakers, given any number of Jolly Ranchers? How might Ms. Hanson draw more attention to this relationship in future lessons?

8. How is Jordan's comment that "you have to do the same thing to both numbers" (para. 25) different from Jerlyn's comment that "you have to add the same amount each time" (para. 11)? How is the use of addition different in the solutions posed by each of these students?

9. In the case, students identify several factor-of-change relationships between different rows of the ratio table (para. 32). Can you find other ways of relating the rows in the table? How many ways can you relate the ratios of 100:260 (the answer to the second problem) and 200:520 (the answer to the third problem) to other ratios in the table? Why are strategies based on a factor-of-change used more frequently in the case than strategies based on the unit rate?

10. Compare additive and multiplicative ways of thinking about the ratio table created by Jerlyn and Kamiko. (Or consider additive thinking versus multiplicative thinking more generally— What would it mean to triple a recipe additively? multiplicatively?) How is the girls' use of repeated addition related to the factor-of-change relationships that students identify later in the lesson? Why does Ms. Hanson want students to recognize the multiplicative relationships between the rows of the table, rather than thinking of the rows being related by consistently adding five more Jolly Ranchers and 13 more Jawbreakers each time?

11. In the case, students justify that the unit rate of 1:2.6 "fits" into the ratio table created by Jerlyn and Kamiko (paras. 30–32). Using graph paper or a graphing calculator, create a coordinate graph for this table and use your graph to show that the unit rate of 1:2.6 and the ratios of 100:260 and 200:520 fit into the ratio table. Make observations about your graph. Why do the data points fall in a straight line? Is it appropriate to connect the data points in this situation? What is the equation generated by the data points? What is the coefficient of x in this equation, and why is this number important?

CONNECTING TO YOUR OWN PRACTICE

In this section, we offer ways to connect the specific ideas investigated in "The Case of Marie Hanson" to a set of larger issues that can be explored in your own classroom. Building on your analysis of "The Case of Marie Hanson," you can use the activities presented below as opportunities for focused reflection on issues that might be important to your own teaching of mathematics.

• In the "Analyzing the Case" section, you identified ways in which Marie Hanson's pedagogy supported students' learning. One aspect of Marie Hanson's pedagogy that appeared to support her students' learning is the way in which she selected and sequenced the candy jar problems. According to Hiebert and colleagues (1997), "Teachers need to select sequences of tasks so that, over time, students' experiences add up to something important. Teachers need to consider the residue left behind by sets of tasks, not just individual tasks" (p. 31).

Design a sequence of tasks to promote students' understanding of ratio and proportion in your classroom. Consider the issues that were important in selecting and sequencing the candy jar problems in Ms. Hanson's classroom: What context will you use? How does the task build on and extend students' prior knowledge? What strategies will the tasks promote? How will you choose the numbers in the problems to encourage specific strategies? How and in what order will students present their strategies to the class? What errors or misconceptions might be expected? How will the tasks advance students' thinking about multiplicative relationships? How and when will you introduce cross-multiplication? (Langrall & Swafford's [2000] discussion of different levels and essential components of proportional reasoning might be helpful in planning the sequence of tasks.)

• Plan a lesson around the sequence of tasks that you have designed. Consider the following: How will you set up the tasks in ways that will allow students to apply a variety of solution strategies? How will you provide opportunities for students to explore the task, and how you will support their learning during this time? How will you conduct a whole-group discussion that will allow the main mathematical ideas to surface and important connections to be made? Teach and reflect on the lesson. In particular, consider which pedagogical moves that Marie Hanson used to support students' learning, and that you identified in the "Analyzing the Case" section, were prevalent in your lesson. Identify specific pedagogical moves that you want to continue work on or explore further.

EXPLORING CURRICULAR MATERIALS

You may want to explore your curriculum for ideas related to ratios and proportions by considering the following questions: Is there a specific unit on ratio and proportion? What ideas are developed in the unit, and how are the ideas developed? What contexts and what type of tasks are used to help students make sense of ratio and proportion? Are the tasks used in ways that promote students' understanding of ratio and proportion? Are the tasks set up in a way that provides opportunities for exploration and discovery, or are they structured to the point of removing the challenge of the task and the complexity of the mathematics? (See Stein et al. [2000] for a discussion on selecting and enacting cognitively challenging tasks.) If the tasks have been over-structured, how might you revise them to provide students with opportunities for high-level thinking and reasoning?

You also may want to explore the mathematical ideas made salient in the case by investigating mathematical tasks drawn from other curricular materials. The following list identifies curricula that contain problems considered to be "mathematically similar" to the task used in Marie Hanson's class.

Billstein, R., & Williamson, J. (1999). *Middle grades math thematics: Book 1*. Evanston, IL: McDougal Littell.

   Of particular interest is an exploration activity (pp. 416–417) in which students use proportions to solve missing-value problems that are situated in real-world contexts.

Education Development Center, Inc. (1998a). *MathScape: Buyer beware: Rates, ratios, percents, and proportions* (*Student guide*). Mountain View, CA: Creative Publications.

   Of particular interest is Lesson 7 (Halftime Refreshments) (pp. 20–21), in which students are asked to solve missing-value problems that are situated in recipe contexts.

Foreman, L. C., & Bennett, A. B., Jr. (1996b). *Visual mathematics: Course II, lessons 21–30*.

   Of particular interest in Lesson 23 (Ratio and Proportion) are Actions 1–3 in the Connector Teacher Activity (pp. 357–358). Students are asked to explore the relationships among a set of discrete objects (red and yellow game markers) and to determine the number of markers in various larger, but equivalent, sets.

Lappan, G. Fey, J. T., Fitzgerald, W. M., Friel, S. N., & Phillips, E. D. (2002). *Comparing and scaling: Ratio, proportion, and percent*. Glenview, IL: Prentice Hall.

   Of particular interest is Problem 6.3 (pp. 68–72), in which students use proportions while working with population data. In addition, Problem 3.2 (p. 29) and Problem 6.2 (p. 67) are contextualized missing-value problems that might be of interest.

The Mathematics in Context Development Team. (1997). *Mathematics in context: Per sense* (*Student guide*). In National Center for Research in Mathematical Sciences Education & Freudenthal Institute (Eds.), *Mathematics in context*. Chicago: Encyclopaedia Britannica.

   Of particular interest are Problems 5–8 (p. 19), in which students are encouraged to solve missing-value problems by using a table.

CONNECTING TO OTHER IDEAS AND ISSUES

If you have additional time, you may want to explore some aspect of the case in more depth. Each of the readings identified at the end of this section can be used to further explore issues that surfaced in "The Case of Marie Hanson." For example, you might: (1) use Boston, Smith, and Hillen (2003) to consider how to use the lesson featured in the case to build an understanding of cross-multiplication; (2) consider how Marie Hanson's students utilized the four common strategies for solving problems involving ratios and proportions (unit rate, factor-of-change, fraction, and cross-product) described in Cramer and Post (1993); (3) use the Lamon (1999) chapter to further explore ratio tables and how they can be used to solve a range of problems; (4) consider how Ms. Hanson selected and sequenced the candy jar problems to elicit the different levels and essential components of proportional reasoning identified by Langrall and Swafford (2000); (5) compare and contrast the ratio tables described in Middleton and van den Heuvel-Panhuizen (1995) with the tables created by Ms. Hanson's students; and (6) consider the ways in which Ms. Hanson might have used the activity described in Parker (1999) with her students prior to the lesson described in the case.

Boston, M., Smith, M. S., & Hillen, A. F. (2003). Building on students' intuitive strategies to make sense of cross-multiplication. *Mathematics Teaching in the Middle School, 9*, 150–155.

   In this article, the authors discuss how the sequence of ratio tasks used in "The Case of Marie Hanson" helps to develop students' abilities to reason proportionally. Suggestions also are provided on how the lesson featured in the case might serve as a springboard for introducing the cross-multiplication algorithm while maintaining a focus on meaning and understanding.

Cramer, K., & Post, T. (1993). Proportional reasoning. *Mathematics Teacher, 86*, 404–407.

   The authors describe types of proportional reasoning problems (missing value, numerical comparison, qualitative prediction, and comparison) and the strategies (unit rate, factor-of-change, fraction, cross-product) that middle school students typically use to solve these types of problems. The authors argue that middle school students are often more successful at solving proportional reasoning problems when they use sense-making strategies, such as finding a unit rate, rather than a cross-multiplication approach.

Lamon, S. (1999). *Teaching fractions and ratios for understanding: Essential content knowledge and instructional strategies for teachers*. Mahwah, NJ: Erlbaum.

   The author argues that ratio tables are a sophisticated strategy and representation for solving proportional problems. Problems and student work that illustrates children's early strategies for creating ratio tables are presented and discussed in Chapter 11 (pp. 163–184). Of particular interest is Problem 12 (p. 183), which asks the reader to build a ratio table.

Langrall, C. W., & Swafford, J. (2000). Three balloons for two dollars: Developing proportional reasoning. *Mathematics Teaching in the Middle School, 6,* 254–261.

The authors draw on relevant literature and on examples of students' thinking from their own research to describe how different types of proportional reasoning problems might be sequenced to develop increasingly sophisticated levels of proportional reasoning in children's thinking. The authors discuss how instruction first should allow students to use informal reasoning and explore a variety of strategies in order to develop the essential components of proportional reasoning.

Middleton, J. A., & van den Heuvel-Panhuizen, M. (1995). The ratio table. *Mathematics Teaching in the Middle School, 1,* 282–288.

The authors define ratio tables as tables in which equivalent ratios can be generated by successive manipulation of numbers in the table. They suggest that studying ratio tables can help prepare middle school students for more advanced proportional reasoning (i.e., observing multiplicative and additive relationships in tables), yet remain accessible to students with limited skills. Several examples of student work using ratio tables are provided.

Parker, M. (1999). Building on "building-up": Proportional reasoning activities for future teachers. *Mathematics Teaching in the Middle School, 4,* 286–289.

The author describes the "building-up" strategy, a strategy that can be used to solve missing-value problems. "Building-up," either additively or multiplicatively, is an important precursor to understanding the multiplicative structure of proportion problems for both preservice teachers and their students. The article concludes with a description of an introductory lesson on ratio that could be used with preservice teachers.

Comparing
Similar Figures

The Case of Marcia Green

This chapter provides the materials to engage you in reading and analyzing the teaching and learning that occur in the classroom of Marcia Green as she and her 7th-grade students enlarge figures using rubber-band stretchers and explore the relationship between the original figure and its enlarged image.

Prior to reading the case, we suggest that you complete the Opening Activity. The primary purpose of the Opening Activity is to engage you with the mathematical ideas and tools that you will encounter when you read the case. The questions in the Opening Activity are nearly identical to ones that Marcia Green's students encounter during the lesson.

Once you have completed the activity, you may want to refer to Appendix C, which contains a set of solutions generated by teachers who completed the Opening Activity as part of a professional development experience that focused on "The Case of Marcia Green." You are encouraged to make sense of the different solutions provided and to consider the relationship between your solution and those produced by others.

OPENING ACTIVITY

Please engage in this activity and its "Solve" and "Consider" questions before reading the case. For this activity, you will need two rubber bands of the same size, a pencil, several pieces of white typing paper, scissors, and tape. Begin by following the diagram in Figure 4.1a and the directions below to create a rubber-band stretcher.

Tie the two rubber bands together by passing one band through the other and back through itself. Pull on the two ends, moving the knot to the center of the bands. You may

need to pull on the knot so that both bands form half of the knot. (Lappan, Fey, Fitzgerald, Friel, & Phillips, 1997, p. 13a)

Next, draw a simple figure approximately 2 inches in height and width on a piece of white paper. The diagram in Figure 4.1b illustrates how to position the figure and the anchor point on opposite sides of the page. The anchor point is needed to enlarge the figure, but does not require precise placement.

Tape the sheet with the picture you want to enlarge to your desk next to a blank sheet of paper. If you are right-handed, put the figure on your left. If you are left-handed, put it on the right. (See Figure 4.1b for models of left-handed and right-handed set-ups.)

The simple figure will be used to practice making an enlargement with the rubber-band stretcher. Enlarge the figure using the following directions and Figure 4.1c as a guide:

With your finger, hold down one end of the stretcher securely to the anchor point. Put a pencil through the other end of the stretcher and stretch the rubber bands until the knot is above part of the outline of the figure. Guide the knot around the original picture while your pencil traces out a new picture on the blank paper. Do not allow slack in the rubber bands. Try to keep the knot floating directly over the outline of the figure as your pencil draws the new figure. The more carefully the knot traces over the original figure, the better your drawing will be. (Lappan et al., 1997, p. 6, 13b)

Practice enlarging your simple figure a few times, until you feel comfortable using the rubber-band stretcher and can produce a fairly neat and accurate enlargement.

Now that you have had the opportunity to practice using the rubber-band stretcher, repeat the process by

FIGURE 4.1. (a) Directions for Creating the Rubber-Band Stretcher; (b) Directions for Positioning the Figure and the Anchor Points; (c) Directions for Tracing the Figure

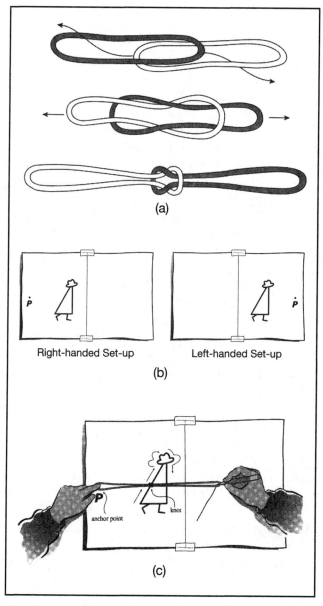

(a)

Right-handed Set-up   Left-handed Set-up

(b)

anchor point   knot

(c)

From *Connected Mathematics: Stretching and Shrinking, Similarity* by Glenda Lappan, James T. Fey, William M. Fitzgerald, Susan N. Friel, and Elizabeth Defanis Phillips © 1997 by Michigan State University. Published by Pearson Education, Inc., publishing as Pearson Prentice Hall. Used by permission.

Solve

- How are the original and enlarged figures the same? How are they different?
- In particular, what do you notice about the lengths of the sides, the perimeters, and the areas of the original figures in comparison to their enlargements?

Consider

- Suppose that the enlargement process was repeated using a rubber-band stretcher made of three rubber bands. What can you predict about the relationship between the original figure and its enlargement?

READING THE CASE

As you read the case, we encourage you to identify points in the lesson where Marcia Green asks what you consider to be good questions and to consider why they are good questions. For example, you might select a question that Marcia Green asks following a student's explanation that you felt served to draw students' attention toward a key mathematical idea, or one that she poses to an individual student that assisted the student's learning while also allowing the mathematics to remain open for exploration.

We encourage you to write down the questions you select and why you think they were good questions to ask. If you have colleagues who also are reading this case, you may want to share the questions each of you have identified and your reasons for selecting them. The list of questions you generate can serve as the basis for a discussion about what makes a good question, for a continued investigation of questions in other cases, or as a starting point for exploration in your own classroom. For example, you may begin to consider the type of questions you ask during a lesson and how these questions influence your students' learning of mathematics. We will discuss additional connections to your own practice at the end of the chapter.

drawing a square and an equilateral triangle (each with side lengths of 2 inches) and then using the rubber-band stretcher to enlarge these figures. Use your original drawings of the square and equilateral triangle and their enlargements to answer the "Solve" and "Consider" questions.

THE CASE OF MARCIA GREEN

1. Marcia Green is a 7th-grade teacher at Dalton Middle School. She has been teaching middle school students for 17 years, almost all of which have been spent in urban classrooms teaching at-risk students. Marcia holds an elementary education degree and is certified to teach grades 4 through 8, but she minored in mathematics in college and has always had a teaching schedule consisting mainly of mathematics classes. Marcia considers herself a mathematics teacher and would choose to teach only mathematics because she enjoys working with the mathematics teachers at Dalton. This is especially true now that Dalton is in its second year of implementing an exciting new curriculum and new methods of teaching that stress learning mathematics with meaning and understanding.

2. Dalton's reform efforts provided time for extensive collaboration among the mathematics teachers. During the first year of the project, the 7th-grade teachers began to realize that their students harbored many misconceptions about the part–whole relationship expressed by the numerator and denominator of a fraction. In an effort to enrich students' understanding of rational numbers and of ratios beyond the part–whole relationships conveyed by fractions, Marcia and her fellow teachers chose proportional reasoning as the focal point of the following year's goals. The contention of the NCTM Curriculum and Evaluation Standards for School Mathematics (1989) that proportional reasoning "is of such great importance that it merits whatever time and effort must be expended to assure its careful development" (p. 82) in the middle school curriculum made the teachers at Dalton confident in this decision.

3. The reform efforts at Dalton also are helping Marcia to make improvements in her own classroom. Marcia feels that her main strength is her ability to motivate students to want to learn. She is convinced that she helps her students experience success by showing a genuine concern for their learning and by initially sparking their interest to engage with new material. Marcia encourages students to actively discuss mathematical ideas. She still struggles, however, to convince her 7th-graders to be respectful of ideas that they do not agree with. Showing respect for the opinions of others continues to be a problem in her classroom.

Marcia Green Talks About Her Class

4. If someone had asked me a few years ago to describe the role of proportional reasoning in middle school, I would have responded that my students study ratio and proportion problems late in May. Although an entire chapter of our text is devoted to various types of ratio and proportion problems, we often have time to tackle only the "unit rate" problems (i.e., finding the best buy). I was always quite pleased to close the year with lessons that were useful in real life, were age-appropriate, and incorporated valuable mathematical skills (such as finding equivalent fractions, using division to find a unit rate, using multiplication to scale-up to a certain number of units, and even the "trick" of cross-multiplying).

5.   Today I would answer that question quite differently. After the first year of implementing the new curriculum and methods of teaching, my colleagues and I decided to give proportional reasoning prime importance in our reform efforts. The 7th-graders at Dalton now encounter proportional reasoning problems throughout the school year in our daily warm-up exercises. These problems often ask students to form ratios and answer questions based on the objects given in a picture. Students have become quite skillful at determining and describing ratios as part–part and part–whole relationships, at finding equivalent ratios, and at devising their own intuitive methods of using rates and proportions to solve problems (such as making a table or drawing pictures).

6.   My 7th-graders have developed many ideas that we are now ready to explore further. We are about to begin a unit that will give students the opportunity to use and refine their intuitive proportional reasoning concepts (i.e., multiplicative thinking and qualitative notions of proportionality). The unit allows the ideas of similarity, scale factor, and ratio and proportion to be developed as students examine transformations that shrink or enlarge figures. Connected by the concept of similarity, each lesson pushes students' intuitive notions a little further. The opening lesson intends for students to: (1) form an intuitive, visual definition of similar figures as those having the same shape but different sizes; and (2) realize that the area of an enlarged figure has increased by a different factor than the lengths of the corresponding sides. Both of these ideas are developed and strengthened throughout the unit.

7.   The initial definition of similarity is enhanced later as students discover properties that similar figures share and that nonsimilar figures do not (namely, that similar figures have equal corresponding angles and have equal ratios between pairs of corresponding sides). Visual representations allow students to see the precise relationship between scale factors and area in similar figures: If the length of the corresponding sides of similar figures are related by a scale factor of x, then the areas are related by a factor of x^2. The closing lessons then provide opportunities for students to utilize the ideas of similarity, scale factors, and proportion to solve real-world problems involving similar rectangles and triangles.

8.   The opening lesson has students enlarging a square and an equilateral triangle using a rubber-band stretcher (two rubber bands knotted together) and requires much time and effort in preparation. We made the rubber-band stretchers at the end of class yesterday to save a little time, but we will still use up some class time today before we can discuss anything mathematical. I need to distribute the rubber-band stretchers, the handouts with the pictures of the figures we are going to enlarge (a smiley face, a square, and an equilateral triangle), blank paper, and tape, and I also need to demonstrate how to use the rubber-band stretcher to enlarge a figure. Once the handout and a blank sheet of paper are taped side-by-side on the students' desks, students finally will be able to practice enlarging figures. While holding down one end of the rubber-band stretcher on an anchor point and putting a pencil through the other end, the students trace an image of the original figure by moving the pencil on the blank paper so that the knot in the rubber-band stretcher floats over the outline of the original figure (as shown in Figure 4.2).

9.   When we compare the image of the squares and triangles with the original figures, students hopefully will offer a description that we can use in forming our initial definition of similar figures. I think students will recognize easily that the lengths of the corresponding sides and the perimeters in the enlarged figures have doubled, and I hope our earlier work with fractions enables students to switch fluently between reciprocal relationships such as "doubled" and "half." I also hope students recognize that the area of the enlarged figure has not doubled, but is actually four times larger than the area of the original. The precise relationship between the areas of similar figures will be revisited later as students think about tonight's assignment and after we have developed more thoroughly the idea of scale factors later in the unit. I really like that this unit incorporates its own assessment by having students apply everything they have learned in earlier lessons to solve application problems in the closing lessons.

10.   Although this lesson seems like a very small step mathematically compared with the time it requires to set up, I am hoping it will spark students' interest enough to get them thinking about similarity, scale factors, and proportions. When we began working with the new materials, I always questioned in the back of my mind whether taking the extra time for activities that allow students to discover new ideas was really worth it (after all, it would take only a couple of minutes to tell students what similar figures are). However, my experience is that telling students about a mathematical idea (which they are supposed to memorize and practice) doesn't optimize learning even if it does optimize time. And I truly believe that initially engaging students with the mathematics will motivate them to learn and to want to participate. I am still concerned, though, that too much time will be consumed by tracing the figures and not enough time will be left to discuss the mathematics.

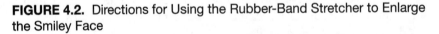

FIGURE 4.2. Directions for Using the Rubber-Band Stretcher to Enlarge the Smiley Face

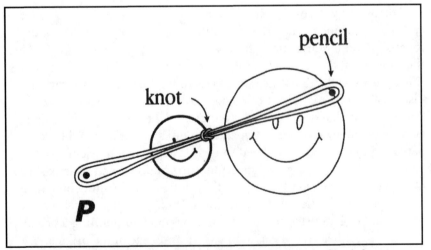

From *Connected Mathematics: Stretching and Shrinking, Similarity* by Glenda Lappan, James T. Fey, William M. Fitzgerald, Susan N. Friel, and Elizabeth Defanis Phillips © 1997 by Michigan State University. Published by Pearson Education, Inc., publishing as Pearson Prentice Hall. Used by permission.

The Class

11.   Distributing the materials, setting up the papers, and getting situated with their partners occupied the first 10 minutes of class. We were finally ready to begin. At the overhead, I asked students to watch what this amazing little machine would do to the smiley face picture. Putting a pencil through the rubber-band stretcher, I demonstrated how to hold down one end of the stretcher to the anchor point while keeping the knot positioned over the outline of the circle and allowing the other pencil to trace out the new figure. I repeated the directions again while tracing the eyes and mouth.

12.   Students watched intently and were eager to try using the stretchers themselves. I asked students to have each partner take a turn tracing the smiley face, then to have one partner trace the square and the other trace the triangle. As students began their drawings, I circulated the room and heard many variations of my directions being repeated among the pairs. After issuing several reminders of how to use the stretchers, I concluded that I could have saved valuable class time by giving a written copy of the directions to each pair of students.

13.   Even with the initial difficulties, most students seemed to be enjoying this activity. A few students had become frustrated because their new figures were quite sloppy, but I encouraged them to try again, telling them to be sure to keep tension in the rubber bands and to focus on keeping the knot above the outline of the original figure. This reminder was enough to convince most students to persevere, although one pair of boys had given up completely and was secretly trying to draw the image freehand. While I was annoyed that they were not following directions, I knew from experience that confronting them hostilely would only cause them to withdraw from the activity even further. As I approached their desks, I said jokingly, "Wow, this is the best one I've seen yet. Markus, since your enlargement came out so neatly, you should trace the square on the overhead." Markus smiled sheepishly and replied, "Ah, Mrs. G., we're busted. We just drew this—I can't make that thing work." I showed Markus how to set up the rubber-band stretcher, and he seemed pretty intent on getting it to work this time. His partner Armando, however, still remained disengaged with the task. I commented to Markus that when he was finished with the square, he should help Armando set up the stretcher to trace the triangle. I heard Armando muttering "whatever" as I walked away, and I made a mental note to try to involve Armando in the discussion at some point in today's lesson.

14.   Once the majority of students had completed their drawings, I chose two students who had made exceptionally neat drawings to enlarge the square and triangle on the overhead sheets. When they had finished, I called students' attention to the overhead. "Okay, let's make some observations about what the rubber-band stretcher did to the original square and triangle." Before I could call on anyone, several students chimed in, "They got bigger," or, "It made them bigger." Jason's hand was the only one still in the air. I called on him, and he began, "I was going to say that the shapes stayed the same"—but before he could finish his sentence, several students were expressing their disagreement—"No, they didn't—they got bigger." I motioned that the class should quiet

down, and I said, "Let's let Jason finish." Jason continued, "Well, yeah, they got bigger but they still stayed the same shape. The square is still a square and the triangle is still a triangle."

15.   Mumblings of "no kidding" and "duh" from the class indicated that students thought that this observation was too obvious to state. I reminded students that we needed to listen to everyone's ideas and that they should always voice their observations, questions, and concerns because you never know when something that seems trivial might be very important. I heard Jason jokingly say, "Yeah guys," to some of his friends. I added, "In fact, there is even an important mathematical term to describe figures that have the same shape but different sizes. We refer to them as *similar figures*." Jason's observation would be validated further in the next lesson as students encountered transformations that did not preserve shape and discussed the characteristics of similar versus nonsimilar figures.

16.   I asked for further observations or questions, and students didn't seem to have any, so I suggested that we list on the overhead what had been said so far. Jessica raised her hand and said, "Same shape, only bigger. And it's not exact. It's the same, but it's like a rough drawing." I made three separate bullets ("same shape," "bigger," and "not exact, a rough drawing"), repeating each as I wrote it down. Jason raised his hand to offer "the old square and the new square are *similar figures*," emphasizing the term as if to say, "I told you so," to his classmates. I added to the list, "the original square and the enlarged square are similar figures" and also "similar figures have the same shape but different sizes."

17.   I continued, "I still have a question. How much larger is the image than the original figure?" Students seemed to be looking over their papers, but no one offered any ideas, so I prompted with, "How might we find this out?" Miguel said, "We could measure!" and I responded with, "Okay, what might we measure?" He suggested that we measure the sides of the squares and triangles. Other students suggested that we also measure the diagonal of the square and the diameter of the smiley face. I told students that, while those were all good ideas, we should begin by measuring the sides of the squares and triangles. "And as you are measuring," I added, "I would like you to think about how the original figure relates to its enlarged image. Please measure in centimeters so that the measurements will be consistent."

18.   I distributed rulers, and most pairs immediately started measuring. I was hoping we could finish the measuring in about 5 minutes, because we were already almost 30 minutes into the period and that would leave us 15 minutes for discussion and to wrap things up. As I began to walk around the room, Jared asked whether they needed to measure all of the sides, since one shape was a square and the other was an equilateral triangle. My reply was, "You decide. Why might it be a good idea to measure all of the sides?" His partner Lacey said, "In case Jared made a mistake the first time," and the pair returned to measuring.

19.   One pair of girls was completely engaged in social talk and appeared completely unengaged with the task. As I approached them, I could see that they didn't have a thing written down and apparently had not even picked up their ruler. I greeted them with, "So I assume you two are

finished measuring and have this all figured out?" Alyssa, definitely the more vocal of the two, responded, "I don't see why we have to measure." This caught me off guard not only because of her tone of voice, but also because Alyssa typically takes the lead in pairwork and is a good student, despite her tendency to socialize. I had thought that speaking to them would be enough to get them back on task, and I did not expect to be challenged. Obviously annoyed, I replied, "You need to measure because I am going to call on you two first. And make sure that you both understand what is going on because I want Katie to be the spokesperson." As I walked away, I could hear Alyssa grumbling, "What are we supposed to measure, anyways?" to which Katie whispered that they could measure the sides of the squares and triangles.

20.   Other pairs of students had already finished measuring and were talking about how the measurements were related. I waited a couple of minutes for Alyssa and Katie to finish measuring, then called the class together. "Okay, Katie would like to come up and write down the measurements for the sides of the squares." Katie wrote 2½ by one side of the original square and 6 by one side of the enlarged square. I asked, "What about the other sides?" and Katie responded, "They are all the same, it's a square." I asked the class if they agreed with these measurements, and several students indicated that the enlarged square was "closer to 5 centimeters than 6." Katie then answered that they actually got 5, 6, 5½, and 4½ for each of the sides, but decided to use 6 since it was the largest. I asked, "If you got different measurements for each of the sides, how do you know that it is supposed to be a square? Squares have all sides the same length." Katie softly replied, "We said the new square was like a bigger picture of the little square. It stays the same shape." Jason blurted out, "Similar figures!" which the class found quite amusing.

21.   I then asked, "If these are supposed to be squares, why did we get different measurements for each of the sides?" Maria said, "Our measurements might not be exact," and Tia added that "the bigger square isn't exact either—it's a rough drawing like we said before. So the angles are not perfectly right angles and that made the sides different." I called on Juan next, since his hand had been in the air for awhile, and he said, "We didn't get exactly 5 centimeters either, but we went with 5 because it's in the middle and that would be a better estimate, since our measurements might be a little too big or a little too small." The class seemed to agree with this, so Katie erased the 6 and wrote a 5 by the enlarged square. I was pleased with students' facility in estimating, since the line segments produced by the rubber-band stretcher were typically quite sloppy. I also was relieved that students had decided on 5 cm for the sides of the enlarged square. We needed this measurement to discover that the lengths had doubled! (In doing the task the night before, I had worried that the lack of precision in measuring would impede students' discovery of the intended relationships unless I directed them toward the "right" measurement.)

22.   I wanted to move the discussion to how the two squares were related. Katie was still at the overhead, so I directed the question at her. "So if we agree that the smaller square has sides of 2½ centimeters and the larger one has sides of 5 centimeters, then how are the two squares related?"

Katie answered that "it's double," and several students voiced their agreement. Then Alyssa suddenly spoke up from her seat. "I still don't see why we needed to measure if all you wanted was the relationship. And I don't see how everyone is saying double, double, double. Just look at the two squares. It's much more than double." Even though Alyssa still had a tone to her voice that I did not like, I finally understood what the trouble was. I asked her to continue. "See that little square?" she said. "To me, it's a fourth of that big one. Four of it will fit into the big one." I asked, "Could you come up and show us what you mean?" Alyssa came up to the overhead (and Katie quickly sat down) and divided the enlarged square into four smaller squares, as shown in Figure 4.3a. She repeated, "Four little squares will fit into this big square."

23.   Alyssa returned to her seat, and I commented that while she had made a very good point, we had interrupted Katie in the middle of saying something important also. I stated, "We seem to have two different ideas up here. Katie said, and many of you seemed to agree, that it has doubled, while Alyssa says that it is four times bigger. Any comments on that?" Juan said, "I know! Take 2½ plus another 2½ and that gives you the 5 centimeters for the sides of the big square. Two little squares fit across the top and two little squares will fit along the side. That gives four little squares, so the big square is four times bigger." I marked the lengths in on Alyssa's diagram as Juan talked (as shown in Figure 4.3b).

24.   "Okay, so we have said that the lengths doubled and that the area is four times bigger. What about the perimeter?" I asked. As I said the words *area* and *perimeter*, I moved my marker on the drawing to remind students what perimeter and area were. Bonita quickly said, "It's doubled, too." I asked her how she knew, and she said that the perimeter of the smaller square was 10, and of the larger one was 20, so it is twice as big.

25.   I added three more bullets to the observation sheet that we had started earlier: The lengths of the sides of the square have doubled, the area has become four times larger, the perimeter has doubled. As I wrote the word "doubled," it occurred to me that not everyone might be thinking about these problems in the same way. Were students thinking of "doubled" as "10 plus 10" or as "10 times 2"? I hoped that students were seeing multiplicative relationships (such as "the area is four times

FIGURE 4.3. (a) Alyssa's Diagram Showing How Four Little Squares Will Fit into the Larger Square; (b) Juan's Description of the Lengths on Alyssa's Diagram

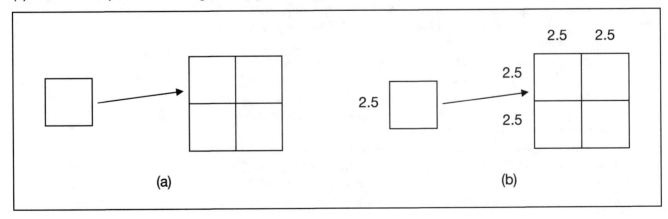

(a)   (b) bigger") rather than only additive relationships ("2½ plus another 2½"), but I couldn't determine whether or not that was the case. Rather than exploring this further at this moment, I decided to move on to the triangles. Tomorrow's lesson would provide me with a better opportunity to assess whether students were using multiplicative reasoning as they encountered the notion of scale factors.

26.   I put up the overhead sheet with the triangles and asked if the same relationships held for the triangles. We needed to look at the measurements first, and Jared said that they got 3 centimeters for each side. For the larger triangle, the class agreed on 6 centimeters for each side since it should still be an equilateral triangle. They quickly decided that the lengths and the perimeter had doubled as was the case with the squares. I asked, "What about the area?" and after a little bit of silence, Tia was the first person to speak up. "It tripled," she said. "Look, I'll show you." She came up to the overhead and drew three little triangles inside the larger one, as shown in Figure 4.4a.

27.   Tia continued, "It's just like before, two triangles fit along the side because the length is double. The bottom is double, too, so one more triangle will fit here." I waited before saying anything, hoping that a student would be able to say it for me. Bonita was the first to respond. "But you haven't covered the whole triangle," she said. "There is a hole in the middle. You could fit another triangle in there." Tia looked confused, so I asked Bonita to come up and show us what she meant. Referring to Figure 4.4b, Bonita said that there would be just enough room for another triangle "turned upside-down because the space was 3 centimeters on each side just like the triangle. So then four small triangles would fit into the larger triangle, just like with the squares."

28.   It was time to wrap up the lesson, and I wanted to give them something to think about for tomorrow. I put the list of observations on the overhead and commented that they had made good observations today that would help us throughout the unit. I read over the list and repeated that we would refer to many of these ideas over the next few days. For homework, I asked students to write down their ideas about what would happen to the lengths of the sides, the perimeter, and the area if we enlarged the figures using three rubber bands knotted together. I wrote the question down on the overhead, repeated it, and added that sketches might be helpful.

FIGURE 4.4. (a) Tia's Diagram That Illustrates That the Area Tripled; (b) Bonita's Use of Tia's Diagram to Explain That the Area Is Actually Four Times Larger

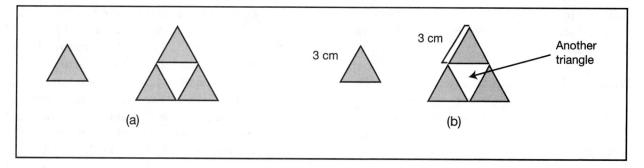

ANALYZING THE CASE

Now that you have had an opportunity to "visit" Marcia Green's classroom and identify what you think are good questions, we invite you to consider how Marcia Green's use of questioning supported her students' learning of mathematics. Here are a few suggestions on how to proceed.

- Review the list of good questions that Marcia Green asks throughout the lesson. For each question, consider: (1) What makes it a good question? (2) What is Mrs. Green's purpose for asking this question? and (3) How did the question advance students' learning?
- Review the list of questions that you have identified and create a list of criteria for a "good" question.
- If you have colleagues who also are reading this case, compare your criteria and possibly generate a master list. Note points of disagreement, as these are likely to be fruitful topics for further discussion. If you are working on this activity alone, we encourage you to refer to Appendix C, which includes a list of criteria for good questions identified by a group of teachers who participated in a professional development experience that focused on "The Case of Marcia Green."

You may wish to continue your analysis of the case by considering the questions in the next section. Alternatively, you can skip the next section and proceed directly to the "Connecting to Your Own Practice" section, in which you are encouraged to relate the analysis of the ideas and issues raised in the case to your own teaching practice.

EXTENDING YOUR ANALYSIS OF THE CASE

The questions listed in this section are intended to help you focus on particular aspects of the case related to teacher decision-making and student thinking. If you are working in collaboration with one or more colleagues, the questions can serve as a stimulus for further discussion.

1. What were Mrs. Green's goals for this lesson? To what extent were these goals met during the lesson? Cite evidence from the case to support your claim. What other models or contexts might be used to develop these same ideas?

2. Mrs. Green never directly connects the lesson to students' earlier work with ratios. Why might this have been a valuable thing to do? Identify opportunities where Mrs. Green could have made connections to students' earlier experiences with expressing ratios of objects in a picture, finding equivalent ratios, and using proportions to answer questions (based on the objects in the picture). Identify opportunities where Mrs. Green could have introduced proportional reasoning terminology and strategies that students would need to describe similar figures more precisely (i.e., using ratios and proportions) in future lessons.

3. Students' explorations of the main mathematical ideas are not completed by the end of the lesson. How will the homework assignment contribute to realizing the goals of the lesson? What mathematical ideas does Mrs. Green need to make salient in the following lesson? What might Mrs. Green do in the following lesson to summarize and solidify the ideas generated here?

4. Describe the structure of Mrs. Green's lesson. What does this indicate about Mrs. Green's perceptions of student learning and of her role in the classroom?

5. Mrs. Green directs students to measure only the sides of the original and enlarged figures (para. 17). What might have been gained by not limiting the attributes students chose to measure? Mrs. Green comments that she is pleased with students' ease in estimating the measurements of the sides of the "roughly" enlarged figures, and also relieved that they decided on 5 cm (para. 21). What might Mrs. Green have done if students' measurements were not accurate enough for them to see the intended relationships?

6. Mrs. Green makes a mental note to return to Armando sometime during the day's lesson (para. 13), but she does not follow through with this. At what point in the lesson would Mrs. Green have had a good opportunity to return to Armando? What would she hope to accomplish in doing so?

7. Mrs. Green eventually comes to realize the source of Alyssa's defiance. How might she have handled her encounter with Alyssa and Katie differently? Are there any other places in the lesson where you would have responded differently than Mrs. Green?

8. In paragraph 24, Mrs. Green asks Bonita how she knew that the perimeter had doubled but does not elicit different strategies or ideas from the rest of the class. What might have been gained by explor-

ing perimeter more thoroughly? Why might Mrs. Green not have wanted to move the class in this direction?

9. Mrs. Green is concerned about students seeing multiplicative relationships rather than just additive relationships (para. 25). Why should Mrs. Green be concerned about this? Does it make a difference in how students approach the task in the case? How would additive thinking impact students' approaches to the problem shown in Figure 4.5?

10. The lesson described in the case took more than a full class period. Why do you think Mrs. Green felt this was a worthwhile task? Do you agree with her decision to spend more than one day on just one lesson?

CONNECTING TO YOUR OWN PRACTICE

In this section, we offer ways to connect the specific ideas investigated in "The Case of Marcia Green" to a set of larger issues that can be explored in your own classroom. Building on your analysis of "The Case of Marcia Green," you can use the activities presented below as opportunities for focused reflection on issues that might be important to your own teaching of mathematics.

According to Hiebert and colleagues (1997), "When we think of how to guide the mathematical activities of the class, teachers are always faced with a dilemma: how to support students as thinkers and creative problem solvers and how to help them learn important mathematics" (p. 39). As teachers, we often face a tension between assisting students' learning while maintaining the challenging aspects of a task. One way that Marcia Green supported students' engagement with the mathe-

matics in the task without removing their opportunities for high-level thinking and reasoning was by asking "good" questions. The following activities are intended to help you consider the nature of questioning in your own classroom.

- In the "Analyzing the Case" section, you considered the nature of questioning in Marcia Green's classroom by identifying "good" questions that she asked and her purposes in asking those questions. Plan a lesson that you will soon be teaching. Begin the planning process by solving the task using all of the strategies that you might expect to see from your students. Consider potential student errors and misconceptions that might arise as students are exploring the task. Using your criteria for a good question and/or the "criteria for good questions" from the chart provided in Appendix C, generate a list of questions that you will ask your students in order to: (1) advance their learning as they work on the task; and (2) highlight important mathematical ideas as they share and discuss their solutions.

- Teach a lesson that requires your students to investigate and make sense of a mathematical idea or relationship. Ideally, this would be lesson that you planned in the activity described above. Record the lesson on videotape or audiotape, or have a colleague observe and take notes. Choose a 15-minute segment of the lesson and list all of the questions you asked during this segment. Then examine the questions you asked, as follows: (1) Identify the questions that you think were good. Why did you ask those questions? What made them good questions to ask? (2) Identify the questions you asked that you do not think were good. What made these questions not as good? and (3) Compare the questions that you identified in lists 1 and 2. How are they the same and how are they different? Which questions appeared to advance students' learning? How do the characteristics of your questions compare with those of Marcia Green's questions?

- Enact a lesson on similarity in which students explore figures that have been enlarged or shrunk (i.e., the activities described by Slovin [2000] or Tracy and Hague [1997], or from the NCTM *Addenda Series* [1994], discussed in the following section) in order to see how your students think about these problems. In what ways was your enactment of the lesson similar to or different from the lesson portrayed in the case? In particular: How

FIGURE 4.5. A Problem That Could Expose Additive Versus Multiplicative Thinking

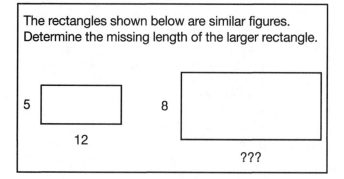

does your students' thinking about similarity and scale factor compare with the students in the case? How does your use of questioning compare with Marcia Green's use of questioning in the case? In what ways did your questions serve to highlight important mathematical ideas and provide students with opportunities for thinking and reasoning?

EXPLORING CURRICULAR MATERIALS

You may want to explore your curriculum for ideas related to similarity by considering the following questions: Is similarity used as a context for developing students' understanding of proportional relationships? If not, could the curriculum be modified so as to provide students with opportunities to consider proportional relationships in a geometric context? In what ways might such experiences strengthen students' understanding of proportional relationships?

You also may want to explore the mathematical ideas made salient in the case, by investigating mathematical tasks drawn from other curricular materials. The following list identifies curricula that contain problems considered to be "mathematically similar" to the task used in Marcia Green's class.

Billstein, R., & Williamson, J. (1999). *Middle grades math thematics: Book 1.* Evanston, IL: McDougal Littell.

Of particular interest is an exploration activity (pp. 424–426), in which students build two trapezoids from pattern blocks and determine whether they are similar figures.

Education Development Center, Inc. (1998c). *MathScape: Gulliver's worlds: Measuring and scaling (Student guide).* Mountain View, CA: Creative Publications.

Of particular interest is Lesson 11 (Gulliver's Worlds Cubed) (pp. 30–31), in which students explore how length, area, and volume change when a figure is enlarged by various scale factors.

Foreman, L. C., & Bennett, A. B., Jr. (1996b). *Visual mathematics: Course II, Lessons 21–30.* Salem, OR: The Math Learning Center.

Of particular interest in Lesson 30 (Similarity and Scaling in 2–D and 3–D) is Action 7 in the Focus Teacher Activity (pp. 479–480). Students are shown how to create enlargements by a scale factor of 2 and reductions by a factor of one-half using a rubber-band stretcher made of two rubber bands. They are then asked to consider several questions, such as whether the size of the rubber bands affects the enlargement/reduction and how to create reductions by fractional factors.

Lappan, G., Fey, J. T., Fitzgerald, W. M., Friel, S. N., & Phillips, E. D. (1997). *Connected Mathematics: Stretching and shrinking, Similarity.* Palo Alto, CA: Dale Seymour.

Problem 1.1 (p. 7) is identical to the problem that appears in "The Case of Marcia Green." Of particular interest is Problem 1.1 Follow-Up (pp. 7–8) in which students are asked to consider whether moving the anchor point when enlarging a figure with the rubber-band stretcher will affect the enlargement.

The Mathematics in Context Development Team. (1998b). *Mathematics in context: Ratio and rates (Student guide).* In National Center for Research in Mathematical Sciences Education & Freudenthal Institute (Eds.), *Mathematics in context.* Chicago: Encyclopaedia Britannica.

Of particular interest are Problems 2–3 (pp. 32–33), in which students enlarge an irregular figure and explore the relationship between the corresponding linear and area measurements of the original figure and its enlarged image.

CONNECTING TO OTHER IDEAS AND ISSUES

If you have additional time, you may want to explore some aspect of the case in more depth. The resources identified below provide some possibilities for broadening the discussion of similarity and scale factor. For example, you might: (1) discuss the types of activities Mrs. Green might want to incorporate into future lessons to avoid the additive reasoning errors discussed in Miller and Fey (2000); (2) discuss how the strategies used by the students described in Slovin (2000) are similar to or different from the strategies used by students in Mrs. Green's class; (3) discuss the ways in which the activities described in NCTM (1994) or Tracy and Hague (1997) also could help students understand similarity and scale and whether these activities might be worthwhile for Mrs. Green's students; or (4) use the Lamon (1999) chapter as a basis for discussing how conceptual work related to similarity provides the underpinnings for developing proportional reasoning.

Lamon, S. (1999). *Teaching fractions and ratios for understanding: Essential content knowledge and instructional strategies for teachers.* Mahwah, NJ: Erlbaum.

In Chapter 15 (pp. 239–254), the author focuses on similar figures and defines them as objects that have the same shape and a multiplicative relationship between corresponding attributes. The distinction between additive and multiplicative reasoning is highlighted via numerous examples and exercises. Of particular interest are Problems 1–11 (pp. 249–253) and Problem 18 (p. 254), which focus on similarity.

Miller, J., & Fey, J. (2000). Proportional reasoning. *Mathematics Teaching in the Middle School, 5,* 310–313.

> The authors report the results of a study in which they compared two groups of 7th-grade students: one group that used a reform curriculum while the other group used a traditional curriculum. The authors then investigated the students' proportional reasoning skills. Students using the reform curriculum were more successful than the other students on a set of proportional reasoning tasks. Several tasks are discussed in the article, including two problems that are set in the context of enlarging photographs. Common errors and misconceptions are discussed, including applying additive strategies to proportional situations.

National Council of Teachers of Mathematics. (1994). *Addenda series grades 5–8: Understanding rational numbers and proportion* (pp. 61–75). Reston, VA: Author.

> This cluster contains two investigations that focus on scale factor and similar figures. The effect of enlarging linear dimensions on an object's area and volume is discussed and student activities that make these ideas salient are provided. The chapter includes worksheets that could be used in class.

Slovin, H. (2000). Moving to proportional reasoning. *Mathematics Teaching in the Middle School, 6,* 58–60.

> The author uses the context of transformational geometry to engage students in the study of proportional reasoning. Three nonnumerical problems that relate to similar figures, scale factor, and percent increase are discussed. Students' strategies for solving these problems also are described and analyzed.

Tracy, D. M., & Hague, M. S. (1997). Toys 'R' math. *Mathematics Teaching in the Middle School, 2,* 140–145, 159.

> The authors describe an activity in which students study proportional reasoning through examining scale-model toys. Students begin by investigating toys such as Matchbox cars that have a known scale factor. Students use this scale to draw a life-size model of the toy in chalk on the playground. To properly enlarge the toy, students must attend to the effects of the scale factor on length, perimeter, and area. The lesson is extended by having students create scale models of toys with unknown scale factors.

Exploring Problems Involving Ratios and Percents

The Case of Janice Patterson

This chapter provides the materials to engage you in reading and analyzing the teaching and learning that occur in Janice Patterson's classroom as she and her 7th-graders use diagrams to solve problems whose quantities are related proportionally.

Prior to reading the case, we suggest that you complete the Opening Activity. The primary purpose of the Opening Activity is to engage you with the mathematical ideas that you will encounter when you read the case. The three problems that are found in the Opening Activity are identical to those found in the case. Although each problem can be solved algebraically, you are encouraged to try an alternative approach. For example, visual approaches, such as those presented in the "Consider" component of the Opening Activity, might help you make sense of the quantities in the problems and highlight their relationships in ways that algebraic approaches do not.

Once you have completed the activity, you may want to refer to Appendix D, which contains some solutions generated by teachers who completed the Opening Activity as part of a professional development experience that focused on "The Case of Janice Patterson." You are encouraged to examine the different solutions provided and to consider the relationship between your solution and those produced by others.

OPENING ACTIVITY

Please solve problems 1 through 3 and respond to the "Consider" question before reading the case. Be sure to show the method you used to find each answer. (See Figure 5.2. for publisher and copyright information).

Solve

1. The ratio of the length of a certain rectangle to its width is 4 to 3. Its area is 300 square inches. What are its length and width?
2. A length of string that is 180 cm long is cut into 3 pieces. The second piece is 25% longer than the first, and the third piece is 25% shorter than the first. How long is each piece?
3. If 50 gallons of cream with 20% butterfat are mixed with 150 gallons of milk with 4% butterfat, what percent butterfat is the resulting mixture?

Consider

Some students correctly solved each of these problems using a diagram. A diagram that was used for each problem is shown in Figure 5.1. Try to make sense of the diagram and to complete the solution to each problem using the diagram.

READING THE CASE

As you read the case, we encourage you to make note of what the students in Janice Patterson's class are doing during the lesson that may have contributed to their learning. (You may want to use a highlighter or Post-it notes to keep track of these as you read the case.) For example, you may notice general features of the students' work (e.g., they solved three problems; they worked in groups; they presented their solution strategies at the overhead) as well as more specific aspects of their ways of working (e.g., they used visual approaches to make sense of the problems; they questioned one another when they did not understand).

We encourage you to write down what students did that may have contributed to their learning. These can serve as topics for discussion with a colleague who also has read the case, as issues to investigate as you read additional cases, or as starting points for exploration in your own classroom. For example, you might wonder whether students in your class would benefit from presenting solutions at the overhead. We will discuss additional connections to your own practice at the end of the chapter.

FIGURE 5.1. (a) Kalla and Robin's Diagram for Problem 1 of the Opening Activity; (b) Cassandra and Alfonso's Diagram for Problem 2 of the Opening Activity; (c) V.J. and Trina's Diagram for Problem 3 of the Opening Activity

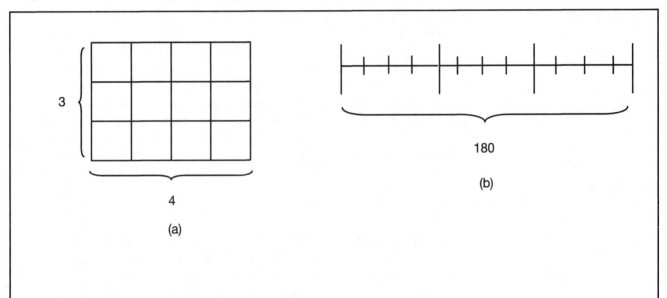

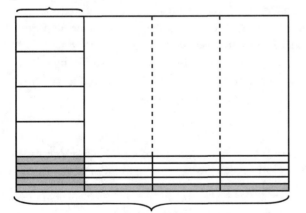

THE CASE OF JANICE PATTERSON

1.   Janice Patterson always considered herself to be a good mathematics
student. She did well in the mathematics courses she took and really
enjoyed the challenge they presented. Although she had wanted to be a
teacher as long as she could remember, it was her success in mathematics
in high school that convinced her that she should teach mathematics.
Once she started teaching, she looked for ways to continue to learn more
mathematics.

2.   In the past 3 years she has found that actually teaching mathematics
to students at Lincoln Middle School has provided her with the opportunity to continue her own learning. Preparing to teach students—many
of whom do not share her love of mathematics and/or have shaky
foundations on which to build—has challenged her to go beyond the
algorithms and rules that previously had been the cornerstone of her
instruction. In the process of trying to see mathematics through the eyes
of her students, she has been asking WHY about things she previously had
taken for granted. As a result, she has come to believe that although
algorithms are important, they are not enough.

3.   Janice is now committed to removing the mystery from doing
mathematics. Her goal is to help students develop strategies that will
help them make sense of mathematics. In doing so, she too has made
connections that she had not considered previously and has developed
new ways of approaching old problems.

Janice Patterson Talks About Her Class

4.   Last week my 7th-grade students began a unit on ratio and proportion. (Although we had done a lot of work with percents during the past
month, we had not used the language of ratio and proportion to describe the relationships.) I began the new unit by introducing the concept of ratio as a way of comparing the number of black pieces with the
number of red pieces in collections (e.g., two black pieces to five red
pieces would be the ratio of 2 to 5). We then moved on to describe other
collections of pieces that had the same basic ratio (e.g., 4 to 10; 6 to 15;
40 to 100). We concluded the introduction by filling in the missing
values in a table, such as the one shown in Table 5.1, and having students
discuss their methods for finding the missing values.

TABLE 5.1. The Table Students Used to Determine the Missing Values
in Collections of Black and Red Pieces

Ratio of Black to Red Pieces	Number of Black Pieces	Number of Red Pieces	Total Number of Pieces
3 to 5			24
	7	12	
2 to 3	10		
	10		40

5.   Although the "pieces" are a good way to help students begin to think about ratios, they have two limitations. First, they represent discrete quantities and therefore are not applicable in modeling situations that involve continuous quantities. The second problem is that they are very abstract and have no connection to the "real world." So, we are now moving on to story problems involving percents and ratios that address both of these issues. The problems involve continuous quantities and two of the three problems are set in a context.

6.   The three problems we will be working on (shown in Figure 5.2) are not all the same type but each problem involves reasoning about quantities and relationships—important components of proportional reasoning. I think it is important to give problems to students in which they have to determine what they know and what they need to figure out, and then develop a plan for doing so. When all the problems are the same type and can be done with a specific rule, there is not much thinking involved once you decide how to solve the first problem. Too often students are asked to do word problems that are of a cookie-cutter variety—they all use the same basic procedure. This set of problems will be different. Solving one problem correctly will not necessarily help students solve the next problem correctly.

FIGURE 5.2. The Three Problems That Janice Patterson Gave to Her Students

---

1. The ratio of the length of a rectangle to its width is 4 to 3. Its area is 300 square inches. What are its length and width?

2. A length of string that is 180 cm long is cut into 3 pieces. The second piece is 25% longer than the first and the third piece is 25% shorter than the first. How long is each piece?

3. If 50 gallons of cream with 20% butterfat are mixed with 150 gallons of milk with 4% butterfat, what percent butterfat is the mixture?

From *Visual Mathematics: Course II, Lessons 21–30* published by The Math Learning Center. Copyright © 1996 by The Math Learning Center, Salem, Oregon. Reprinted by permission.

7.   In today's lesson, I am going to stress how diagrams and sketches can help students solve the problems they encounter. We have used these forms of representation throughout our work on fractions, decimals, and percents, so this will not be a new idea for my students. I think that the value of diagrams and sketches is that they help students to make sense of situations and to communicate their thinking.

The Class

8.   I distributed the problem set and asked students to work in pairs to solve the problems. I suggested that they start with the first problem and told them that I will check in with them in a few minutes to see if they are ready to discuss it. I encouraged them to go on to the second problem if they completed the first one before we were ready to discuss it as a

class. Since working together is standard practice in my classroom, the students immediately got to work—reading the problem, making sketches to help in understanding the problem, and discussing possible strategies for solving it. As they worked, I checked in with the pairs and asked them to explain the rationale for a particular approach, to propose alternative approaches, or to provide evidence that a proposed solution met the conditions stated in the problem. About 10 minutes into the class, it appeared that most pairs had completed the first problem. I decided to have a few pairs present their work on the first problem before they continued work on the remaining problems.

Considering the First Problem

9.   A number of pairs volunteered to share their solution to the first problem, and I chose Lamont and Richard since they had not shared a solution in the past few days. After briefly restating information given in the problem, Lamont indicated that 3 times 4 was equal to 12, and they needed "a number that both 3 and 4 would go into." When I asked why they had multiplied 3 and 4, the pair indicated that the ratio of the length to the width initially was given as "4 to 3." Lamont and Richard (with Lamont doing most of the talking for the pair) went on to say that they had determined that "3 goes into 15 five times and 4 goes into 20 five times, too." Since 15 times 20 is equal to 300, the area of the given rectangle, they concluded that these numbers represented the width and length of the rectangle, respectively.

10.   At the conclusion of their presentation, I asked the class if they had any questions for Lamont and Richard. Tashika commented that she did not understand their solution, particularly where the 12 had come from. Neither Lamont nor Richard was able to explain why they had multiplied 3 and 4 or how the result of that multiplication (12) connected to their thinking in obtaining the solution. I indicated that I, too, had wondered how they had obtained the 15 and 20. Lamont and Richard declared that they had been looking for a number "that both 3 and 4 went into." At this point I asked the pair how they had obtained the number 5. Lamont and Richard responded that 5 was what "3 and 4 go into." At this point Sarah asked, "Did you guys just guess and check?" to which Lamont and Richard responded in unison, "Yeah!"

11.   Although Lamont and Richard's answer to the problem was correct, their explanation of their "guess-and-check" strategy clearly left the class confused about the relationship between the information given in the problem, the strategy used, and the answer obtained. I was concerned about students being confused by the presented solution, but I did not want to step in and explain the solution myself. So, I asked the class if anyone had another way to look at the problem that they would like to share. Kevin and Maria said that they would show their way, but that it was "sort of" like Lamont and Richard's.

12.   Maria began by saying that they knew that the length and width really weren't 4 and 3 because 4 × 3 was not 300 and you needed two numbers that would multiply to get 300. "But," she said, "you needed to multiply both 3 and 4 by some other number that would give you numbers that

TABLE 5.2. Kevin and Maria's Table for the First Problem

Width	Length	Area
3 × 2 = 6	4 × 2 = 8	48
3 × 3 = 9	4 × 3 = 12	108
3 × 4 = 12	4 × 4 = 16	192
3 × 5 = 15	4 × 5 = 20	300

would multiply to get 300." At this point I was a bit confused, but asked the pair if they could show us what they meant. Kevin said that they had made a table (shown in Table 5.2).

13.   "In the first column," he explained, "you multiply 3 by a number to find the width, in the next column you multiply 4 by the same number to find the length, and in the last column you multiply the width and length to find the area." He continued, pointing to the first row of the table, "So, if you multiply 3 and 4 by two you get a width of 6 and a length of 8, which gives you 48. This is not enough. Then you multiply 3 and 4 by three in the second row. You just keep doing this until you get the answer." He then asked if anyone had any questions. Tanya asked why they multiplied by 2, 3, 4, and 5. Maria said that if they needed to find numbers that had the same ratio as 3 to 4 and that if they just kept multiplying 3 and 4 by larger and larger numbers, they would finally get the one that worked. Kevin jumped in, "You need to multiply 3 and 4 by the same number so that the ratio stays the same. So, like 6 to 8, 9 to 12, 12 to 16, and 15 to 20 are all the same ratio as 3 to 4. They all reduce down to 3 to 4." Claudia asked, "How do you know when it works?" Kevin responded, "It works when you get 300!"

14.   I thought that Kevin and Maria's solution made sense. It provided a more systematic approach to the guess-and-check strategy, and it showed the importance of using the same factor when finding the lengths and widths of new rectangles in order to keep a constant ratio. I wanted students to also see an approach that did not rely on guessing. I asked if anyone had solved the problem another way. Robin said that she and Kalla had done it differently. I asked them to come up and present their solution.

15.   Kalla began by making a sketch of a rectangle, labeling the length 4, the width 3, and the area 300 square inches. She explained that the 4 and 3 represented the ratio of the length to the width rather than the actual length and width of the rectangle. Continuing the presentation, Robin indicated that there would be 12 squares in the interior of the rectangle, because 3 × 4 was equal to 12. Therefore, the pair concluded, the 300 square inches that made up the area of the rectangle must be equally distributed among the 12 squares. By dividing 300 by 12, they determined that each of the 12 squares would contain 25 square inches. Robin then put a 25 in each square in order to make this point clear (as shown in Figure 5.3a).

16.   Robin then explained that, in order to find the length and width of the original rectangle, they had to determine the length of the side of

each inside square. If the area of each inside square was 25, she argued, then the side of each square would be 5 inches. Erasing the 3 and 4 she previously had written on the diagram, she wrote in 5 inches to represent the side of each square as shown in her revised diagram (shown in Figure 5.3b). She then explained that the length of the entire rectangle would be 20 inches, since it contained the sides of four squares, and that the width of the rectangle would be 15 inches, since it contained the sides of three squares.

17.   At the conclusion of their presentation, one student commented that the solution and strategy that Kalla and Robin had presented was "cool." Another student pointed out that their answer was identical to the one given by the other two pairs. I noted that their answer was indeed the same, but that they had used a different approach to solve the problem.

Continuing with the Second Problem

18.   At this point I thought we should move on to the remaining problems since we were about halfway through the class. I told students that I wanted them to continue working on Problems 2 and 3 and that I would continue to check on their progress. The students did not seem to be having any trouble with the second problem. It was interesting to see that several students immediately began drawing diagrams to represent the lengths of string. When I learned to do problems of this type, I set up an equation where x was the length of the first piece of string (i.e., $x + x + .25x + x - .25x = 180$), solved for x, and then found the lengths of the other two pieces. Although this was an efficient way to get an answer, I am not sure how much I understood about what I was doing. Also, I was in high school before I ever saw problems like this, not in 7th grade.

19.   Although less than 10 minutes had passed, everyone seemed to be done with the second problem, so I indicated that we were ready to discuss it. Rather than asking for volunteers to present the solution and

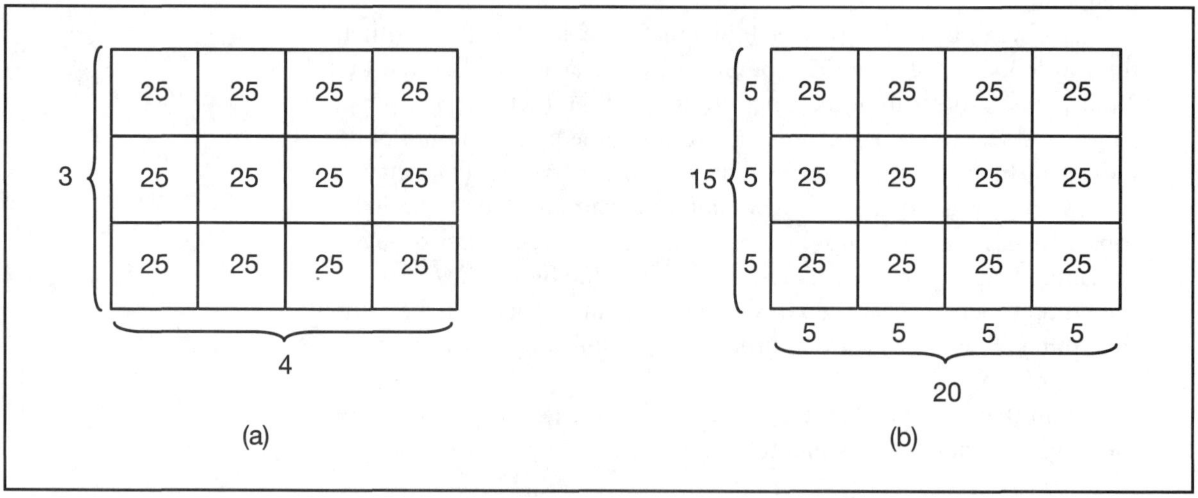

FIGURE 5.3. (a) Kalla and Robin's Initial Diagram for the First Problem; (b) Kalla and Robin's Revised Diagram for the First Problem

method, this time I decided to invite Sasha to share her approach with the class. I had noticed that Sasha made extensive use of the diagram and I wanted students who had not considered this method to have an opportunity to do so. Also, I wanted to avoid going through the guess-and-check approach to this problem, which several students had used. Although it is a fine strategy, especially in the early stages of problem-solving, we were reaching the point where I felt it was time for students to be using more sophisticated approaches.

20.   Sasha proceeded to the overhead and immediately began to draw. I asked her if she would explain as she went along what she was doing. She began, "The piece of string was 180 centimeters long and it was cut in three pieces. So, I drew a line and labeled it 180 centimeters." (See Sasha's drawing in Figure 5.4a.)

21.   She continued, "Then, I divided 180 by 3 and got 60. So that if the three pieces were equal they would each be 60 centimeters." (See Figure 5.4b.)

22.   At this point Elizabeth had her hand waving. I alerted Sasha that Elizabeth had a question. Sasha called on Elizabeth. Elizabeth said, "But they are not equal so they can't all be 60." Sasha responded that she wasn't done yet. She had just used the 60 to get started. Sasha resumed her explanation: "So then it says the second piece is 25 percent longer and the third piece is 25 percent shorter. So, I divided each piece into four sections so I could see how big 25 percent was. (See Figure 5.4c.) So

FIGURE 5.4. (a) Sasha's Initial Diagram for the Second Problem; (b) Sasha's Diagram for the Second Problem with Additional Detail; (c) Sasha's Diagram for the Second Problem That Shows Each Piece Divided into Four Sections; (d) Sasha's Final Diagrams for the Second Problem.

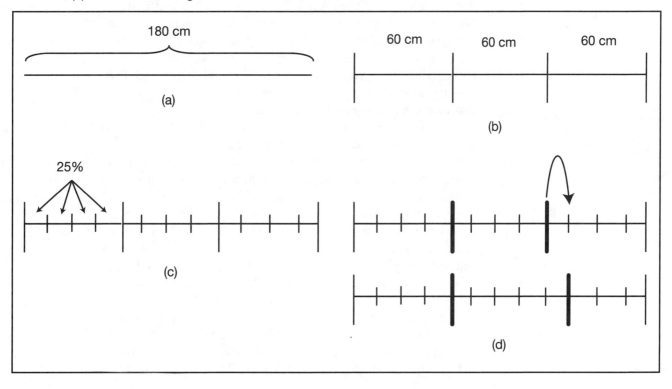

then I made the second piece 25 percent longer and the third piece 25 percent shorter by moving the line over." (See Figure 5.4d for Sasha's final diagram.)

23.   "So finally, I had to figure out how many centimeters each piece was. The first piece is 60 because it was 60 to begin with and I never changed it. Each section of the piece is 15 centimeters because 60 divided by 4 is 15. So, the second piece is 75 because there are five sections, and the third piece is 45 because there are three sections. And 60 plus 75 plus 45 is 180, so that's it."

24.   I asked the class if they had any questions for Sasha. David asked, "How did you know that each of the sections of the first piece was equal to 15 centimeters?" Sasha explained, "Well, if the piece is 60 centimeters and each of the parts is equal, then I tried to find a number that times 4 was 60. So I divided 60 by 4." Leon added, "You can just multiply 60 by .25 and that gives you 15, too." Sasha appeared to think about Leon's alternative approach and then added, "Yup. Leon's right. You could do that too." Kyle asked, "But how did you know to divide the piece into 4 sections?" Sasha responded that 25% was the same as ¼ and that she wanted to see how big 25% would be so that she could make the second piece that much bigger and the third piece that much smaller.

25.   I thanked Sasha for her presentation and the class for their good questions. I decided not to ask for another way to do this problem. I knew that the third problem was going to take some time and I wanted my students to begin work on it.

Beginning Work on the Third Problem

26.   Students set to work on the final problem. I suspected that this problem would be difficult. When I listened into the conversation of the first pair I visited, my suspicion was confirmed. One of the students, Jason, was arguing that the answer was 24%, "because you just add the two percents together." His partner Angela, however, countered with, "You can't just add them. It was 20 percent of 50 gallons. So, it would be a smaller percent if you mixed it into 200 gallons." Although I was hearing some interesting points being raised by the pair, I was concerned that they were talking past one another.

27.   With less than 10 minutes left in class and considerable confusion about how to proceed, I thought that a whole-class discussion of the issues that were being raised by Jason and Angela would be helpful. I asked Jason if he would like to explain how he and his partner were thinking about the problem. I wasn't looking for a solution at this point, just a starting point for the discussion of the problem.

28.   Jason began by saying that he had thought it was 24% but that Angela said that it would be smaller. David asked, "Why would it have to be smaller?" Angela explained, "It's 4 percent of 150. That's a little percent of a big amount. It's 20 percent of 50. That's a big percent of a smaller amount. So if you mixed the 50 gallons and the 150 gallons together, you get 200 gallons. The 20 percent that was in the 50 gallons is now mixed in the whole amount." David then asked, "So what percent would it be if it is not 24 percent?" Angela said that she didn't know yet but that it had to be more than 4% but less than 20%. I asked Angela if the answer

would be closer to 4% or to 20%. She responded, "I think it will be closer to 4 percent because the 150 gallons has only 4 percent butterfat now, so when you mix in the 50 gallons of cream, the 20 percent butterfat gets stirred into the whole mixture. So now that 20 percent gets spread out over the whole mixture of 200 gallons. It will give you more butterfat than the 4 percent, but it has to be a lot less than 20 percent."

29.   I asked the class if what Angela said made sense to them. I saw most of the 25 heads in the room nodding in the affirmative. "Okay," I said, "now that we know that the answer needs to be in the range of 4 percent to 20 percent, and maybe closer to 4 percent, how can we figure it out?" At this point Dametris said, "We have two different percents and two different amounts so we gotta make them alike somehow." I said that this sounded like a good suggestion and asked if anyone had any ideas about how to make them alike. Crystal said, "We could find out how much 20 percent and 4 percent is gallon-wise." I asked her to explain what she meant by "gallon-wise." She went on to say that we should find how many gallons of butterfat were in 50 gallons of cream and in the 150 gallons of milk before we mix them together.

30.   I asked her how she thought we could do this. Crystal said that she would draw a diagram. I invited her to the overhead to do so. She began by drawing a rectangle, as shown in Figure 5.5, and indicating the rectangle represented all 50 gallons of cream. She then explained, "It says that 20 percent is butterfat. That is one-fifth, so I divided the rectangle into five equal pieces and shaded the amount of butterfat."

31.   "Each of these pieces must contain 10 gallons. So there are 10 gallons of butterfat in the 50 gallons of cream." I asked if anyone had any questions for Crystal. Leon said, "Can't you just multiply 50 times .20 without a picture of it? I did it that way and I got 10 gallons, too. I don't

FIGURE 5.5. Crystal's Diagram for the Third Problem

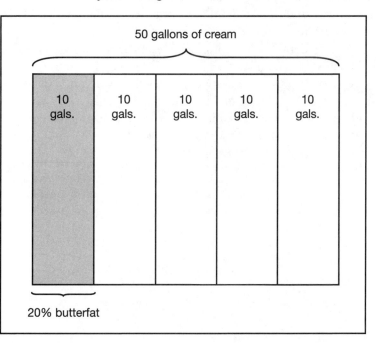

see why you need a picture." Crystal responded by saying that maybe you didn't need the picture to multiply, but that she needed the picture in order to figure out what to do. At this point I said that I wanted students to go back to their pairs for the remaining 5 minutes of class and see if they could discuss how they could finish the problem by building on Crystal's or Leon's approaches or by trying some other approach to the problem. For homework, I explained, they were to complete the problem and provide an explanation of how they solved it.

Reflection

32.   I thought class went reasonably well and that students did a good job with the problems. I knew the last problem would be the most difficult, but I really thought they would be able to reason their way through it. Crystal's initial effort suggests that this was true for some students, although I think her diagram may have been confusing to some. I hope that my students actually will think about how to use Crystal's reasoning to determine the percent of butterfat in the 200-gallon mixture. I have found that using rectangles to represent quantities can really help you to see the relationship between the quantities and to make sense out of the situations presented. I see this visual approach as providing a really good foundation for students. Once they understand "how things work," students will be prepared to deal with algebraic/symbolic methods later on. The benefit of the symbolic approach is that it works equally well for "nice" or "messy" numbers, and it is fast and efficient. When my students do encounter symbolic approaches, I hope that they will be able to relate these new approaches to more conceptual ways of thinking about problems. So developing Crystal's method, or any visual method, at this point makes sense since it will provide the conceptual underpinnings that are necessary in order to make meaning of more symbolic approaches.

33.   Tomorrow I am going to start class by asking the pairs to form groups of four and to talk about their progress on the problem. During this time I can look around and see how students solved the problem and hopefully identify a few who can share their work. Crystal and Leon seem like possible candidates. I also will be looking for solutions that use other types of diagrams. I will suggest a few if they do not come out of the discussion naturally. I often introduce such examples by saying that a student in another class solved it this way, and inviting students to critique the proposed method.

ANALYZING THE CASE

Now that you have had an opportunity to "visit" Janice Patterson's classroom and note what her students were doing during the class that may have contributed to their learning, we invite you to consider the teacher's role in the lesson. Specifically: Did Janice Patterson really teach? She seemed to do and say very little during this class. What was her role in this lesson? Here are a few suggestions on how to proceed.

- Review the list you created during your initial reading of the case in which you identified what students in Janice Patterson's class were doing during class that may have contributed to their learning. For each item on your list indicate *how* this may have contributed to students' learning and what the teacher did (or may have done) before or during the class to create or facilitate this opportunity. Be sure to cite specific evidence (i.e., paragraph numbers) from the case to support your claims.
- Consider Janice Patterson's role as the teacher in this lesson by reviewing the list of teacher actions identified above. How would you characterize her role? What are the most important facets of this role? Cite specific evidence from the case to support your argument.
- If you have colleagues who also are reading this case, compare and contrast the ideas in your individual lists and possibly generate a master list. Note points of disagreement since these are likely to be fruitful topics for further discussion and debate. If you are working on this activity alone, we encourage you to refer to Appendix D, which includes a list that was produced by teachers who participated in a professional development experience that focused on "The Case of Janice Patterson." You may want to note points of agreement and disagreement and flag issues that you wish to investigate.

You may wish to extend your analysis of the case by considering the questions in the next section. Alternatively, you can skip the next section and proceed directly to the "Connecting to Your Own Practice" section, in which you are encouraged to relate the analysis of the ideas and issues raised in the case to your own teaching practice.

EXTENDING YOUR ANALYSIS OF THE CASE

The questions listed in this section are intended to help you focus on particular aspects of the case related to teacher decision-making and student thinking. You may want to focus on one that addresses an issue with which you have been grappling. If you are working in collaboration with one or more colleagues, one or more of the questions can serve as a stimulus for further discussion and debate.

1. Mrs. Patterson structures her lesson around challenging problems that incorporate proportional reasoning concepts but are very different in content and in structure. What does it mean to teach mathematics *through* problem-solving or to center a lesson around a challenging task in the way that Mrs. Patterson did? Would it be possible for all of Mrs. Patterson's lessons to look like this one? Why or why not?
2. Mrs. Patterson appears to have established a problem-solving environment in her classroom. How might Mrs. Patterson have created such an environment? What experiences and opportunities would students need in order to engage in the lesson in the way that Mrs. Patterson's students did?
3. Mrs. Patterson intends for students to strengthen their proportional reasoning skills by engaging in problems that require multiplicative thinking. What evidence can you find that Mrs. Patterson's students are reasoning proportionally?
4. Mrs. Patterson intends for students to gain experience in using visual diagrams to solve problems. In what ways did visual diagrams help support her students' thinking?
5. Although Lamont and Richard admit to using a guess-and-check strategy for Problem 1, they want to explain how their solution connects back to the conditions in the problem. Why might the boys feel compelled to give an explanation rather than sharing their guess-and-check strategy? What do Lamont and Richard seem to understand? Do any of their comments make sense, or could they be rephrased to make sense?
6. For Problem 2, compare part-to-part to part-to-whole relationships by determining the percent of the whole string that each piece represents. Is the first string 25% larger than the shortest string? Is the first string 25% smaller than the largest string? Why do these answers seem inconsistent?

7. How might Angela's comments (para. 28) relate to V.J. and Trina's diagram for Problem 3 (shown in Figure 5.1c)?
8. Could Mrs. Patterson's students have solved the first two problems successfully without using their visual approaches? What other strategies might they have used?

CONNECTING TO YOUR OWN PRACTICE

The activities described in this section are designed to help you consider the ways in which issues identified in Mrs. Patterson's classroom have implications for your own teaching of mathematics. Alternative views of teaching and learning mathematics place teachers and students in much different roles than they previously might have played. In particular,

> [I]nstead of acting as the main source of mathematical information and the evaluator of correctness, the teacher now has the role of selecting and posing appropriate sequences of problems as opportunities for learning, sharing information when it is essential for tackling problems, and facilitating the establishment of a classroom culture in which pupils work on novel problems individually and interactively, and discuss and reflect on their answers and methods. (Hiebert et al., 1997, p. 8)

Here are a few activities that will help you move from consideration of Janice Patterson's teaching to a focus on your own classroom practices.

- In the "Analyzing the Case" section, you considered ways in which Janice Patterson's role in the classroom constituted "teaching" mathematics. Teach a lesson (using the task from "The Case of Janice Patterson" or another task that has the potential to foster students' thinking and reasoning) and record the lesson using videotape or audiotape, or have a colleague observe and take notes. As you reflect on the lesson consider the following questions: What was your role in the lesson? What was the role of your students in the lesson? How do your role and that of your students compare with the roles of the teacher and students in Mrs. Patterson's classroom? What might you do differently the next time you teach (to further enhance students' learning and/or to help students understand their role in the lesson)?
- Review the list you created during the case analysis in which you indicated what Janice Patterson did

(or may have done) before or during the lesson to create or facilitate students' learning opportunities. Select one of the teacher "moves" from this list that you feel has implications for your own teaching. Plan and teach a lesson in which you purposefully address the identified pedagogical issue. For example, you may be curious about the ways in which Mrs. Patterson used Jason and Angela's disagreement about how to solve Problem 3 to launch a whole-class discussion. You might then plan and teach a lesson in which you make a concerted effort to promote discourse by having students consider two different arguments. If possible, audiotape or videotape the lesson, or have a colleague observe and take notes. As you go back over the lesson, reflect on the changes you made and the impact these changes appeared to have had on students' learning. Also indicate what you still need to work on with respect to this pedagogy.

EXPLORING CURRICULAR MATERIALS

You may want to explore your curriculum for ideas related to proportional reasoning by considering the following questions: Do students have the opportunity to engage in solving story problems involving percents and ratios that are not of a cookie-cutter variety? If not, could the curriculum be modified so as to include such problems? In what ways might working on problems of this type strengthen students' understanding of proportionality? What role could diagrams and sketches play in helping students develop this understanding?

You also may want to explore the mathematical ideas made salient in the case, by investigating mathematical tasks drawn from other curricular materials. The following list identifies curricula that contain problems considered to be "mathematically similar" to the task used in Janice Patterson's class.

Foreman, L. C., & Bennett, A. B., Jr. (1998). *Math alive! Course III, Lessons 13–17.* Salem, OR: The Math Learning Center.
Of particular interest in Lesson 13 (Modeling Situations) are Actions 1–11 in the Focus Teacher Activity (pp. 341–345). Students use diagrams to solve problems that typically are solved algebraically (e.g., Find the two numbers whose sum is 40 and whose difference is 14).
Foreman, L. C., & Bennett, A. B., Jr. (1996b). *Visual mathematics: Course II, Lessons 21–30.* Salem, OR: The Math Learning Center.
Of particular interest in Lesson 22 (Picturing Percentage Problems) are Actions 1–6 in the Focus Teacher

Activity (pp. 347–351). Students are asked to not only use diagrams to model mathematical situations but also explain how to reason from them. One of the problems in Lesson 22 is identical to the second problem used in "The Case of Janice Patterson."

The Mathematics in Context Development Team. (1998a). *Mathematics in context: Decision making (Student guide).* In National Center for Research in Mathematical Sciences Education & Freudenthal Institute (Eds.), *Mathematics in context.* Chicago: Encyclopaedia Britannica.

Of particular interest are Problems 1–2 (p. 15). Students could solve these coin situation problems using a variety of strategies and representations.

CONNECTING TO OTHER IDEAS AND ISSUES

If you have additional time, you may want to explore some aspect of the case in more depth. The resources identified below provide some possibilities for exploring the mathematical and pedagogical issues raised in the case. For example, you might: (1) discuss how the problems described in Barb and Quinn (1997) could be solved using visual diagrams; (2) compare Janice Patterson's role in the lesson to Hiebert and colleagues' (1997) description of the role of teacher; (3) use J. P. Smith's (1996) "new moorings for efficacy" (pp. 396–397) and/or the key elements identified in M. S. Smith (2000, p. 382) to analyze Janice Patterson's teaching and discuss whether or not she has established new moorings for herself and her students; (4) discuss how the definition of teaching you created in your analysis of the case is similar to or different from the definition created by teachers in the course described in Smith (2001).

Barb, C., & Quinn, A. L. (1997). Problem solving does not have to be a problem. *Mathematics Teacher, 90,* 536–542.

The authors briefly review the history of the role of problem-solving in the curriculum. They propose to help students develop problem-solving skills by building on their prior knowledge and helping them to refine their own strategies. The authors then argue that students should solve traditional algebra word problems (e.g., mixture problems) in ways that make sense, that is, by using multiple strategies and/or representations instead of using algebra. The authors conclude with a discussion of how a mixture problem (similar to Problem 3 in the case) could be solved using visual approaches rather than algebraic ones.

Hiebert, J., Carpenter, T. P., Fennema, E., Wearne, D., Murray, H., Olivier, A., & Human, P. (1997). *Making sense: Teaching and learning mathematics with understanding.* Portsmouth, NH: Heinemann.

In Chapter 3 (pp. 29–41), the authors describe two responsibilities of the teacher: providing direction for the mathematical activities of the class and guiding the development of the classroom culture. The final chapters (7–10) of the book offer glimpses of several elementary mathematics classrooms in which teachers promote learning with understanding by taking on these responsibilities.

Smith, J. P. (1996). Efficacy and teaching mathematics by telling: A challenge for reform. *Journal for Research in Mathematics Education, 27,* 387–402.

The author briefly summarizes the literature on teacher beliefs and, in particular, teachers' beliefs about what it means to be successful and know they have achieved success. The author discusses how current reform efforts challenge teachers and the community to develop new measures of teacher success, and concludes by suggesting new measures for teacher efficacy.

Smith, M. S. (2000). Redefining success in mathematics teaching and learning. *Mathematics Teaching in the Middle School, 5,* 378–382, 386.

The author describes how one teacher revised her definition of success—for herself and her students—during the course of a school year. The teacher's new moorings for success are described in detail.

Smith, M. S. (2001). Using cases to discuss changes in mathematics teaching. *Mathematics Teaching in the Middle School, 7,* 144–149.

The author describes her use of "The Case of Janice Patterson" in a mathematics methods course for preservice elementary and secondary teachers. Of particular interest are the issues raised by participants as they discussed what it means to teach.

PART II

FACILITATING LEARNING FROM CASES

In Part II of this book (Chapters 6–10), we turn our attention to providing support for case facilitators. Chapter 6 serves as an opening to this section of the book and describes how to facilitate learning from the cases. Chapters 7 through 10 provide support materials intended to assist facilitators in utilizing the cases and related materials provided in Chapters 2 through 5. Part II is intended primarily for those readers who will be facilitating discussions around the cases and related materials found in Part I. These facilitators may include any professionals who contribute to improving the quality of mathematics teaching and learning through their work in diverse settings such as schools (e.g., teacher leaders, coaches, mentors, administrators); school district offices (e.g., curriculum coordinators, staff developers); regional intermediate units and state agencies; or colleges and universities (e.g., instructors of mathematics or methods courses).

Using Cases to Support Learning About Teaching

The cases found in Part I of this book embody a vision of mathematics teaching and learning that is very different from how most teachers have learned mathematics and learned to teach mathematics. The vision calls for students who can think and reason about challenging and complex problems that give rise to significant mathematical understandings. It also calls for teachers who can appropriately scaffold and support students' learning by creating environments that foster communication, inquiry, and investigation. It is now widely accepted that meeting these goals and standards will require a great deal of learning on the part of teachers, the vast majority of whom were taught and learned to teach under a paradigm in which memorization, repetition, and speed were of paramount importance.

The kind of learning that is required of teachers has been described as transformative (i.e., sweeping changes in deeply held beliefs, knowledge, and habits of practice) as opposed to additive (the addition of new skills to an existing repertoire) (Thompson & Zeuli, 1999). Teachers of mathematics cannot successfully develop their students' thinking, reasoning, and communication skills simply by adopting a new curriculum or by using more hands-on materials. Rather, they must thoroughly overhaul their thinking about what it means to know and understand mathematics and how they can best support their students in the struggle to learn deeper and more complex mathematics.

One approach to helping teachers transform their practice involves situating the professional education of teachers "in practice" (Smith, 2001). In a seminal paper on this topic, Ball and Cohen (1999) argue that "teachers' everyday work could become a source for constructive professional development" (p. 6) through the development of a curriculum for professional learning that is grounded in the tasks, questions, and problems of practice. They propose that teachers' instructional practice be seen both as a site for professional learning and also as a stimulus for developing inquiry into practice from which many teachers could learn. To accomplish this goal, they argue that records of authentic practice—curriculum materials, narrative or video summaries of teachers planning for and/or engaging in instruction, samples of student work—should become the core of professional education, providing a focus for sustained teacher inquiry and investigation.

This book represents such an approach to teacher education. The materials and activities in Part I encourage teachers to construct knowledge central to teaching by engaging in activities that are built around artifacts of classroom practice. Cases—the centerpiece of the materials—provide the opportunity to analyze how teacher and student interactions in the classroom influence what students learn. The instructional tasks that appear in the Opening Activities (which are drawn from actual classroom practice) invite teachers to explore important mathematical ideas. Finally, activities such as the comparison of the cases and/or instructional tasks to teachers' own practice, or to other curricular materials, provide yet more opportunities for teachers to learn about practice from the actual work of practice.

WHY CASES?

Similar to many other teacher educators, we have been drawn to cases because they capture the complexity and situatedness of instructional practice. Unlike theories, propositions, principles, or other abstractions, the particularities of cases vividly convey the profusion of events, actions, and thought that constitute the moment-by-moment lived experience of a classroom lesson. As such, we have found that teachers resonate with cases in a way that they do not with educational theories or methods textbooks. Told through the voice of the classroom teacher, our cases offer the additional advantage of allowing the reader to "listen in" as the teacher in the case struggles with the multitude of decisions and dilemmas that constitute the lived experience of the middle school mathematics classroom. Cases are also an effective medium for capturing the *interdependence* of teachers' knowledge of mathematics, pedagogy, and students. By exposing how these different kinds of knowledge are accessed and used in the decisions that teachers make, cases portray how teachers simultaneously think about and pull from mathematical knowledge, pedagogical expertise, and knowledge of how students learn mathematics, in order to reach an instructional goal.

LEARNING FROM CASES

In order to learn from cases, teachers must do more than simply read them. We have found it useful to distinguish between two classes of activities in which teachers engage in order to learn from cases: analysis and generalization. Analysis involves the careful examination of a teacher's decisions and interactions with students in light of the goals that the teacher wishes to accomplish with respect to student learning. Generalization involves viewing the particularities of case-based episodes as instantiations of a broader set of ideas about mathematics, about teaching, and about learning. Each of these is discussed in more detail below.

Analysis

Analyzing instructional practice involves the interpretation of teacher thinking and action in the context of the overall lesson. For example, one might be interested in analyzing how a teacher's questions influenced students' opportunities to learn. This would involve paying attention to not only the frequency and kinds of questions asked by the teacher, but also when, of whom, and about what she asked those questions. In this way, the analysis goes beyond simply counting the frequency of, for example, higher- versus lower-order questions, to a focus on examining why a particular question asked of a particular student at a particular moment in the lesson may have led to opportunities for significant student learning. For example, we frequently have used "The Case of Marcia Green" (Chapter 4) to help teach-

ers learn to analyze teacher questioning. After teachers identify "good questions" asked by Marcia, they are encouraged to discern what makes the questions they have identified effective. Invariably, this leads to teachers' recognition of the importance of what else is going on at the point in the lesson at which the "good question" was asked. For example, in one case discussion, teachers commented on how questions asked earlier in the lesson (and students' responses to those questions) actually laid the groundwork for the next set of "good questions."

Because they appear as narratives in print form, the cases in this book represent a controlled way for teachers to learn these skills of lesson analysis. Unlike observations of real teaching, teachers can "stop" the action at any moment to ponder the implications of a particular decision. They can even revisit a particular part of the lesson in order to check the facts and deepen their analysis. Finally, narrative cases allow the reader to more easily keep the entire lesson in view while interpreting the teacher's action at a given point in the lesson.

Generalization

The ultimate goal of reading and analyzing cases is for teachers to be able to formulate ways of acting and interacting in *their own classrooms* that are thoughtful, principled, sharable, and effective (Shulman, 1992). In order to achieve this goal, teachers must learn to connect the specifics of deeply contextualized, case-based moments with a broader set of ideas about mathematics, about teaching, and about learning. Generalizing allows teachers to view the specific incidents within the cases as instantiations of larger patterns and principles—patterns and principles that will have applicability to their own practice as well.

To foster the development of this kind of skill, our cases are situated within a larger, more general set of mathematical and pedagogical ideas that we intend for teachers to ultimately understand and utilize to make sense of new situations that they will encounter in their own practice. Toward this end, well-conducted case discussions are crucial because they highlight the question, "What is this a case of?" thus stimulating learners "to move up and down, back and forth, between the memorable particularities of cases and powerful generalizations and simplifications of principles and theories" (Shulman, 1996, p. 201).

Our goal is for teachers, through reading and discussing cases, to connect the events depicted in the cases to an increasingly elaborated knowledge base of mathematics, teaching, and learning, and to their own practice. For example, in "The Case of Marie Hanson" (Chapter 3), teachers are exposed to Marie's thought processes as she monitors student work and decides which students to call on to present their solution strategies to the whole class and in what order. Marie decides to first call on a student who has solved the problem using an incorrect additive approach in order to air that misconception and then to move on to a student whose response was correct and accessible to other students in the class. In the case discussion, the facilitator can help teachers to view Marie's thinking and decisions as an instance of using student responses in a pedagogically productive way, a skill that applies in situations other than the specific situation in which Marie Hanson found herself.

WHAT CAN BE LEARNED FROM OUR CASES

In addition to learning the skills of analyzing and generalizing, there is also specific content that teachers can learn through engagement with our cases. As noted in Chapter 1, the cases were designed to instantiate a broader set of ideas about mathematics—in this volume, rational numbers and proportionality—and about ways in which teachers may support or inhibit students' learning in the context of cognitively challenging mathematical tasks. Each of these is discussed briefly below.

Rational Numbers and Proportionality

Despite strong consensus that proportional reasoning is central to the development of solid mathematical proficiency in the middle grades, there is much evidence that this domain is exceptionally challenging for students. Moreover, some teachers have difficulty differentiating situations in which the comparison between quantities is multiplicative rather than additive, tend to use additive strategies when multiplicative approaches would be appropriate, and do not recognize ratios as a multiplicative comparison (Post, Harel, Behr, & Lesh 1991; Simon & Blume, 1994; Sowder et al., 1998). Situations aimed at encouraging teachers to revisit and question their own understanding of rational number and proportionality have been purposefully built into the cases in this volume. We have embedded multiple opportunities for teachers to actively grapple with and make sense of quantities that are related multiplicatively. These include situations in which teachers are encouraged to develop a range of strategies for solv-

ing problems that require proportional reasoning (e.g., factor-of-change strategies, unit rate strategies, and ratio tables, in addition to cross-multiplication); situations in which teachers are encouraged to develop the flexibility that allows them to appropriately select from and use the particular strategy that is most efficient for a given problem; and situations in which teachers are encouraged to make use of a variety of representational forms (e.g., tables, diagrams, symbols) as a way of developing a robust understanding of the relationships and ideas that appear in various proportional reasoning tasks. Teachers are expected to develop deeper understandings of proportionality by encountering the above situations in our cases again and again, in different contexts, and in slightly different forms.

Ways of Supporting and Inhibiting Student Learning

After years of focusing on the mastery of nonambiguous, procedurally oriented skills—skills that are easy to mimic and apply successfully without much thought—many students find high-level tasks intimidating and anxiety provoking. As increasing numbers of middle schools have taken up the challenge of using more ambitious tasks, it has become clear that many teachers need assistance in learning how to support students' capacities to engage with and successfully complete these tasks. Those who are most effective are able to both retain high-level expectations for how students should tackle such tasks and provide the right kind and amount of assistance to allow students to succeed. Less effective teachers either supply too much assistance, essentially taking the difficult thinking away from the students and doing it for them, or fail to provide enough direction and assistance, allowing students to flounder in unsystematic and nonproductive ways.

Situations aimed at encouraging teachers to identify and understand ways of supporting students' learning of complex mathematical ideas have been purposefully built into the cases. We have embedded multiple opportunities for teachers to notice and analyze how student thinking can be supported during a lesson. These include situations in which the teachers in the cases keep expectations high by pressing students to explain and justify their thinking and reasoning; situations in which the case teachers assist students as they try to make connections between different solution paths, ways of representing a mathematical idea, or between a concept and a procedure; and situations in which the case teachers uncover and use student responses to problems in pedagogically productive ways for all students. As with the mathematical ideas, teachers are expected to develop deeper understandings of ways of supporting student thinking by encountering these ideas in our cases again and again, in different contexts, and in slightly different forms.

PREPARING FOR AND FACILITATING CASE DISCUSSIONS

Although we recognize that individual teachers may elect to use the cases on their own (and Part I is written to allow them to do so), we feel that engaging teachers as a group around the central ideas of the cases has even greater potential to lead to robust learning and improved practice. The success of group sessions, however, is directly dependent on the skill and preparedness of the facilitator. In this section, we describe how facilitators can prepare for and carry out effective learning experiences with groups of teachers using our cases.

Preparing for Case Discussions

Similar to the wisdom of teachers preparing for lessons by anticipating how their students will approach planned instructional tasks, it is a good idea for facilitators to prepare for case discussions by reading and thinking about the case from the perspective of teachers. We encourage facilitators to begin their preparations by completing the problems presented in the Opening Activity that precedes each case and then by reading the case itself. By keeping in mind how the specific group of teachers with whom they will be working might approach the Opening Activity and case, the facilitator often can predict what issues will arise and prepare to deal with them. The next preparation step is to study the facilitation materials that have been prepared for each case (found in Chapters 7–10 of Part II). These materials have been designed specifically to help facilitators assist teachers as they interact with the case materials. As the facilitation chapters were being written, we were keenly aware that the cases would be used in a variety of settings and with teachers at different points in their careers. Moreover, we expect that facilitators will have a variety of backgrounds and will be pursuing a multitude of important and worthwhile goals. Accordingly, the facilitation chapters do not prescribe certain formats or routes through case discussions. Rather they have been designed to make explicit what is embedded in the cases so that facilitators can make their own de-

cisions regarding how to connect learning opportunities in the cases to the particular group of teachers with whom they are working and the goals that they have for their work.

The heart of each facilitation chapter is the "Case Analysis." This section indexes the main ideas embedded in the cases; more specifically, it allows the facilitator to prepare for case discussions that connect particular, case-based incidents to larger, more generalizable sets of ideas. The "Case Analysis" has two major components. First, the key mathematical ideas are more fully described, and, for each idea, the specific places in the case that contain incidents related to that idea are listed. These incidents are identified by their paragraph numbers in the case and by a short explanation of how the incident relates to the mathematical idea. Next, the key pedagogical ideas are identified, accompanied by, as in the mathematics section, a list that provides markers of specific places in the case that contain incidents related to those ideas and a brief explanation of how the incident relates to the pedagogical idea.

A complaint sometimes raised about case discussions is that they can be "all over the board," with the facilitator appearing to have only loose control over what gets talked about and how. Becoming familiar with the materials in the "Case Analysis" section of a facilitation chapter will enable facilitators to avoid this pitfall and to lead a focused and productive case discussion. By studying both the mathematics and pedagogy sections of the "Case Analysis," facilitators will become familiar with the big ideas of the case and exactly where examples of those ideas are embedded in the case. This knowledge will help them to recognize when teachers are grappling with case incidents that have the potential to lead to deeper insights, to encourage teachers to consider specific episodes of the case at opportune moments, and to help teachers to look across various instances to surface the big ideas.

Other sections of a facilitation chapter will help the facilitator to prepare for activities related to the case discussions. For example, a section entitled "Facilitating the Opening Activity" provides suggestions for orchestrating teachers' learning during the Opening Activity—a mathematical problem-solving session that utilizes a task related to the mathematical task that is featured in the case. In "Facilitating the Case Discussion," suggestions are provided for how to have participants prepare for case discussions and various strategies for conducting the discussion. Finally, in "Extending the Case Experience," we provide facilitators with ideas regarding how they might extend teachers' explorations of the mathematical and pedagogical ideas on which the cases are based.

Facilitating Case-Based Experiences

We recommend having teachers work on the problems in the Opening Activity prior to reading the case. In our experience, having teachers complete and reflect on ways of solving the tasks in the Opening Activity is critical to a rich and successful case discussion. By grappling with the mathematics in the tasks, teachers become familiar and confident with the underlying mathematical ideas in the case and are therefore better prepared to think flexibly about the solution strategies that students produce as the case unfolds.

The role of the facilitator during the Opening Activity is to elicit a variety of solution strategies to the problems and, to the extent possible, help teachers to identify how those strategies are both similar to and different from one another. We have found it useful to have teachers work on the tasks first individually, then in small groups, and finally to participate in a large-group discussion in which various solution strategies are made public.

We also have found that case discussions are most productive when teachers have read the case on their own time prior to the session in which it will be discussed. In this regard, reading the case with a guiding question in mind appears to lead to more "active" reading of the case and more thoughtful and focused participation in the case discussion. Toward this end, we have provided suggestions in each facilitation chapter for ways to focus teachers' initial reading of the case.

Facilitating the case discussion itself is a learned skill. Not unlike classroom teachers, facilitators must listen intently to the participants and learn how to steer the conversation in useful directions. Toward this end, it is important for the facilitator to have specific teacher learning goals in mind for the case discussion. With respect to "The Case of Marie Hanson" (Chapter 3), for example, a facilitator may want teachers to be able to learn how to interpret and selectively use various student-generated solution strategies in whole-class discussions. To accomplish this goal, the facilitator would not only pose tasks that provided opportunities for teachers to notice how Marie Hanson used student responses, but would also listen carefully during the case discussion to the teachers' analyses of what occurred in Marie Hanson's class. A good facilitator would highlight and reinforce those comments that related to Marie

Hanson's productive use of student responses, would acknowledge but not extend or elaborate those comments that took the discussion in different directions, and would summarize across relevant comments in order to drive home the points that could be taken from the case related to her goal.

Extending Case-Based Experiences

Finally, facilitators sometimes choose to extend the case-based experiences by providing teachers with additional opportunities to explore the mathematical and pedagogical ideas on which each case is based. By moving beyond the specifics of a case and task, teachers can begin to examine their own practice in light of new understandings about mathematics, instruction, and student learning. The three types of activities presented below suggest ways in which you might extend the case experience.

Connecting to teachers' practice. Several suggestions are made in Chapters 2 through 5 in the section entitled "Connecting to Your Own Practice." You may wish to assign one or more of these activities as follow-up assignments for teachers to explore in their own classrooms.

You also might consider asking teachers to identify an issue that the case raised for them and collect these ideas into a master list of issues with which your particular group of teachers are grappling. You might then ask teachers to identify one issue that they would like to work on and begin working collaboratively on planning a lesson in which the issue can be addressed. By focusing on an issue, teachers will be able to base the lesson on whatever mathematical content they currently are teaching.

Exploring the mathematical ideas in curricular materials. You may want to have participants examine the manner in which the mathematical ideas portrayed in the case "play out" in their own curriculum. Ask teachers to identify tasks and the kind of thinking required to solve them, how the tasks build on students' prior knowledge, and how the tasks collectively shape students' learning of the mathematical content.

Alternatively, you may want to ask teachers to compare two different curricula. By comparing and contrasting curricula, teachers have the opportunity to see how different texts develop a particular mathematical idea or set of ideas and to analyze the extent to which the texts are designed to engage students in mathematical thinking and reasoning. (If you are working with preservice teachers, you may want to have them compare the curriculum that is used in the school in which they will be doing their student teaching with one that reflects an alternative view of mathematics teaching and learning.)

You also may want to have teachers engage in solving additional mathematical tasks. The tasks identified and described in the section entitled "Exploring Curricular Materials" in Chapters 2 through 5 are mathematically similar to the tasks featured in each case.

Using professional readings to enhance and extend learning. In the section entitled "Connecting to Other Ideas and Issues" in Chapters 2 through 5, several suggestions are made for how to use the resources that are identified and described. You may wish to assign one or more of the suggested activities and readings as follow-up assignments in order to help teachers broaden or deepen their understanding of rational number and proportionality and/or the teaching of those topics.

PUTTING THE PIECES TOGETHER

Based on our own experiences in using the cases and the experiences of colleagues, we can recommend their use in preservice mathematics methods and content courses, as well as in professional development efforts for practicing teachers. However, it is important to note that the cases in this volume are not meant to represent a complete curriculum for middle school mathematics teacher education.

Depending on one's circumstances, the cases can be used in a variety of ways. For example, facilitators may want to build a focused course around all four cases in this volume. We have designed and offered such a course on proportional reasoning to practicing and prospective elementary, middle school, and high school teachers using the cases in this volume as the backbone and supplementing them with related readings and activities. Details about this course can be found at *www.cometproject.com.* This website provides information regarding the goals for the course, specific activities used in the course, and the sequencing of course activities. In addition, the website contains instruments that we developed to measure what teachers learned about proportionality from the course as well as references to papers that describe what teachers appeared to learn. In other situations, facilitators may want to select one or two specific cases to blend into an existing teacher education agenda in order to address an identified need. Whatever the situation, in the chapters that follow facilitators will find the support that they need to make optimal use of each of the cases.

Facilitating Learning from The Case of Randy Harris

"The Case of Randy Harris" portrays the work of a 7th-grade teacher and his students at Stevenson Middle School as they work over 2 days using rectangular grids to represent quantities expressed as fractions, decimals, and percents, and to connect different representations of the same quantity. Although Mr. Harris's students struggle at times to reason from and with the rectangular grids, Mr. Harris continues to press students to use the diagrams to solve the problems and to focus their attention on the ways in which the diagrams can help them make sense of the situation. He supports his students as they work through the problems, by soliciting multiple ways of solving the problems and recording these methods so that students can refer to them in their ongoing work. At the conclusion of the lesson, students are left with the task of solving the last problem in Set B in as many ways as they can.

CASE ANALYSIS

In this section, we provide a detailed analysis of the mathematical and pedagogical ideas that are found in the case. These analyses may help you in determining which aspects of the case you wish to highlight during the discussion.

Considering the Mathematics in the Case

The mathematics in this case unfolds largely through students' attempts to solve Problem Sets A and B. Randy Harris assigns these problems to help his students deepen their understanding of the relationships among fractions, decimals, and percents. In Set A students encounter a variety of different rectangular grids that are partially shaded. As the students find the fraction, decimal, and percent of the area shaded in each grid, they begin to make connections among these three different rational number representations. In Set B students are asked to begin by shading a given decimal, fraction, or percent of the total area in a given rectangular grid and then to represent the shaded area in two other ways.

Below we identify several important mathematical ideas that surface in the case, and we provide examples of where these ideas appear.

Connections among fractions, decimals, and percents. In Problem Sets A and B, students must determine the fraction, decimal, and percent represented by a shaded portion of a given rectangular grid. Using a diagram, students can visually verify the equivalence of the fraction, decimal, and percent representations in each problem because they represent the same shaded portion of the given whole. The list that follows provides examples of connections among fractions, decimals, and percents that arise in the case.

- Mr. Harris mentions using a 10 × 10 grid as a way to visualize the equivalence of fractions and decimals, and plans to link these two representations with percent. He also indicates that he wants students to be able to move flexibly among the three representations. (paras. 5–6)
- Deanna is the first student to derive the decimal and percent equivalent of a given fraction by finding an equivalent fraction with a denominator of 100. She finds a fraction equivalent to $^{34}/_{80}$ with 100 in the denominator because she says, "It makes it easier to find the percent if you can make it per hundred." (para. 15)
- Michael reduces a fraction first and then finds the

equivalent fraction with a denominator of 100 (Method 2). (para. 20)

- Denise uses equivalent fractions to find the percent. (para. 23)
- Denise uses the 10×10 grid to explain the difference among 0.45, 45%, and 0.45%. She first equates 0.45 with 45% on the 10×10 grid. She then makes an enlargement of one square, or 1%, to show how 0.45% looks just like 0.45 but is 100 times smaller because it is really 0.45 of one small square, which is $1/100$ of the total rectangular grid. (paras. 24–25)
- Mr. Harris helps students relate the decimal 0.725 to 72.5% of the 10×8 rectangular grid, and students eventually see that 72.5% is the same as $58/80$ or $29/40$. (paras. 33–34)
- Kendra reasons that one row is $1/10$ or 0.10 or 10% of the total area of the 10×8 rectangular grid; she is aware that all three labels are appropriate for representing the area of one row of the diagram. (para. 35)
- Devon relates the fraction $3/8$ to 37.5% of the area shaded in his diagram. (para. 39)
- Darlene uses Devon's reasoning to relate $1/8$ to 12.5% in her diagram. (para. 40)

Unit rate. Using a unit rate strategy involves determining a relationship between one quantity and a unit of another quantity (Lamon, 1999). In other words, unit rates answer the question, "How many (or how much) for one?" (Lamon, 1999, p. 207). This strategy is used in Mr. Harris's class when the students find the percent value corresponding to each individual square in a given rectangular grid. Once the unit rate is determined, it can be used to find the total percent associated with a given shaded area or to determine how many squares in a rectangle should be shaded in order to correspond to a given percent of the total area. The list that follows identifies instances in which the notion of unit rate surfaces in the case.

- Beverly and Rashid explain that if there are 80 squares in the grid then each square represents $1\frac{1}{4}$%; then Joe uses this unit rate to determine the percent for 34 squares. (paras. 17–18)
- Denise incorporates unit rate into her explanation, "Each square is worth 1 percent . . . so each column is worth 10 percent." (para. 24)
- Mr. Harris encourages the use of this strategy through his questioning. (para. 24)
- Mr. Harris leads Marilyn to use Method 3 from Day 1 to find the percent of the total represented by each square in the rectangular grid; Marilyn uses this unit rate to determine how many squares she needs to shade in order to cover 72.5%. (para. 33)

Chunked quantities. This general strategy involves identifying convenient clusters within complex quantities and using them to solve problems (Lamon, 1999). Some of Mr. Harris's students partition the grid into conveniently sized sections and rename the sections as fractions representing shaded portions of the entire area. Some students also reason about the quantities using chunks comprising rows and/or columns in the grid. The list that follows indicates some ways in which the notion of "chunked quantities" appears in the case.

- Peter lets a 4×4 square be the unit and recognizes that there are four such units in the original square; therefore, ¾ of the square is shaded. (para. 21)
- Denise incorporates chunked quantities into her explanation, "Each column is one-tenth of the square so that is 0.10. So if I have 4 columns shaded, this would be 0.40." (para. 24)
- Kendra views the rectangle as 10 columns that are each worth 0.10, which is convenient for shading 0.70 of the figure. Then she needed to divide the columns into new chunks (such as 4 squares covering 5% and 2 squares covering 2.5%) in order to shade in .025. (para. 35)
- Devon divides the rectangle into 8 parts, renaming them as eighths. With Mr. Harris's help, Devon determines that each of these chunks represents 12.5% of the whole, which helps him reason what percent is shaded. (paras. 38–39)
- Darlene uses horizontal rows, reasoning that each row is worth $1/8$ of the total area, and then follows Devon's reasoning to find her final answer. (para. 40)

Considering How Student Thinking Is Supported

Randy Harris believes that developing conceptual understanding of mathematics is facilitated through the use of visual diagrams. In his view, diagrams provide students with a tool for making sense of situations. He also thinks that diagrams can be used to help students develop an understanding of mathematical procedures. Mr. Harris wants his students not only to be able to perform routine procedures but also to understand what they are doing and why they are doing it. Although Mr. Harris has made considerable progress in transferring these beliefs into his practice, he is not always consistent in this regard.

Below we identify several pedagogical moves that Randy Harris made that may have influenced his students' opportunities to engage in high-level thinking, reasoning, and communication during the lesson, and we provide examples of where these ideas appear in the case.

Building on students' prior knowledge and experiences. Mr. Harris accomplishes this in at least two ways: (1) by selecting a task that builds on students' prior knowledge and experiences; and (2) by encouraging students to refer to previous work or strategies that may be useful in solving the task at hand. The list that follows identifies ways in which Mr. Harris builds on students' prior knowledge and experiences.

- Students have had experiences relating fractions to decimals using a 10 × 10 grid; Mr. Harris now wants students to link fractions and decimals to their equivalent percents. He also wants students to apply what they have learned in the context of 10 × 10 grids to problems with rectangular grids that are not 10 × 10. (paras. 5, 6, and 10)
- Mr. Harris reminds students of the usefulness of remembering the decimal and percent equivalents of unit fractions. (para. 12)
- Mr. Harris mentions that Michael used Method 2 (which had been used and recorded previously). (para. 20)
- Mr. Harris suggests that Denise use the familiar 10 × 10 grid to address Ramon's question. (para. 23)
- Mr. Harris notices that students' previous work with 10 × 10 grids is interfering with their ability to shade 72.5% of the 10 × 8 grid. He sets out to guide students toward making sense of the problem by clarifying what the unit whole is and what "percent" means. He refers students to the previously recorded methods from Day 1 to select a method for solving the problems. (paras. 20 and 33)
- Mr. Harris prompts Devon to build on what he already knows about unit fractions and their equivalent percents in order to finish his solution. (para. 39)

However, Mr. Harris sometimes assigns tasks without providing students with enough resources to complete them in the ways that he expects (i.e., using visual approaches), as shown by the examples that follow.

- On Day 1, Mr. Harris does not himself model or have students model solving the problems in ways that connect to the diagram. (paras. 11 and 12)
- At the beginning of Day 2, Mr. Harris decides to introduce Set B without doing an example, although it is not clear that the work done on Day 1 will help students with this new set of tasks. (para. 29)

Encouraging nonalgorithmic explanations and justifications. Mr. Harris wants students to make sense of the relationships among fractions, decimals, and percents, rather than only being able to perform conversion procedures. Toward this end, he tries to make sure that a nonalgorithmic approach is explained for most problems. With some problems, he initiates discussion of a nonalgorithmic solution, while in other instances the explanations are initiated by students. Examples of how Mr. Harris encourages nonalgorithmic explanations and justifications are provided in the list that follows.

- Mr. Harris recognizes that Natalie's and Deanna's justifications rely primarily on symbolic algorithms and do not make use of the diagram. He prompts the class to work through an explanation of a solution method that does make use of the diagram. (paras. 15–18)
- Mr. Harris introduces Method 3 as a way to solve the problems without relying on algorithms and procedures. (paras. 16 and 17)
- Even though Michael has already explained a correct solution to the problem, Mr. Harris allows Peter to share another solution that turns out to make sense of the diagram. (para. 21)
- Mr. Harris asks students not to use Method 1 in solving the remaining problems. (para. 26)
- Mr. Harris helps Marilyn use and explain Method 3 to find 72.5% of the 10 × 8 grid. (para. 33)
- Mr. Harris solicits more solutions, and Kendra explains her method that uses the diagram to make sense of the problem. (para. 35)
- Mr. Harris recaps two nonalgorithmic methods to help students remember and use these methods for solving the remaining problems. (para. 36)
- On Day 2, Mr. Harris invites Devon to share his nonalgorithmic approach to Problem 2. (para. 37)
- On Day 2, Mr. Harris encourages Darlene to present her visual approach to Problem 2. (para. 40)

However, Mr. Harris does not consistently encourage students to use the diagrams, nor does he always communicate that visual approaches are valued. Some of examples of these instances are identified in the list that follows.

- Mr. Harris allows Danielle, Sheryl, and David to use algorithms to solve the first problem, even though he was "hoping for an explanation that relied less on memory or procedure." (paras. 11–12)
- When Michael and Peter present their solutions to the third problem, Mr. Harris comments that both solutions are "good," without pointing out the differences in using Peter's visual approach versus Michael's algorithmic approach. (para. 21)
- Mr. Harris allows Denise and Devon to use algorithms to find the decimal equivalents to the shaded areas. (paras. 23 and 39)
- The homework assignment on Day 1 is to complete the remaining problems in Set A without using Method 1, implying that Methods 2 and 3 may be used, even though neither uses a visual approach. (para. 26)
- Mr. Harris does not press Kendra to explain her visual approach to the problem nor does he validate her solution. (para. 35)

Encouraging communication. Mr. Harris encourages communication in at least three ways: (1) by incorporating the production of explanations into the explicit goals of a task, (2) by allowing students to work in pairs or groups on problems, and (3) by asking students to come to the overhead projector to explain and justify their solutions to a task. The list that follows identifies ways in which Mr. Harris encourages communication throughout the lesson.

- Mr. Harris asks students to provide explanations and, in many cases, probes their explanations or asks for further elaborations. (paras. 23–25)
- Mr. Harris stresses the importance of explaining solution strategies as a goal for the task. (para. 13)
- Mr. Harris encourages student-to-student interaction when he asks Ramon to question Denise and then asks Denise to further address Ramon's question. (para. 23)
- Mr. Harris requires students to explain their solutions to homework in writing. (para. 26)

Recording solution strategies. Mr. Harris physically records different solution strategies on the blackboard, allowing both himself and his students to refer to the

list in subsequent work. Mr. Harris also verbally recaps effective strategies that have been used by students, in order to help students remember them for use on subsequent problems. Moments at which Mr. Harris records or recaps different solution strategies are shown in the list that follows.

- Mr. Harris records the methods used to solve the problems on Day 1. (para. 19)
- Mr. Harris verbally recaps several solution strategies before asking students to complete the last two problems. (para. 36)

However, Mr. Harris also misses several opportunities to add students' strategies to the list of methods. These occasions are identified in the list that follows.

- Mr. Harris does not add Peter's strategy to the list of methods on Day 1. (para. 21)
- Mr. Harris does not provide a written record of Kendra's, Devon's, and Darlene's strategies on Day 2. (para. 41)

Modeling high-level performance. Mr. Harris often provides class time for students to share their solution strategies, and therefore model high-level performance. In most instances, this modeling of high-level performance is accompanied by discussion or questioning (by Mr. Harris and/or other students in the class). The list that follows indicates ways in which Mr. Harris has students model high-level performance.

- Mr. Harris notes to the class that both Michael and Peter used "good" methods. (para. 21)
- Denise explains the difference between 0.45 and 0.45% in response to Ramon's question. (para. 25)
- Mr. Harris notices Devon's nonalgorithmic solution and invites him to share it with the class. (para. 37)
- Mr. Harris notices Darlene's nonalgorithmic solution and asks her to share it with the class. (para. 40)

Encouraging multiple solution methods. Mr. Harris encourages students to use multiple solution methods, in at least two ways: (1) by emphasizing the need for multiple methods as part of the explicit goals for the task, and (2) by asking for more solutions or other ways of looking at the problem even after a correct solution method has been presented. The list that follows provides instances in which Mr. Harris encourages students to use multiple solution methods.

- Mr. Harris tells students that he wants them to come up with different ways of solving the problems. (para. 13)
- Mr. Harris asks whether anyone looked at the problem another way, and allows students to explain their alternative approaches. (paras. 34–35)
- Mr. Harris introduces, records, and highlights alternative solution methods. (paras. 19 and 36)

Providing an appropriate amount of time. Mr. Harris tries to provide an appropriate amount of time for students to explore a task, to think, and to make sense of the mathematics for themselves, in at least three ways: (1) by choosing to spend two class periods on problems that encourage students to use the visual diagrams even though they already know procedures for converting among fractions, decimals, and percents; (2) by allowing students time within each class period to work on the problem sets in small groups, as well as time for giving or listening to explanations of multiple solution strategies in a whole-class setting; and (3) by allowing mathematical detours in a discussion when appropriate. The list that follows provides examples of the ways in which Mr. Harris provides an appropriate amount of time for students to explore the task.

- In order to give students time to struggle with the problems themselves, Mr. Harris decides to stop whole-class discussion of Problem 1 in Set A even though he is not satisfied with the results. (para. 12)
- Mr. Harris gives students time to work on the problems in groups before the class discusses them. (para. 13)
- Mr. Harris encourages Denise to address Ramon's question even though it is not directly about solving any of the problems in the task. (para. 23)

Although Mr. Harris generally provides students with an appropriate amount of time, at other times he does not provide students with enough time to engage in the tasks. In particular, on Day 1, Mr. Harris does not give students any time to grapple with the first problem. (para. 11)

Monitoring students' mathematical performance. Mr. Harris monitors students' mathematical performance both formally and informally during the 2 days of instruction, as shown by the examples in the list that follows.

- Mr. Harris reviews homework. (paras. 13 and 27)
- Mr. Harris observes students as they work in groups. (para. 30)
- Mr. Harris gives a formal assessment at the end of the 2 days. (para. 41)

Maintaining complexity of task. Mr. Harris tries to keep the task at a high level in at least two ways: (1) by allowing students to grapple with the problems in pairs (Day 1) or in groups (Day 2); and (2) by encouraging students to take responsibility for their learning by asking them to reflect on their work. Examples of the ways in which Mr. Harris maintains the complexity of the task are provided in the list that follows.

- On Day 2, Mr. Harris decides to let students begin Set B without an example. (para. 29)
- Mr. Harris asks Marilyn what the problem is asking her to do. (para. 33)
- Mr. Harris asks Marilyn to compare her original answer with her new answer. (para. 33)

However, at other times during the lesson, Mr. Harris simplifies a task by asking leading questions that do not allow students to grapple with the mathematics on their own. These instances are shown in the list that follows.

- Mr. Harris leads the class through the process of finding a unit rate (Method 3) by asking leading questions. (paras. 17–18)
- Mr. Harris engages Marilyn in a rapid question-and-answer exchange that leads her to solve the problem using Method 3, finding a unit rate. (para. 33)

FACILITATING THE OPENING ACTIVITY

The primary purpose of the Opening Activity is to engage teachers with the mathematical ideas that they will encounter when they read the case. The three problems that are found in the Opening Activity (see the section entitled "Opening Activity" in Chapter 2) are identical to those found in Problem Set B in the case. In solving the three problems, participants face a challenge: They are asked to solve the problems in ways that utilize the diagrams and do not rely merely on arithmetic procedures for equating fractions, decimals, and percents. This is especially challenging since the grids provided are not 10×10 grids. In this section, we provide suggestions for using the Opening Activity.

1. Begin by having teachers work individually to solve the three problems for 5 to 10 minutes and then continue to work on the task with a partner or in a small group. (We have found that beginning with "private think time" ensures that each participant has a chance to grapple with the task prior to engaging in collaborative work.) You may want to provide each group with transparencies of the three grids used in the problems (for recording their solutions).

2. Assist teachers in their work on the task if they appear to be having difficulty. Consider the following suggestions:

   • If some participants are unable to think about the problems in ways that utilize the diagrams, help focus their attention on rows, columns, or other subsections of the grid (e.g., in Problem 1, recognizing that each column of the grid represents $1/10$, 0.10, or 10% of the total grid; in Problem 2, recognizing that two rows of the grid represent 25% of the total grid).

   • If some participants have difficulty getting started, ask one or two successful pairs or groups to present and explain their solution to the first problem. This often helps those who are stuck, and it makes the demonstrated strategies available for others to use on subsequent problems, if appropriate.

   • Watch for a common misconception—treating the grids as if they were 10×10. If participants produce incorrect solutions that suggest this misconception (e.g., shading 72½ squares in Problem 1), try to help them focus on the total number of squares in the grid and the relative number of those squares that are shaded. For example, in the grid given for Problem 1, there are 80 squares, rather than 100. If 72.5 squares are shaded in the grid, then the shading appears in more than 7 out of every set of 8 squares. This must correspond to more than 0.725 or 72.5%, which would correspond to only about 7 out of 10 squares shaded.

3. Orchestrate a whole-group discussion to allow participants to share various solution strategies and approaches. During the discussion you may want to:

   • Solicit responses that portray general solution strategies that will be found in the case (e.g., chunking—partitioning the grid into convenient sections, such as rows or columns; using a unit rate—finding the percent corresponding to each square in a grid). (If you asked the small groups to record their solutions on an overhead transparency, this would facilitate the presentation of solutions during the whole-group discussion.) It is helpful to discuss at least one nonalgorithmic approach, but it may not be necessary or desirable to create an exhaustive list. (A list of different solution methods we have seen teachers use to solve these tasks can be found in Appendix A. This may help you prepare for the emergence of methods you might not have used when you solved the problems.)

   • Discuss the relative strengths and weaknesses of various approaches and methods (e.g., a unit rate approach works well on Problem 1, because you can easily distribute 100% over 80 squares to see that an individual square corresponds to 1.25%. However, on Problem 2, this approach is difficult because it is not so easy to distribute 100% over 96 squares—in this case an individual square corresponds to 1.041666666%).

   • Ask participants to discuss any difficulties they experienced in solving the task and to brainstorm ways in which they could provide support to students who encountered similar difficulties.

4. Discuss the "Consider" portion of the Opening Activity, in which participants are asked to think about how the three problems relate to proportional reasoning. The "Case Analysis" identifies the aspects of the case that relate to proportional reasoning, and this section should help you prepare for a general discussion of proportional reasoning as it applies to this case. (Alternatively, you might want to postpone a discussion of proportional reasoning until after participants have read and discussed the case. At that time you could approach the topic by asking participants to consider Randy Harris's comments in paragraph 7 of the case.)

FACILITATING THE CASE DISCUSSION

The case discussion is intended to help participants analyze the mathematical and pedagogical ideas in the case. The "Case Analysis" should be of assistance in identifying the key ideas in the case and how each idea "plays out" in the details of the case. Although it is likely that you will begin by examining specific aspects of

Randy Harris's teaching practice, you should consider how to connect the specific events that occur in his class with more general ideas about mathematics teaching and learning. In this section we provide suggestions for launching and facilitating the case discussion, and for various follow-up activities that you may wish to pursue.

1. If possible, have participants read and reflect on the case before meeting as a group to discuss the case. As participants read the case, we suggest that you ask them to identify what they see as the key pedagogical moves made by Randy Harris during the lesson. (This activity is described in more detail in the section of Chapter 2 entitled "Reading the Case.") This individual activity will help participants to think deeply about the pedagogy in the case and to prepare for the small- and large-group discussions. Alternatively, you may want to select one of the questions found in Chapter 2 (see the section entitled "Extending Your Analysis of the Case") to guide the reading of the case.

2. Have teachers work in groups of three or four to create a two-column support-and-inhibit chart. Teachers should begin this process by reviewing the lists of pedagogical moves that they created while reading "The Case of Randy Harris" and determining whether a specific move should be placed in the "support" or "inhibit" column (or perhaps in neither). When completing this task, group members should be encouraged to reach consensus on what is placed in their group's chart and to cite specific evidence from the case (using paragraph numbers) to support each idea recorded in their charts.

3. During the whole-group discussion, you may want to develop a support-and-inhibit chart that combines the work of the individual groups. You might begin building this master chart by asking the groups to identify the pedagogical move in their chart that they feel had the greatest impact on what Randy Harris's students learned. These "greatest impact" moves could then be added to the master chart and discussed by the whole group. Encourage participants to argue respectfully if they do not agree that an identified move served the stated purpose. This can lead to a rich discussion that draws on evidence used to support the claims being made. After each group has contributed one move to the list, open the conversation up by asking if there are any other moves that should be included. Two "support-and-inhibit" charts are included in Appendix A (one that we developed in preparation for a discussion of "The Case of Randy Harris" and one that was created by a group of teachers). We encourage you to develop your own chart prior to reviewing the ones we have provided.

    You may wish to end the discussion by asking teachers what lessons can be learned from Randy Harris's teaching that can be applied to other teaching situations. This will help teachers to move beyond the particular events that occurred in the case and to begin to see them as instantiations of more generalizable ideas about mathematics teaching and learning.

4. Once you have completed a discussion of supporting and inhibiting factors, you may want to raise additional questions for consideration. The questions in Chapter 2 (see the section entitled "Extending Your Analysis of the Case") may be useful for this purpose. Alternatively, you may wish to ask teachers to investigate a specific mathematical or pedagogical idea that was discussed in the case analysis.

5. Following the discussion, you may want to have participants reflect individually by writing about some aspect of the case experience. This could involve having participants consider what Mr. Harris should do the next day, what Mr. Harris could have done differently, or whether Mr. Harris accomplished his goals for the lesson.

EXTENDING THE CASE EXPERIENCE

If you have additional time, you may want to provide teachers with opportunities to consider their own practice and continue to explore the mathematical and pedagogical ideas on which the case is based. The section entitled "Extending Case-Based Experiences" in Chapter 6 suggests three types of activities you might want to assign teachers for these purposes.

Facilitating Learning from The Case of Marie Hanson

"The Case of Marie Hanson" focuses on 2 days in the classroom of a 6th-grade teacher and her students at Freemont Middle School. In the case, Ms. Hanson and her students explore several "missing-value" proportion problems using strategies that make sense to students. Ms. Hanson believes that this lesson, and others like it, will help develop students' abilities to reason proportionally before they are introduced to formal notation and symbolic solution methods in later grades. Students in the case generate a variety of strategies for thinking about proportions, including making a table, using a factor-of-change, and finding a unit rate. As they present their ideas to the class and consider the approaches used by their classmates, students have the opportunity to examine multiplicative relationships between quantities and to use these relationships to make connections between different strategies.

CASE ANALYSIS

In this section, we provide a detailed analysis of the mathematical and pedagogical ideas that are found in the case. These analyses may help you in determining which aspects of the case you wish to highlight during the discussion.

Considering the Mathematics in the Case

The "Jawbreakers and Jolly Ranchers" problems selected by Marie Hanson require students to reason about quantities by thinking in terms of multiplicative relationships. Questions A and B of the first problem are identical to problems posed in earlier lessons, and require students to determine a ratio and to generate equivalent ratios. The Jawbreakers and Jolly Ranchers

problems are more difficult than earlier ones, however, because the numbers form a unit rate that is not an integer. The second and third problems can be thought of as "missing-value" proportion problems, although students are not provided with any algorithms or set procedures for solving these problems. Instead, students in Marie Hanson's class develop a variety of strategies to reason about the situations presented in each problem—strategies that they can "make sense of every step of the way." Ms. Hanson provides several opportunities for students to explore multiplicative relationships throughout the discussion of the second and third problems, and chooses the fourth and final problem to allow students to apply their understanding of ratios to a new situation.

Below we identify several important mathematical ideas that surface in the case, and we provide examples of where these ideas appear.

Ratio and equivalent ratios. Ratios express multiplicative relationships between quantities. The first two problems require students to attend to the part-to-part ratio of Jolly Ranchers to Jawbreakers, and the third problem involves the part-to-whole ratio of Jolly Ranchers to total candies. Students in the case frequently use multiplicative relationships in reasoning through their solution strategies as they attempt to increase the total number of candies while keeping the ratio constant. Students' comments throughout the case seem to indicate that they have developed a solid understanding of the concepts of ratio and equivalent ratios. The list that follows provides specific examples of how these ideas "play out" in the case.

- Ms. Hanson informally defines ratio to her students as a "comparison between two sets of things."

She chooses to postpone formal notation and allows students to express ratios in any way that makes sense to them. (paras. 5–6)

- In this and previous lessons, students are asked to write a ratio and generate equivalent ratios to express the relationship between the numbers of objects shown in a picture. (paras. 5, 8)
- In earlier lessons, most students had successfully determined ratios of Twinkies to boxes and of stick figures to lollipops. Ms. Hanson comments that students easily determined the ratio of five Jolly Ranchers to 13 Jawbreakers. (paras. 7, 9)
- Comments by several students indicate that they have grasped the concept of ratio as a multiplicative relationship between quantities. (paras. 12, 26, 28)
- Jerlyn and Kamiko use the ratio of 5:13 to create equivalent ratios in their table. (paras. 10–11)
- Students use the 5:13 ratio and the 1:2.6 ratio in their strategies for solving subsequent problems. (paras. 22, 26, 27)
- Students determine whether two ratios are equivalent. (paras. 19, 25–28)

Multiplicative versus additive relationships. Multiplying both quantities in a ratio by the same constant generates an equivalent ratio (i.e., it maintains the multiplicative relationship between the original numbers in the ratio). Repeated addition, as used by Jerlyn and Kamiko in the case (para. 11), also preserves the original ratio because it has the same effect as multiplying by a constant. Students in the case frequently use multiplicative relationships to "grow the quantities at the same rate"—the ratio of Jolly Ranchers to Jawbreakers in the original candy jar is held constant even though the quantity of each candy has been changed. By contrast, adding the same amount to each quantity does not maintain the original ratio. As shown by Jordan's strategy in the case (paras. 24–25), the Jolly Ranchers appear to "catch up" to the Jawbreakers. Middle school students frequently apply additive strategies to reason incorrectly about proportional situations (Hart, 1988; Karplus, Pulos, & Stage, 1983a, 1983b; Tournaire & Pulos, 1985). Instances in which multiplicative and additive reasoning surface in the case are provided in the list that follows.

- Jerlyn and Kamiko apply repeated addition to create a table of equivalent ratios. They consistently add five more Jolly Ranchers and 13 more Jawbreakers to generate each new row of the table. (para. 11)

- Jordan adds 95 Jolly Ranchers and 95 Jawbreakers, asserting that he had to do the same thing to both quantities. (para. 25)
- Sarah questions Jordan's strategy, pointing out that the two candies are "almost even" in the new jar. Jerry also states that the ratio in Jordan's new jar did not stay the same. (paras. 25–26)
- Ms. Hanson uses students' comments to conclude that adding the same amount to each quantity will not keep the ratio constant. (paras. 29–33)
- Thinking about how the rows of the ratio table are related, students conclude that multiplying both quantities by the same number will keep the original ratio constant. (paras. 32–33)

Proportional reasoning using a unit rate. A unit rate compares how many (or much) of one quantity per one unit of the other quantity (Lamon, 1999). In the case, students use a diagram to determine the unit rate of 2.6 Jawbreakers to 1 Jolly Rancher. However, students in the case do not directly apply a unit rate strategy to solve the problems and also do not recognize the unit rate relationship in the table created by Jerlyn and Kamiko (para. 10). That is, students do not recognize that multiplying the number of Jolly Ranchers by 2.6 will give the corresponding number of Jawbreakers. While students had recognized unit rate relationships in earlier problems, unit rate strategies are not prevalent in this lesson primarily because the unit rate has a noninteger value—the quantity of "2.6 Jawbreakers" does not make sense in the context of the problems. The list that follows provides specific examples of how the unit rate relationship arises in the case.

- In previous problems, students circled combinations of objects that illustrated a unit rate and were encouraged to do so by Ms. Hanson. In this problem, students cannot circle a whole number of Jawbreakers for each Jolly Rancher. (paras. 6, 9)
- Students' comments that "you couldn't divide them evenly" and "you can't get back to one" indicate that the numbers in the problem make it difficult to determine a unit rate. (para. 12)
- April's strategy and diagrams, and contributions from her classmates, lead her to develop the unit rate of 2.6 Jawbreakers to 1 Jolly Rancher. (paras. 13–17)
- Students question whether the new ratio of 1:2.6 fits into the ratio table created by Jerlyn and Kamiko. Students later determine that it does fit because multiplying both numbers by 5 gives the original ratio of 5:13. (paras. 19 and 30–33)

- In solving the second problem, Jerry applies a factor-of-change to the unit rate of 2.6 Jawbreakers to 1 Jolly Rancher. However, using a unit rate strategy would require that students multiply the number of Jolly Ranchers by 2.6 to obtain the number of Jawbreakers. (para. 26)

Proportional reasoning using a factor-of-change. A factor-of-change, or scale factor, is a constant that can be used to generate equivalent ratios. Using a factor-of-change strategy, students generate the desired equivalent ratio by multiplying both terms of the original ratio by the same constant. Students also might multiply by a series of constants until they recognize a ratio that can easily be "scaled-up" to the desired ratio. The first two problems in the case elicit factor-of-change strategies because of the numbers in the problems—the scale factor needed to obtain the new ratio is a whole number. Finding equivalent fractions by multiplying the numerator and denominator by the same constant is another example of a factor-of-change strategy. The examples in the list that follows indicate how factor-of-change relationships are used in the case.

- Students use two different factor-of-change strategies for the second question. Jerry begins with the unit rate of 1:2.6 and multiplies both terms by 100, and Owen begins with the ratio 5:13 and multiplies both terms by 20. (paras. 26–27)
- Students settle the question of whether 1:2.6 fits into the ratio table when Sarah notices that you can get from the first row in the table to the second row by multiplying by five. Students then identify factors-of-change between other rows of the ratio table. (para. 32)
- Ms. Hanson comments that about half of the students used a factor-of-change strategy to solve the third problem and selects Danielle to explain this strategy to the class. (para. 37)
- Joshua uses a "scaling-up" strategy to solve the homework problem. (para. 38)
- Ms. Hanson uses equivalent fractions to relate Angelica's cross-multiplication strategy to Danielle's strategy. (paras. 42–43)

Proportional reasoning using a ratio table. Using a table to organize equivalent ratios is often helpful in reasoning about proportional situations. In the case, the ratio table facilitates Joshua's "scaling-up" strategy and provides several connections between strategies based on repeated addition and strategies based on multipli-

cation. Jerlyn and Kamiko's table was created through repeated addition, and it is used later in the lesson to illustrate multiplicative relationships between quantities. (Although not explored in the case, ratio tables also can facilitate creating coordinate graphs or generalizing rules to express proportional relationships. See Middleton and van den Heuvel-Panhuizen [1995] for further discussion of how ratio tables support middle school students' development of proportional reasoning concepts.) The list that follows provides instances in which ratios tables are used in the case.

- Jerlyn and Kamiko create a ratio table by repeatedly adding five more Jolly Ranchers and 13 more Jawbreakers. (paras. 10–11)
- Ms. Hanson adds 1:2.6 to the ratio table. However, students are still viewing the table additively and are not sure whether this new ratio fits in. (para. 18–19)
- Ms. Hanson summarizes why Jerlyn and Kamiko's use of repeated addition in creating the ratio table preserves the original ratio. (para. 33)
- Students discuss how different rows of the table are related, and conclude that "you are always multiplying the two different sides of the table by the same amount." Once Sarah points out the factor-of-change relationship between 1:2.6 and 5:13, other students begin to identify factor-of-change relationships between other rows of the table. (paras. 32–33)
- Ms. Hanson mentions that students attempted to extend Jerlyn and Kamiko's table by continuing to add five Jolly Ranchers and 13 Jawbreakers. Since using additive strategies to extend ratio tables often becomes tedious in dealing with large numbers, she solicits more efficient, multiplicative strategies. (paras. 36–38)
- To solve the third problem, Joshua begins by creating a table and then realizes that he can scale-up from 180 total candies to 720 total candies by multiplying by 4. (para. 38)

Proportional reasoning using cross-multiplication. Cross-multiplication is an efficient algorithm for solving missing-value proportion problems, especially when problems cannot be solved easily and directly using equivalent fractions (i.e., whenever the multiplicative relationships or the numbers in the problem are noninteger values). However, cross-multiplication often is applied mechanically without any underlying understanding or connection to meaning. Hence it can be misapplied, either by setting up the proportions incorrectly or by attempting to cross-multiply in inappropriate situations (such as when multiplying fractions or when dealing with nonproportional quantities). Because cross-multiplication is an easy procedure to use but a rather difficult one for which to develop a deep understanding, Ms. Hanson favors solution methods that students can "make sense of every step of the way" as a precursor to cross-multiplication. The list that follows provides instances in which cross-multiplication arises in the case.

- Ms. Hanson's experiences in learning proportional reasoning consisted mostly of memorized procedures such as cross-multiplication. By contrast, she and her colleagues are working to provide their students with a solid understanding of ratio and proportion and with a variety of strategies to apply to proportional situations. (paras. 1–3)
- With her father's help, Angelica uses cross-multiplication to solve the homework problem. (para. 39)
- Ms. Hanson clarifies the cross-multiplication algorithm presented by Angelica by relating it to the context of the problem and to Danielle's strategy. (paras. 42–43)

Considering How the Teacher Supports Student Thinking

Ms. Hanson provides students with a series of problems that have the potential to elicit high-level thinking and reasoning about ratios and proportions. Ms. Hanson has selected the problems to build on students' earlier experiences with ratios and has sequenced the problems in a way that helps students to develop increasingly sophisticated proportional reasoning strategies. Through her participation in professional development activities, Ms. Hanson has heightened her awareness of how students learn to reason proportionally. She believes that it is very important to expose students to a variety of strategies for thinking about proportional relationships.

Below we identify several pedagogical moves that Marie Hanson made that may have influenced her students' opportunities to engage in high-level thinking, reasoning, and communication during the lesson, and we provide examples of where these ideas appear in the case.

Building on students' prior knowledge and experiences. Ms. Hanson selects problems that build on students' earlier work with ratios. She sequences these

problems in a way that builds upon the ideas generated throughout the class discussions and that promotes students' understanding of multiplicative relationships. Specific examples of how and when this occurs in the case are provided in the list that follows.

- Ms. Hanson describes students' earlier work with ratios. (paras 5–7)
- Questions a and b of the first problem are identical to the problems posed in earlier lessons. As noted by students, this problem is more difficult because one number is not a factor (or multiple) of the other. (para. 12)
- Using large numbers in the second and third problems encourages the use of strategies based on multiplicative relationships because determining equivalent ratios through repeated addition would become tedious. (paras. 20, 34)
- Ms. Hanson decides to postpone the question of whether the unit rate of 1:2.6 fits into the table until students are better prepared to engage in the discussion. (para. 19)
- By choosing to expose an incorrect strategy based on additive relationships first, Ms. Hanson sets up an opportunity for students to discover that multiplicative relationships are the "way to go." (paras. 23 and 28)
- Ms. Hanson considers the ideas generated during class as she chooses subsequent problems for both classwork and homework. Because of her inservice training on proportional reasoning, Ms. Hanson is able to anticipate the strategies and types of thinking that student will apply to the different types of problems that she has created. As a way of summarizing one of the big ideas of the lesson, she chooses a final problem that will cause students to attend to multiplicative relationships between equivalent ratios. (paras. 34, 45–46)
- Ms. Hanson explains cross-multiplication by relating it to Danielle's strategy, which students encountered earlier. (paras. 42–43)

Providing an appropriate amount of time. Ms. Hanson provides students with ample time to explore the problems she has chosen for this lesson. Because students are expected to produce more than just an answer, Ms. Hanson designates significant amounts of class time for students to develop their own strategies and to explain their ideas to the class. She provides time in class for students to make sense of the main mathematical ideas and to make connections between different solution methods, as evidenced by the examples in the list that follows.

- Ms. Hanson devotes all of Thursday's class time to exploring two problems. (paras. 8, 20)
- Ms. Hanson is uncertain whether the first solution makes sense to students, so she takes time to ask students why this problem seems more difficult than previous problems. (para. 12)
- Ms. Hanson allows a significant amount of time for April and others to work through the unit rate strategy. (paras. 13–17)
- Ms. Hanson takes time to revisit the question of whether the unit rate fits into the table. Once students determine that it does fit, Ms. Hanson uses this opportunity to highlight the multiplicative relationships in the table. (paras. 30–33)
- Ms. Hanson elicits another solution method to the homework problem because she cannot tell whether students understand the strategy presented by Danielle. (para. 38)
- Ms. Hanson is concerned that Angelica (and the rest of the class) is not sure of what she did or why she did it, and takes time to explain cross-multiplication and relate it to other strategies. (paras. 40–43)

Pressing students to provide explanations. Ms. Hanson consistently requests that her students provide explanations for their solutions and ideas, and often allows students to use the overhead projector at the front of the room in order to do so publicly. She also takes advantage of opportunities for students to extend and/or clarify ideas presented by their classmates. Instances in which Ms. Hanson presses students for explanations are provided in the list that follows.

- Ms. Hanson asks students to explain their ideas and solution methods. (paras. 11, 27, 32, 37, 38)
- Ms. Hanson asks students to further explain ideas presented by others. (paras. 15, 18, 27)

Modeling high-level performance. Ms. Hanson and several students in her classroom model and explain a variety of strategies for thinking about proportional relationships. As she observes students' work, Ms. Hanson notes specific strategies and ideas that she would like to have presented to the class in order to make these approaches available for all students to apply to subsequent problems. Examples of how high-level performance is modeled in the case are provided in the list that follows.

- Ms. Hanson asks Jerlyn and Kamiko to present their ratio table because this strategy had not been used previously. (para. 10)
- With "a little coaxing," April presents her diagram, which models a unit rate strategy, to the class. (para. 13)
- For the second problem, Jerry uses a strategy based on multiplicative relationships to counter Jordan's approach of adding 95 to both terms of the ratio. Jerry's notation is adopted by Ms. Hanson to illustrate the ideas offered by Jerlyn and Owen. This notation highlights the factor-of-change between equivalent ratios. (paras. 26–27)
- Ms. Hanson chooses Danielle to present a strategy that involves using a factor-of-change approach. (para. 37)
- Ms. Hanson asks Joshua to present a solution method based on "scaling-up" from the ratio table. (para. 38)
- Ms. Hanson models how equivalent fractions can be used to solve the homework problem and to connect cross-multiplication to Danielle's strategy. (paras. 42–43)

Encouraging communication. Ms. Hanson encourages mathematical discourse by providing opportunities for students to develop mathematical ideas as a community. She often steps out of the spotlight and allows students to address one another directly and to build off of one another's ideas. Examples of these instances are identified in the list that follows.

- Students are expected to question each other directly. Ms. Hanson often asks the class whether they have any questions for the student who has just offered an explanation. (paras. 16, 25, 40)
- April, Jerry, and Sharee build off of one another's ideas to develop a unit rate strategy. The only input from Ms. Hanson is to ask whether other students have questions or can add to an idea. (paras. 15–16)
- Rather than correct Jordan herself, Ms. Hanson allows the class to determine that using an additive constant does not work. (paras. 25–27)
- Ms. Hanson sets up a conversation in which students determine that the ratios in the table are related by multiplicative constants. (para. 32)

Scaffolding students' thinking. Ms. Hanson scaffolds students' thinking by asking guiding questions and providing opportunities for students to make conceptual connections and analyze mathematical relationships. The list that follows provides examples of when and how Ms. Hanson scaffolds students' thinking.

- Ms. Hanson asks students to connect the unit rate to the ratio table. When the class returns to this question, they discover other multiplicative relationships in the table as well. (paras. 18, 30–32)
- Ms. Hanson wants students to explore and develop a variety of strategies for reasoning about proportional relationships. She comments that even though some of the students' strategies are inefficient, they seem to make sense to students, which will help build a foundation of proportional reasoning concepts. (paras. 36, 44)
- When Ms. Hanson asks students to reflect on Jordan's new candy jar versus Jerry's, she sets up a situation in which students could reason through an erroneous strategy based on additive relationships and reject it in favor of strategies based on multiplicative relationships. (para. 27)
- Ms. Hanson summarizes or rephrases students' ideas in order to make important concepts salient to the class. (paras. 28–29)
- Ms. Hanson compares Jordan's use of an additive constant to Jerlyn and Kamiko's use of repeated addition in creating their table. (para. 30)
- Ms. Hanson connects cross-multiplication to Danielle's factor-of-change strategy. (paras. 42–43)

FACILITATING THE OPENING ACTIVITY

The primary purpose of the Opening Activity is to engage teachers with the mathematical ideas that they will encounter when they read the case. The three problems in the Opening Activity (see the section entitled "Opening Activity" in Chapter 3) are a subset of those encountered by Marie Hanson's students during the lesson featured in the case. The problems are intended to highlight important aspects of proportional reasoning (e.g., additive versus multiplicative relationships, equivalent ratios, scale factors) and to allow teachers to develop strategies that make sense (e.g., using a ratio table, finding a unit rate, applying a scale factor). The "Consider" portion of the Opening Activity challenges teachers to solve each problem in a different way and to explore relationships between different strategies. In this section, we provide suggestions for using the Opening Activity.

1. Begin by having teachers work individually for 5 to 10 minutes, and continue to work on the problems with a partner. (We have found that beginning with "private think time" ensures that each participant has a chance to grapple with the task prior to engaging in collaborative work.) You may want to provide teachers with manipulatives such as square tiles and round chips (to model the problem situation) and calculators. You also may want to provide selected pairs with newsprint (for recording their solutions).

2. Assist teachers in their work on the problems if they appear to be having difficulty. Consider the following suggestions.

   - If some participants have difficulty getting started, you may want to ask them first to focus on the number of Jolly Ranchers compared to the number of Jawbreakers in the candy jar and then to think about how to increase the number of candies while keeping the same ratio of Jawbreakers to Jolly Ranchers. You may want to have them model the situation with concrete materials and to note what happens as they "grow" the jar but keep the ratio constant.
   - If some participants solve the problems using cross-multiplication, suggest that they revisit the task as students who do not know this procedure.
   - Watch for a common misconception—attempting to increase the number of candies by adding a constant value to each number in the original ratio (i.e., for the first problem, participants might reason as Jordan did in the case [paras. 24–25] that 95 Jawbreakers should be added to the new candy jar because there are 95 more Jolly Ranchers). If participants use this incorrect additive strategy, you may want to ask them to consider the relationship between the Jawbreakers and Jolly Ranchers in each jar (e.g., What can you say about the relationship in the original jar? Does this same relationship hold true in your new jar? Should it?). This might help participants to realize that adding a constant value to each term of the original ratio does not produce an equivalent ratio.

3. Orchestrate a whole-group discussion to allow participants to share various solution strategies and approaches. During the discussion you may want to:

   - Solicit responses that portray solution strategies that will be found in the case (e.g., unit rate, reasoning from a ratio table, factor-of-change, cross-multiplication). If you asked some pairs to record their solutions on newsprint, this would facilitate the presentation of solutions during the whole-group discussion. (A list of different solution methods we have seen teachers use to solve these problems can be found in Appendix B. This may help you prepare for the emergence of methods you might not have used when you solved the problems.)

- Post the solution methods used by the participants for each problem in the Opening Activity and discuss the relative strengths and weaknesses of various approaches and methods (e.g., the numbers in the original ratio make it difficult to use strategies based on a unit rate because the unit rate is not an integer; having 100 Jolly Ranchers in the first problem makes it easy to use a scale factor of 20). You might consider asking participants to solve a few additional missing-value problems and have them note the strategies they used to solve each problem. For example:

  A) 5 Jolly Ranchers to 20 Jawbreakers = 7 Jolly Ranchers to ? Jawbreakers

  B) 3 Jolly Ranchers to 5 Jawbreakers = 6 Jolly Ranchers to ? Jawbreakers

  Question A has a unit rate of 1 Jolly Rancher to 4 Jawbreakers, which is much easier to work with mentally than the scale factor of 1.4. Conversely, the scale factor of 2 in Question B is easier to apply than the unit rate of 0.6 Jolly Rancher to 1 Jawbreaker. Participants may find it interesting to consider how their preferred strategy changes according to the numbers in the problem.

- Ask participants to discuss any difficulties they experienced in solving the task, identify what difficulties they might anticipate students having, and brainstorm ways in which they could provide support to students who encountered difficulties.

4. Discuss the "Consider" portion of the Opening Activity, in which participants are asked to solve the problems in a different way, and note the relationship between the strategies. You may want to have teachers compare the various strategies that have been posted and discuss ways in which different strategies are related. (A discussion of how the different strategies are related can be found in Appendix B.) If a variety of solution methods have not emerged during participants' work on the Opening Activity, you may want to have participants read the case and then examine the strategies used by Ms. Hanson's students. We have found that allowing participants to work in groups while analyzing a specific strategy brings out important ideas about ratio and proportion and provides a chance to look closely at students' thinking. You may want to assign each group a specific strategy from the following list.

- Jerlyn and Kamiko's strategy for solving the first problem, using a table (paras. 10–11)
- April's strategy for determining the number of Jawbreakers for each Jolly Rancher (paras. 13–17)
- Jordan's additive strategy for solving the second problem (paras. 24–25)
- Jerry's, Jerlyn's, and Owen's strategies for solving the second problem (paras. 26–27)
- Danielle's factor-of-change strategy for solving the third problem (para. 37)
- Joshua's strategy for solving the third problem (para. 38)
- Angelica's cross-multiplication strategy for solving the third problem (para. 39)
- Ms. Hanson's explanation that relates Danielle's strategy to Angelica's strategy (paras. 42–43)

Ask the groups to describe the strategy, explain why the strategy works (or why it does not work), apply the strategy to another problem, and/or consider what the students who used the strategy seem to know and understand about proportional relationships. You also might ask participants to relate the strategies to procedures for solving missing-value problems (i.e., finding equivalent fractions, finding a unit rate, using cross-multiplication). You may want to allow time for a whole-group discussion in which each small group presents its specific strategy and discusses its responses to the above questions. Once a sufficient number of strategies have been presented, you might want to revisit the portion of the "Consider" question that asks how the different strategies are related, as participants may have gained new insights.

FACILITATING THE CASE DISCUSSION

The case discussion is intended to help participants analyze the mathematical and pedagogical ideas in the case. The "Case Analysis" should be of assistance in identifying the key ideas in the case and how each idea plays out in the details of the case. Although it is likely that you will begin by examining specific aspects of Marie Hanson's teaching practice, you should consider how to connect the specific events that occur in her class with more general ideas about mathematics teaching and learning. In this section we provide suggestions for launching and facilitating the case discussion, and for various follow-up activities that you may wish to pursue.

1. If possible, have participants read and reflect on the case before meeting as a group to discuss it. As participants read the case, we suggest that you ask them to identify ways in which Marie Hanson's pedagogy supported students' learning of mathematics. (This activity is described in more detail in the section of Chapter 3 entitled "Reading the Case.") This individual activity will help participants to think deeply about the pedagogy in the case and to prepare for the small- and whole-group discussions. Alternatively, you may want to select one of the questions found in Chapter 3 (see the section entitled "Extending Your Analysis of the Case") to guide the reading of the case.

2. Have teachers work in groups of three or four to create a two-column chart: One column should specify the pedagogical moves made by Marie Hanson that supported her students' learning of mathematics, the other should list *how* each of the identified pedagogy supported students' learning. Teachers should begin this process by reviewing the lists of supportive pedagogy that they created while reading "The Case of Marie Hanson" and determining whether a specific move should be placed in the group's chart. Once a list of supportive pedagogy has been made, teachers can complete the chart by filling in the second column. In completing this task, group members should be encouraged to cite specific evidence from the case (using paragraph numbers) to support each idea recorded in their charts.

3. During the whole-group discussion, you may want to develop a master chart that combines the work of the individual groups. You might begin building this master chart by asking groups to identify the pedagogical move in their chart that they feel best supported student learning and to provide a rationale for their selection. Encourage participants to argue respectfully if they do not agree that an identified move served to support student learning of mathematics. This can lead to a rich evidence-based discussion. A sample chart that was created by a group of teachers is included in Appendix B. We encourage you to develop your own list prior to reviewing the one provided.

You may wish to end the discussion by asking teachers what aspects of Marie Hanson's pedagogy could be used in other teaching situations. This will help teachers to move beyond the particular events that occurred in the case and to begin to see them as instantiations of more generalizable ideas about mathematics teaching and learning.

4. Once you have completed a discussion of how Marie Hanson supported students' learning, you may want to raise additional questions for consideration. The questions in Chapter 3 in the section entitled "Extending Your Analysis of the Case" may be useful for this purpose. Alternatively, you may wish to ask teachers to investigate a specific mathematical or pedagogical idea that was discussed in the case analysis.

5. Following the discussion, you may want to have participants reflect individually by writing about some aspect of the case experience. This could involve having participants: (1) determine what Marie Hanson should do on the day following the one portrayed in the case; (2) consider whether they would have liked to have been a student in Marie Hanson's classroom and explain why or why not; (3) compare Marie Hanson with a teacher from another case, such as Randy Harris, and consider how the two teachers are the same and how they are different.

EXTENDING THE CASE EXPERIENCE

If you have additional time, you may want to provide teachers with opportunities to consider their own practice and continue to explore the mathematical and pedagogical ideas on which the case is based. The section entitled "Extending Case-Based Experiences" in Chapter 6 suggests three types of activities you might want to assign teachers for these purposes.

Facilitating Learning from The Case of Marcia Green

"The Case of Marcia Green" portrays the work of a 7th-grade teacher and her students at Dalton Middle School as they use rubber-band stretchers to enlarge a square and an equilateral triangle in order to explore the relationship between the dimensions, perimeter, and area of the original figure and its enlarged image. Students are eager to use the rubber-band stretchers and share their observations with their classmates. During the lesson, Mrs. Green questions students in order to clarify aspects of their observations and to refocus a disagreement between two students. Mrs. Green believes that the time spent on the rubber-band activity is worthwhile because the task captures students' interest and provides a basis for the development of proportional reasoning concepts such as ratio, scale factor, and similarity.

CASE ANALYSIS

In this section, we provide a detailed analysis of the mathematical and pedagogical ideas that are found in the case. These analyses may help you in determining which aspects of the case you wish to highlight during the discussion.

Considering the Mathematics in the Case

This lesson is the first in a unit that is intended to develop students' proportional reasoning skills through an exploration of the properties of similar figures. The task in the lesson is intended to provide students with the opportunity to develop initial ideas about similar figures. These ideas will be refined and strengthened in future lessons. In particular, students discover that the scale factor relating the lengths of the sides of similar figures (i.e., a figure and its enlarged image) is not the same as the scale factor relating the areas. This lesson and the homework question equip students to investigate the relationship between the two different scale factors more thoroughly in upcoming lessons.

Below we identify several important mathematical ideas that surface in the case, and we provide examples of where these ideas appear.

Similar figures. A figure and its enlarged image are similar figures. Students observe that the rubber-band stretcher preserves the shape of the figures that are being enlarged. Students form an intuitive definition of similar figures—they have "the same shape but different sizes." In future lessons, students will refine this definition as they discover that similar figures have equal corresponding angles and equal ratios between pairs of corresponding sides. The list that follows identifies instances in the case in which the topic of similar figures arises.

- Forming an intuitive understanding of the properties of similar figures is a main goal of the lesson. Mrs. Green comments that comparing the original figure with its enlargement should lead students to discover that the figures have the same shape but different sizes. (paras. 6, 9)
- Mrs. Green notes that students will refine their concept of similarity as they discover other properties of similar figures in future lessons. (paras. 7, 9, 15)
- Students observe that the rubber-band stretcher has enlarged the original figure. Jason comments that the figures "got bigger but they still stayed the same shape." (para. 14)
- Mrs. Green introduces the term "similar figures" to describe figures that have the same shape but different sizes. (para. 15)

- The introduction to the case and comments by Mrs. Green state the importance of developing proportional reasoning concepts in middle school. (paras. 2, 5)
- Mrs. Green comments that this unit will enable students to strengthen their ideas about ratios, equivalent ratios, and using proportions to solve problems. (para. 6)
- Mrs. Green notes that this lesson intends to build a foundation of proportional reasoning concepts, such as similarity and scale factor, which will be developed further in later lessons. (paras. 6–7)
- Students note that the squares are the same shape but different sizes (similar figures). This intuitive, visual sense of proportionality will be explored and quantified in future lessons. (paras. 14–15)
- Students' comments such as "double," "four times larger," and "one-fourth" provide opportunities to introduce proportional reasoning concepts and language. However, Mrs. Green does not take advantage of these opportunities in this lesson. (paras. 22–27)

Creating visual diagrams to discover and communicate mathematical relationships. Students create sets of similar figures using the rubber-band stretchers. They then use their drawings to make observations and reason about the relationships between the original figures and their enlarged images. Several students also use the diagrams at the overhead to explain or justify their ideas more thoroughly. The drawings thus serve as visual tools that facilitate students' discovery of the properties of similar figures intended by the lesson. The list that follows provides examples of how students use visual diagrams in the case.

- Students, especially Jason, make observations about the figures that generate an initial definition of similar figures. (paras. 14–16)
- Alyssa has visually determined that the area has quadrupled and does not see the need to measure the sides of the figures. She asks the class to "look at the two squares" to see that the relationship is "much more than double." (paras. 19, 22)
- Although students enlarged the figures at their seats, Mrs. Green also asks for the square and triangle to be enlarged at the overhead. Several students use the diagrams at the overhead to explain their thinking. (paras. 14, 22–23, 26–27)
- Mrs. Green suggests that sketches might be helpful in thinking about the homework question. (para. 28)

Measurement and estimation. Students measure the sides of the squares and equilateral triangles to explore Mrs. Green's question of how the original figure relates to its enlarged image. The rubber-band stretcher does not produce exact enlargements, and straight lines and angle measures are not perfectly preserved. Students therefore must estimate the dimensions of the enlarged square and equilateral triangle and must make appropriate estimations in order to observe that the dimensions have doubled. Mrs. Green has allowed estimation skills to develop as needed in the context of other activities, and she is pleased with students' reasoning in estimating the dimensions of the enlarged square. The list that follows identifies specific places in the case that pertain to measurement and estimation.

- Mrs. Green asks students to measure the sides of the original figure and their enlarged images in order to discover the relationship among the dimensions, perimeter, and area. (para. 17)
- Jessica comments that the enlargements are "not exact . . . like a rough drawing." Later in the lesson, Maria restates Jessica's idea and Tia adds that "the angles are not perfectly right angles and that made the sides different." (paras. 16, 21)
- Jared asks if they need to measure each side of the square and equilateral triangle. His partner, Lacey, comments that it would be a good idea, in case they made a mistake in measuring the first side. (para. 18)
- Katie's group uses 6 cm for the side of the enlarged square "because it was the largest," but the class feels that 5 cm is more appropriate because it is "in the middle." (paras. 20–21)
- Alyssa does not see the need to measure the sides of the figures because she has relied completely on visual estimation to determine that the area had quadrupled. (paras. 19, 22)

Considering How Student Thinking Is Supported

Marcia Green has selected a task that is intended to provide students with the opportunity to explore some initial ideas about similar figures that will be refined and strengthened throughout the upcoming unit. Mrs. Green believes that it is worth spending time on this activity because the task captures students' interest and provides a basis for the development of proportional reasoning concepts such as ratio and scale factor. Throughout the lesson she encourages students to

- Students' initial observations and the definition of similar figures are added to the class list. (para. 16)
- Students recognize that the shape of the figures has been preserved as they assert that the enlarged figure should still be a square (or equilateral triangle) even though they obtained different measurements for the lengths of each of the sides. (paras. 20, 26)

Relationships between similar figures. When a figure is enlarged so that the lengths of its sides have increased by a scale factor of x, its area increases by a factor of x^2. In the lesson, students discover that the lengths of the sides and the perimeter of the enlarged square have doubled while the area has become four times larger. Mrs. Green attempts to move students toward generalizing this relationship by asking if it also will hold true for the triangles and by posing a homework question that intends for students to determine that the area will be nine times larger when the lengths have tripled. The precise generalization will be discovered in future lessons that draw students' attention to scale factors. The list that follows provides instances in which relationships between similar figures are addressed in the case.

- A main goal of the lesson is for students to realize that the area of the enlarged figure has increased by a different factor than the lengths of the sides. (paras. 6, 9)
- Mrs. Green comments that the homework question and future lessons will prompt students to generalize the precise relationship between the areas of similar figures. (paras. 7, 9)
- Students discuss how the lengths have doubled while the area has become four times larger. (paras. 22–24, 26–27)
- Students note that the perimeters also have doubled, but this notion is not explored thoroughly in the lesson. (paras. 24, 26)
- The homework assignment asks students to consider what will happen to the lengths of the sides, perimeter, and area if three rubber bands are used to enlarge a figure. (para. 28)

Scale factors and multiplicative reasoning. Thinking in terms of scale factors indicates that students can see multiplicative relationships—an important aspect of being able to reason proportionally. This lesson provides a context in which to develop students' ideas about scale factors. Students describe length and area

relationships between a figure and its enlarged imag[e] being "doubled" and "four times larger," respectiv[ely]. However, Mrs. Green is concerned that students m[ay] not be seeing multiplicative relationships even tho[ugh] they state that the lengths have doubled. Students c[ould] be thinking of doubling as adding "the length plus [the] length" rather than as multiplying "the length ti[mes] two." She comments that students' notions about m[ul]tiplicative versus additive relationships will be m[ade] more salient as the class focuses on scale factors in [future] lessons. Attending to scale factors is also essenti[al to] discovering the relationship between the areas of [simi]lar figures. The list that follows provides exampl[es of] how the ideas of scale factors and multiplicative re[ason]ing play out in the case.

- The lesson intends for students to form initial [ideas] about scale factor that will be developed more [fully] explicitly in future lessons. (para. 6)
- Students need to think in terms of scale factor[s to] discover the x to x^2 relationship between the f[actors] of the lengths and the areas of enlarged figure[s.] (para. 7)
- Students using the word *doubled* might be thi[nking] of additive relationships or of multiplicative [ ] relationships. Juan's statement, "2½ plus ano[ther] 2½," indicates that he is thinking of doubling [as an] additive relationship. (paras. 22–24, 27)
- Describing the area as "four times bigger" pr[ovides] an easy transition to thinking of the area as in[creas]ing by a factor of 4. (paras. 22–24)
- Mrs. Green is concerned that students might [not be] recognizing multiplicative relationships whe[n] comparing the lengths of the figures. (para. 2[ ])

Ratio and proportion. Although the ideas [of ratio] and proportion are not discussed explicitly in [the les]son, they are central to the task and arise im[plicitly] throughout the discussion. Students' comme[nts that] the sides of the original figure have "doubled" [and that] the area of an enlarged figure is now "four time[s bigger"] provide opportunities to encourage proportiona[l reason]ing (e.g., the lengths are related by a ratio [of 1 to 2;] the lengths have increased by a scale factor o[f 2; the] lengths of both the square and the triangle inc[rease at] a rate of 1 to 2; the increase in dimensions betw[een the] original and the enlarged square are proport[ional to] the increase in dimensions between the origi[nal and] the enlarged triangle). The list that follows i[ndicates] where ideas related to ratio and proportion ari[se in the] case.

analyze the relationships between the two figures and to make and support their conjectures.

Below we identify several pedagogical moves that Marcia Green made that may have influenced her students' opportunities to engage in high-level thinking, reasoning, and communication during the lesson, and we provide examples of where these ideas appear in the case.

Providing an appropriate amount of time. Marcia Green provides an appropriate amount of time for students to explore the task and discover mathematical relationships for themselves. Mrs. Green also provides time in class for students to think about the problem with a partner and share ideas in a whole-class setting. The list that follows identifies instances in which Mrs. Green uses time appropriately.

- Mrs. Green comments that although this task seems like a small step mathematically compared with the time it consumes, she feels that the lesson provides an interesting, visual context for students to begin thinking about similarity, scale factor, and proportions. (para. 10)
- Mrs. Green gives students time to work in pairs to draw the enlarged figures. Students then discuss their observations as a class and form an initial definition of similar figures. (paras. 12, 14–15)
- Following the first discussion, Mrs. Green gives students time to measure the sides of the squares and triangles with their partners and to look for relationships between the original and enlarged figures. (paras. 18–20)
- Students (in particular, Alyssa, Juan, Tia, and Bonita) are given time to explain, clarify, and demonstrate ideas. (paras. 22–23, 26–27)

Building on students' prior knowledge and experiences. Mrs. Green uses a task that builds on students' prior knowledge of ratios. As the first activity in the unit, this task serves as a transition from the informal proportional reasoning problems students had encountered throughout the year (i.e., forming ratios from objects in a picture) to the comprehensive explorations of similarity, scale factor, and proportionality contained in this unit. Mrs. Green also has provided students with a background of mathematical ideas and skills (such as measurement, estimation, and fractions) that are necessary to explore the task and discover the intended relationships. The list that follows provides examples of how Mrs. Green builds on her students' prior knowledge.

- Students in Marcia Green's class have previously encountered problems involving ratios, equivalent ratios, and proportions. Mrs. Green comments that this unit will allow students to refine and strengthen the proportional reasoning ideas that they have been developing throughout the year. (paras. 5–7)
- Mrs. Green notes that earlier work with fractions, measurement, and estimation should help students explore the task and discover relationships. (para. 9)
- The homework assignment builds on prior knowledge by extending many of the ideas generated during the lesson. (para. 28)

Encouraging communication. Marcia Green wants to establish a classroom environment that encourages mathematical discourse. She does this by creating opportunities for students to interact with one another and share ideas in both small-group and whole-class settings. Mrs. Green indicates that she values students' ideas by recording and displaying their comments on the overhead. Mrs. Green also expects students to respectfully critique the ideas of others. The list that follows provides examples of ways in which Mrs. Green encourages mathematical communication in her classroom.

- Students explore and discuss the task with a partner twice during the lesson, first to enlarge the figures and then to measure the figures and look for relationships. (paras. 12, 18)
- Mrs. Green takes advantage of opportunities to promote student-to-student interaction (among Alyssa, Katie, and Juan, and between Tia and Bonita) during the whole-class discussion. (paras. 22–23, 27)
- Mrs. Green displays students' ideas on an observation sheet on the overhead. (paras. 16, 28)
- Mrs. Green reminds students to be respectful of the ideas of their fellow classmates (such as Jason and Katie). (paras. 15, 23)

Pressing students to explain and justify ideas. Mrs. Green continually presses students to explain and justify their ideas and to make sense of the ideas of others. Students are expected to share their ideas with a partner and in a whole-group discussion and to determine the validity of ideas proposed by others. Examples in which Mrs. Green presses students to explain and justify their ideas are shown in the list that follows.

- Mrs. Green asks individual students (such as Jason, Katie, Alyssa, and Bonita) to further explain or justify their ideas. (paras. 14, 20, 22, 24, 27)
- Mrs. Green asks the class to determine the validity of an idea that has been presented, or to elaborate on ideas that are likely to generate differing positions. (paras. 20–21, 23)

Guiding students' thinking through questioning. Marcia Green often asks questions intended to press students to analyze mathematical relationships. These questions attempt to make the central mathematical ideas salient and to connect or clarify important concepts. Mrs. Green frequently poses questions that build on students' ideas and serve to guide students' thinking toward the goals of the lesson. The list that follows provides examples of questions that Marcia Green poses that serve these purposes.

- Mrs. Green asks students to make observations about what the rubber-band stretcher did to the original figures and uses Jason's observation to introduce the term *similar figures.* Forming an initial definition of similar figures was a goal of the lesson. (paras. 14–15)
- Mrs. Green asks students to consider how the original square relates to its enlarged image, and later asks if the same relationships also hold true for the triangles. (paras. 17, 22, 24, and 26)
- Mrs. Green's questioning about how students know that the enlarged figure is still a square connects the discussion back to the idea of similar figures. (para. 20)
- Mrs. Green asks students to address the two different ideas presented by Katie and Alyssa. Realizing that the lengths increased by a different factor than the area was a goal of the lesson. (para. 23)
- The homework question that Mrs. Green poses will help students generalize the relationship between scale factors and area in similar figures. (para. 28)

FACILITATING THE OPENING ACTIVITY

The primary purpose of the Opening Activity is to engage teachers with the mathematical ideas that they will encounter when they read the case. The task in the Opening Activity (see the section entitled "Opening Activity" in Chapter 4) asks teachers to create sets of similar figures with rubber-band stretchers and to explore the relationships between the original figures and their enlarged images, as Marcia Green's students do in the case. This exploration is intended to help teachers determine that the lengths of the corresponding sides are related by a scale factor of x, and the areas are related by a factor of x^2 (para. 7). The task is challenging because teachers are asked to explore the relationship without any specific direction regarding what to explore or how to explore it. In this section, we provide suggestions for using the Opening Activity.

1. Begin by having participants build their own rubber-band stretchers. You may want to model how to build and use the rubber-band stretcher and then walk participants through the process. (This process is described in more detail in the section entitled "Opening Activity" in Chapter 4.) You may want to have each participant practice using the rubber-band stretcher by enlarging a practice figure (such as a smiley face) before beginning the Opening Activity. Each participant should enlarge the figures on his or her own, but you may want to have participants work in pairs or small groups to explore the relationships between the original figures and the enlargements and to respond to the "Consider" question in the Opening Activity.

   The following materials are required for the Opening Activity: blank paper (for creating the enlargements), tape (for taping the paper to the desk or table); rubber bands (to build the stretchers). (We have found that size 30, 31, 32, or 33 rubber bands work well for this task.) You may also want to provide participants with the following materials: rulers (for measuring the dimensions of the figures); scissors (for cutting out the figures); and/or calculators (for calculating the area of the figures). We have found that making such materials available allows participants to replicate strategies that may be used by students and does not narrow the range of pathways that can be pursued.

2. Assist participants in their work on the task if they appear to be having difficulty. Consider the following suggestions.

   - In order for their enlargements to be more accurate, encourage participants to keep the rubber-band stretchers taut and to keep the rubber band close to the tip of the pencil.
   - If participants are having trouble making accurate enlargements, suggest that they use the stretcher to plot the vertices of the figure and

then use the straight edge of a ruler to complete the enlargements.

- If participants are having trouble determining the relationships between the original figure and its enlargement because some of their enlargements are inaccurate, suggest that the group select their neatest enlargement and use that to investigate and approximate the relationships.

- You might want to encourage participants to make connections between numeric or algebraic strategies and visual strategies. For example, you might ask participants who compared numeric values of length and area to explain why the four little squares fit in the bigger square, or to verify the result of the formulas for area and perimeter in a visual-geometric way. Similarly, you might ask participants who used a visual approach if they can verify their results using the formulas.

3. Orchestrate a whole-group discussion to allow participants to share various approaches and observations in response to the "Solve" questions. During the discussion you may want to:

- Solicit responses that portray general solution strategies that will be found in the case. It is helpful to discuss at least one solution method that does not involve measuring. You also may want to ask participants to make connections between a visual approach and a numeric approach. (A list of different solution methods we have seen teachers use to solve these tasks can be found in Appendix C. This may help you prepare for the emergence of methods you might not have used when you solved the problems.)

- Solicit responses that address general characteristics of similar figures (e.g., shape and angle measure are preserved) as well as observations that focus on relationships between particular attributes of the figures (e.g., side length, perimeter, area).

4. Discuss the "Consider" portion of the Opening Activity, in which participants are asked to make conjectures about enlargements created with a three-rubber-band stretcher, and consider what generalization is suggested about the relationship between: (1) the number of rubber bands and the scale factor relating the side lengths of the original and enlarged figures, and (2) the scale factor for the side lengths of the original and enlarged figures and the scale factor for the areas of the original and enlarged figures. Consider the following suggestions.

- If participants are having difficulty answering the "Consider" question, you might suggest that they explore the task using a three-rubber-band stretcher and then conjecture about a four-rubber-band stretcher and consider the generalization that is suggested.

- You might ask participants to organize their data into a table and look for patterns in the ratios of the side lengths of the original figures and the enlargements (i.e., $1:x$ where x is the number of rubber bands), in the ratios of the areas of the original figures and the enlargements (i.e., $1:x^2$ where x is the number of rubber bands), and in how these two ratios are related to each other (i.e., the ratio of the areas of similar figures is the square of the ratio of the side lengths).

FACILITATING THE CASE DISCUSSION

The case discussion is intended to help participants analyze the mathematical and pedagogical ideas in the case. The "Case Analysis" should be of assistance in identifying the key ideas in the case and how each idea plays out in the details of the case. Although it is likely that you will begin by examining specific aspects of Marcia Green's teaching practice, you should consider how to connect the specific events that occur in her class with more general ideas about mathematics teaching and learning. In this section we provide suggestions for launching and facilitating the case discussion, and for various follow-up activities that you may wish to pursue.

1. If possible, have participants read and reflect on the case before meeting as a group to discuss it. As participants read the case, we suggest that you ask them to identify what they consider to be "good questions" asked by Marcia Green. (This activity is described in more detail in the section of Chapter 4 entitled "Reading the Case.") This individual activity will help participants to think deeply about the use of questioning by the teacher in the case and to prepare for the small- and whole-group discussions. Alternatively, you may want to select one of the questions found in Chapter 4 (see the section entitled "Extending Your Analysis of the Case") to guide the reading of the case.

2. Begin by having teachers work in small groups to share the good questions they identified. You might suggest that each person in the small group share one to three of the questions identified and explain: (1) What makes it a good question? (2) What is Mrs. Green's purpose for asking this question? and (3) How did the question advance students' learning?

3. Once each small-group member has had the opportunity to share the selected questions, you may want to ask the small groups to select one to three of the good questions they identified to write on newsprint and post in the room. You then might ask each small group to generate a list of criteria for good questions that would apply to all of the good questions that have been identified.

4. After the small groups have posted their questions and have generated a list of criteria for a good question, begin the whole-group discussion by focusing on the questions which appear on several of the lists. Ask the groups that selected these "popular" questions to justify their selections. You may then want to discuss one or two questions that appeared less frequently.

   Participants should also be asked how the identified questions exemplify the criteria for good questions that they generated in their small groups. You may want to make a list of the criteria for good questions on chart paper or on an overhead transparency. Additional questions can then be reviewed in light of the criteria.

   The goal of the whole-group discussion is to make salient that a good question is one that helps advance students' engagement with and understanding of the mathematical ideas. A list of all the questions that Marcia Green asked during the lesson is included in Appendix C. In this list, we

have placed an asterisk next to questions that were identified as good questions by a group of teachers with whom we worked. In addition, Appendix C contains a chart of teacher-generated criteria for good questions. We encourage you to make your own list of good questions and develop your own set of criteria for good questions prior to reviewing the sample lists provided.

You may want to conclude the whole-group discussion by asking teachers what lessons can be learned about questioning from Marcia Green's class that can be applied to teaching more broadly. This will help teachers to move beyond the particular events that occurred in the case and to begin to see them as instantiations of more generalizable ideas about mathematics teaching and learning.

5. Following the discussion, you may want to have participants reflect individually by writing about some aspect of the case experience. This could involve asking participants to share what they think Mrs. Green did to prepare for this lesson or to consider how Mrs. Green might build on this lesson to further develop students' understanding of similar figures, scale drawings, or multiplicative relationships.

EXTENDING THE CASE EXPERIENCE

If you have additional time, you may want to provide teachers with opportunities to consider their own practice and continue to explore the mathematical and pedagogical ideas on which the case is based. The section entitled "Extending Case-Based Experiences" in Chapter 6 suggests three types of activities you might want to assign teachers for these purposes.

10

Facilitating Learning from The Case of Janice Patterson

"The Case of Janice Patterson" focuses on a 7th-grade teacher and her students at Lincoln Middle School as they use visual diagrams to solve a set of three challenging problems. While the problems differ in context and structure, as a set they provide students with the opportunity to apply proportional reasoning skills to a variety of situations. Students are actively engaged during the lesson as they explore the problems in pairs and share their work with the class. Throughout the lesson, Mrs. Patterson solicits multiple ways of solving the problems and encourages students to use nonalgorithmic strategies that utilize diagrams. She supports students as they work through the problems by recognizing when they are struggling and by asking questions to scaffold their thinking.

CASE ANALYSIS

In this section we provide a detailed analysis of the mathematical and pedagogical ideas that are found in the case. These analyses may help you in determining which aspects of the case you wish to highlight during the discussion.

Considering the Mathematics in the Case

As a set, the three problems that Mrs. Patterson presents to her students have the potential to elicit high-level thinking about the relationships between quantities. Mrs. Patterson has selected these problems because they are each quite different in structure and context, and can be solved using various approaches—thus giving all of her students the opportunity to engage with the mathematical ideas at some level. Because Mrs. Patterson has not provided students with specific pro-cedures to solve these types of problems, students explore a variety of strategies and create diagrams to support their reasoning. The problems also allow students to apply previous knowledge about ratios among discrete quantities to problems involving continuous quantities.

Below we identify several important mathematical ideas that surface in the case, and we provide examples of where these ideas appear.

Multiplicative relationships. Reasoning about multiplicative relationships between quantities is a common feature of the problems in this lesson. Problem 1 requires students to recognize that the 3 to 4 ratio expresses a multiplicative relationship between the length and width of the desired rectangle. Multiplicative relationships are expressed as percents in Problems 2 and 3. In each of these problems, students find the percent of a quantity and relate percents to fractions and ratios. Problem 3 involves reasoning about two different percents of two different quantities. Students come to realize that although the two quantities can be added together to find a total quantity, the two percents cannot be added together to find a total percent. Students must attend to the relative size of each percent, considering both the amount of fat each percent represents and how this amount compares with the total mixture. The list that follows provides specific examples in which the notion of multiplicative relationships arises in the case.

- Solutions for Problem 1 indicate that students recognize that the 3 to 4 ratio must be maintained when determining the length and width of the rectangle with an area of 300 square inches. (paras. 9 and 12–13)

- Kalla describes 3 and 4 as the *ratio* of length to width rather than the *actual* length and width. (para. 15)
- Students find the percent of a quantity for Problems 2 and 3 both by multiplying the percent by the quantity and by relating percents to fractions. (paras. 20–24 and 30–31)
- In solving Problem 3, students discuss why they can't "just add the two percents," and why the mixture's fat content should be closer to 4% than to 20%. (paras. 26 and 28)
- Dametris notes that Problem 3 involves comparing "two different percents and two different amounts so we gotta make them alike somehow." Crystal suggests that they determine how much the percents represent "gallon-wise." (para. 29)

Ratio and scale factor. Janice Patterson's students have had previous experience with expressing ratios of sets of discrete objects. Students also have had opportunities to determine equivalent ratios, which is essential in solving Problem 1. To determine the length and width of the rectangle with an area of 300 square inches, several students seem to realize that the same number must be multiplied by both 3 and 4 to maintain the 3 to 4 relationship. This thinking incorporates an intuitive notion of scale factor, although the term "scale factor" is not explicitly discussed. The list that follows provides specific examples of where students work with ratio and scale factor during the lesson.

- Mrs. Patterson discusses students' previous work with ratios and finding equivalent ratios, and how this new set of problems extends students' thinking. (paras. 4 and 6)
- For Problem 1, Lamont and Richard seem to realize that 3 and 4 must be multiplied by the same number (i.e., a scale factor) in order to keep the 3 to 4 ratio constant (although they are not able to articulate this idea clearly). (paras. 9 and 10)
- In explaining why he and Maria multiplied by 2, 3, 4, and 5 in Problem 1, Kevin informally defines scale factor as a number you multiply 3 and 4 by so that the ratio stays the same. (para. 13)
- Mrs. Patterson comments that Kevin and Maria's solution for Problem 1 showed the importance of using the same factor in order to keep a constant ratio when finding the lengths and widths of new rectangles. (para. 14)

Creating visual diagrams to make sense of problem situations and communicate mathematical thinking. Because students are not given specific procedures for solving the three problems, this lesson provides an opportunity for students to create diagrams in order to make sense of problem situations. Several students create diagrams to help them think about the relationships between quantities in each of the problems. Students in the case also use diagrams as a tool to clearly communicate their mathematical ideas to others. The list that follows provides specific examples of students using visual diagrams during the class and the importance Mrs. Patterson places on such approaches.

- Mrs. Patterson discusses the value of creating diagrams to make sense of problem situations and to communicate ideas to others. (para. 7)
- For Problem 1, Robin and Kalla draw a rectangle partitioned into square units. (para. 15)
- Mrs. Patterson invites Sasha to share her approach to Problem 2 because Sasha has made extensive use of a diagram in thinking about the problem. (para. 19)
- Crystal draws a diagram for Problem 3 and explains that she needed a picture in order to figure out what to do. (paras. 30–31)
- Mrs. Patterson reflects on how the diagrams supported students' thinking throughout the lesson, and how diagram use is helpful in providing the conceptual underpinnings of symbolic methods. (para. 32)

Problem-solving. Students in Janice Patterson's classroom learn mathematics through solving challenging mathematical tasks. Mrs. Patterson frequently poses tasks that provide opportunities for students to experience a variety of problem-solving strategies in the process of examining important mathematical ideas. In this lesson, she uses three challenging problems both to strengthen students' proportional reasoning skills and to encourage students to create diagrams to solve problems. Her students employ different problem-solving strategies (e.g., guess-and-check, making a table, creating diagrams, deductive reasoning) while engaging with a variety of mathematical ideas (e.g., multiplicative relationships, ratio and scale factor, area, relating fractions, percents, and decimals). The list that follows provides specific examples of students engaging in problem-solving during the class and the importance Mrs. Patterson places on problem-solving.

- Mrs. Patterson describes the benefits of using three problems that address proportional reasoning concepts but are not similar in structure. (para. 6)
- Students work in pairs to explore Problems 1 and 3 as Mrs. Patterson visits each group to facilitate their problem-solving efforts. (paras. 8 and 26)
- Students use different strategies for Problem 1. Lamont and Richard use a guess-and-check strategy but do not approach the problem systematically. Maria and Kevin use a guess-and-check strategy but organize their thinking in a table. Robin and Kalla use deductive reasoning based on the information in the problem and their understanding of area. (paras. 9–10, 12–13, and 15–16)
- Mrs. Patterson invites Sasha to present her solution to Problem 2 because it makes use of a diagram. (para. 19)
- Mrs. Patterson's own experiences with mathematics were dominated by symbolic solution methods. By contrast, she wants her students to solve problems in which they must "determine what they know and what they need to figure out, and then develop a plan for doing so." (paras. 6 and 18)
- Problem 1 requires students to know how to determine the area of a rectangle. Robin and Kalla's diagram serves to reinforce students' understanding of the concept of area. (paras. 15–16)
- Through the discussion of Sasha's solution for Problem 2 and Crystal's diagram for Problem 3, students are given the opportunity to relate fractions, decimals, and percents. (paras. 24 and 30)

Considering How Student Thinking Is Supported

Janice Patterson provides an opportunity for students to explore mathematical ideas in the context of problem-solving by structuring her lesson around three challenging problems. She intends for students to gain experience using multiplicative thinking and visual diagrams as they engage with this set of difficult, yet accessible, problems. Mrs. Patterson maintains a classroom environment in which students can explore and make sense of mathematical ideas and question one another's thinking.

Below we identify several pedagogical moves that Janice Patterson made that may have influenced her students' opportunities to engage in high-level thinking, reasoning, and communication during the lesson, and we provide examples of where these ideas appear in the case.

Providing an appropriate amount of time. Mrs. Patterson provides an appropriate amount of time for students to explore the problems, to think, and to discover mathematical relationships for themselves. She also provides time within the lesson for students to think about each problem with a partner and to share ideas in a whole-class setting. The list that follows provides specific examples of how Mrs. Patterson provides appropriate amounts of time for students to engage in each portion of the lesson.

- Mrs. Patterson gives the class 10 minutes to explore Problem 1 with a partner. When most pairs have completed the problem, she asks students to share their ideas with the class. Mrs. Patterson allows for the presentation of three solution methods to this problem because she is looking for a strategy that does not rely on guess-and-check. (paras. 8–9, 11, and 14)
- The class has worked on Problem 2 for less than 10 minutes when Mrs. Patterson notes that everyone seems to be finished. Since most students used a guess-and-check strategy, Mrs. Patterson elicits only one solution to this problem (which uses a diagram rather than guess-and-check) to allow more time for Problem 3. (paras. 19 and 25)
- Mrs. Patterson notes that less than 10 minutes remain in the class period and students have made little progress on Problem 3. Rather than rushing through a solution to the problem, Mrs. Patterson elicits ideas that will help the students complete the problem for homework. Students continue to think about the problem with their partner for the last 5 minutes of class. (paras. 27–31)

Building on students' prior knowledge and experiences. Mrs. Patterson chooses problems that build on students' prior knowledge of ratios and finding equivalent ratios of discrete objects. The problems she presents are intended to extend students' ideas to situations involving continuous quantities and contextualized settings. The problems increase in difficulty in order for students to experience some success before grappling with the most challenging problem (Problem 3). Students must draw upon prior knowledge in finding and understanding area; in relating fractions, decimals, and percents; and in using diagrams to support their thinking. Mrs. Patterson also has prepared her students to engage with these problems by establishing an environment in which exploration, discussion, and sometimes frustration are the norm. The list that follows provides specific examples of how the lesson builds on students' prior knowledge.

- Mrs. Patterson discusses students' earlier work with ratios. (paras. 4–5)
- Mrs. Patterson notes that students previously had used diagrams to support their thinking about fractions, percents, and decimals. Two students (Sasha and Crystal) provide examples of this in the case. (paras. 7, 24, and 30)
- Students immediately begin exploring Problem 1 with their partners, indicating that exploring mathematics problems with others is the norm in Mrs. Patterson's classroom. (para. 8)
- Mrs. Patterson provides a homework assignment that builds on ideas generated in class. (para. 31)

Encouraging communication. Mrs. Patterson has established a classroom environment that encourages mathematical discourse. She creates opportunities for students to discuss mathematical ideas with a partner and to present these ideas during whole-group discussions. She expects students to be able to justify their own ideas and to make sense of the ideas of others. Thus, students question each other rather than relying on the teacher as the sole mathematical authority in the classroom. The list that follows provides specific examples of how Mrs. Patterson promotes student communication during the lesson.

- Students are given the opportunity to explore the problems with a partner. (paras. 8, 26, and 31)
- Mrs. Patterson asks the class whether they have questions for the students who are presenting solutions. (paras. 10, 24, and 31)
- Students ask questions of their classmates in order to make sense of the ideas being presented. Some of these questions follow Mrs. Patterson's requests (above) and some are initiated by students. (paras. 10, 13, 22, 24, 28, and 31)

Modeling of high-level performance. Mrs. Patterson takes advantage of opportunities for students to model high-level performance. She observes students exploring the problems with their partners and selects specific students to present ideas that exemplify her goals for the lesson. For example, Mrs. Patterson elicits solution strategies that incorporate diagrams and do not rely on guess-and-check. She also chooses a pair of students to talk about their ideas for Problem 3 who, after an initial disagreement, were beginning to make sense of the quantities and relationships in the problem. The list that follows provides specific examples of how Mrs. Patterson solicits students to model high-level performance.

- Mrs. Patterson elicits ways of thinking about Problem 1 that did not rely on guess-and-check methods. (paras. 11 and 14)
- Mrs. Patterson invites Sasha to present her solution for Problem 2 because she has made extensive use of a diagram. (para. 19)
- Mrs. Patterson asks Jason and Angela to share their ideas about Problem 3. She notes that this pair raised issues about the problem that might be helpful to others. (para. 27)
- Mrs. Patterson invites Crystal to the overhead to share her diagram for Problem 3. (para. 30)

Continuing to press students for explanation and meaning. Mrs. Patterson presses students to explain their thinking and make sense of their solution methods. Students are expected to share their ideas and solution strategies with a partner and in a whole-group discussion. Once an idea or solution method has been presented, it is an established routine that students explain their reasoning and answer questions from Mrs. Patterson or from classmates. For example, students such as Lamont and Richard, Kalla and Robin, and Sasha present their strategies to the class, explain their reasoning, and answer questions from Mrs. Patterson or from other students. (paras. 10, 16, and 20–24)

FACILITATING THE OPENING ACTIVITY

The primary purpose of the Opening Activity is to engage teachers with the mathematical ideas that they will encounter when they read the case. The three problems that are found in the Opening Activity (see the section entitled "Opening Activity" in Chapter 5) are identical to those that Mrs. Patterson's students solve in the case. Although participants might be familiar with algebraic procedures for solving these types of problems, the problems become challenging when participants are asked to reason through the problems using diagrams, as Janice Patterson asks of her students (para. 7). The "Consider" portion of the Opening Activity challenges teachers to make sense of students' diagrams and to complete the problems using these diagrams. In this section, we provide suggestions for using the Opening Activity.

1. Begin by having teachers work individually on the problem set for 5 to 10 minutes and then continue to work on the problems with a partner. (We have found that beginning with "private think time" ensures that each participant has a chance to grapple with the task prior to engaging in collaborative work.) You may want to provide teachers with grid paper (for drawing diagrams) and overhead transparencies (for recording their solutions).

2. Assist teachers in their work on the task if they appear to be having difficulty. Consider the following suggestions.

   - If some participants have difficulty getting started, suggest that they draw a picture or diagram to represent what is given or known, and then ask questions that will support their work. For example, on Problem 1, you might suggest that they draw a rectangle that has an area of 300, and then ask questions that will help them focus on the relationship between the length and width (e.g., What do you know about the length and width of the rectangle you are trying to find? What does it mean for the ratio to be 4 to 3? What would some rectangles that have this relationship look like? How can you find the one you are looking for?)

   - If some participants provide only algebraic solutions to the problems, ask them how they think students who are not familiar with these techniques might solve the problems. (You also might point participants to the "Consider" section of the Opening Activity, in which they are asked to complete three student solutions, each of which features a diagram.)

   - Watch for a common misconception—solving Problem 3 additively. If participants solve the problem by adding the percents together (i.e., 20% + 4% = 24% butterfat—similar to Jason's thinking in the case), have them share their thinking with another participant who solved the problem proportionally. Ask the pair if either solution is reasonable, and why. This question might help teachers who are thinking additively to reconsider their solution, as Angela does in the case (paras. 26 and 28).

3. Orchestrate a whole-group discussion to allow participants to share various solution strategies and approaches. During the discussion you may want to:

   - Solicit responses that portray general solution

strategies found in the case (e.g., visual-geometric approaches and arithmetic-algebraic approaches). If you ask some pairs to record their solutions on an overhead transparency, this will facilitate the presentation of solutions during the whole-group discussion. (A list of different solution methods that we have seen teachers use to solve these tasks can be found in Appendix D. Reviewing this set of solutions may help you prepare for the emergence of methods you might not have used when you solved the problems.)

   - Discuss the approaches used by students in Figure 5.1 if these have not already been suggested. You may want to encourage participants to make connections between the visual approaches and the more algebraic approaches (e.g., How are Solutions C and F [shown in Appendix D] for Problem 3 related?).

   - Ask participants to discuss any difficulties they experienced in solving the task and to brainstorm ways in which they could provide support to students who encountered similar difficulties.

FACILITATING THE CASE DISCUSSION

The case discussion is intended to help participants analyze the mathematical and pedagogical ideas in the case. The "Case Analysis" should be of assistance in identifying the key ideas in the case and how each idea plays out in the details of the case. Although it is likely that you will begin by examining specific aspects of Janice Patterson's teaching practice, you should consider how to connect the specific events that occur in her class with more general ideas about mathematics teaching and learning. In this section we provide suggestions for launching and facilitating the case discussion, and for various follow-up activities that you may wish to pursue.

1. If possible, have participants read and reflect on the case before meeting as a group to discuss it. As participants read the case, we suggest that you ask them to make note of what the students in Janice Patterson's class are *doing* during the lesson that may have contributed to their learning. (This activity is described in more detail in the section of Chapter 5 entitled "Reading the Case.") This individual activity will help participants think deeply about the pedagogy in the case and help

them prepare for the small- and whole-group discussions. Alternatively, you may want to select one of the questions found in Chapter 5 (see the section entitled "Extending Your Analysis of the Case") to guide the reading of the case.

2. Ask small groups to consider the question: Did Janice Patterson really teach? Since Mrs. Patterson does not appear to do or say very much during the lesson, this question will provide participants with the opportunity to consider what it means to "teach" and to determine whether or not Janice Patterson was actually teaching.

   As the groups begin to grapple with this question, encourage them to discuss the lists they created during their initial reading of the case in which they identified what students in Janice Patterson's class were doing that may have contributed to their learning. For each item on their list, participants should indicate how this may have contributed to students' learning and what Janice Paterson did (or may have done) before or during the lesson to create or facilitate this learning opportunity. In completing this task, participants should be encouraged to cite specific evidence (using paragraph numbers from the case) to support their claims.

3. The whole-group discussion should focus explicitly on the question "Did Janice Patterson teach?" and on Mrs. Patterson's role during the lesson. Each group should be encouraged to identify specific actions taken by Mrs. Patterson that they feel count as teaching and to justify why these actions are important in providing students with opportunities to learn mathematics. Encourage participants to argue respectfully if they do not agree that an identified teacher action supported student learning. This can lead to a rich discussion that draws on evidence used to support claims being made. The list that we developed in preparation for a discussion of "The Case of Janice Patterson" is included in Appendix D. We encour-

age you to develop your own list prior to reviewing the one provided. (We also have included a list in Appendix D that was created by a group of teachers.)

You may want to conclude the whole-group discussion by asking teachers to consider the aspects of Janice Patterson's way of teaching that may be important for other teachers to consider if they want students to learn to make sense of mathematics. This will help teachers to move beyond the particular events that occurred in the case and to begin to see them as instantiations of more generalizable ideas about mathematics teaching and learning.

4. Following the discussion, you may want to have participants reflect individually by writing about some aspect of the case experience. This could involve asking teachers to consider the role of visual approaches in Janice Patterson's classroom: Why might these approaches be helpful to students? What type of instruction would facilitate the development of such approaches? Alternatively, you may want to ask teachers to consider the roles of teacher and student in Janice Patterson's classroom: What does one need to know and be able to do in order to teach like Mrs. Patterson? What does one need to know and be able to do in order to be a student in Mrs. Patterson's classroom? What are the costs and benefits of assuming these new classroom roles?

EXTENDING THE CASE EXPERIENCE

If you have additional time, you may want to provide teachers with opportunities to consider their own practice and continue to explore the mathematical and pedagogical ideas on which the case is based. The section entitled "Extending Case-Based Experiences" in Chapter 6 suggests three types of activities you might want to assign teachers for these purposes.

APPENDIX A

Sample Responses to The Case of Randy Harris

TEACHER-GENERATED SOLUTIONS TO THE OPENING ACTIVITY

Teachers who participated in a professional development experience that focused on "The Case of Randy Harris" generated the solutions presented in this section. Although there may be other ways of solving the problems, these are the solutions that appeared with greatest frequency.

Problem 1

Randy Harris's students present two possible solutions to this problem. Kendra's solution (para. 35) requires considering each column of the grid to be a "chunk" that is equivalent to 10% or 0.10 of the total grid, and Marilyn's solution (para. 33) requires "unitizing"—finding out what percent each square is worth.

There are two additional solutions that we have seen teachers generate that were not produced by students in Randy Harris's classroom. Solution A involves considering two rows as a chunk and recognizing that each chunk has a value of 25%. Solution B involves a more conventional approach of first changing the decimal to a fraction and then shading the number of squares. Although this approach does not take the diagram as a starting point, it does make a connection between an algorithm and the visual representation.

Solution A. As illustrated in Figure A.1, there are eight rows in the grid. Therefore, four rows are 50%, half of that (or two rows) is 25%, and each individual row is 12.5%. Since there are 10 squares in each row, each individual square is 1.25%. From this point, a number of next steps are possible to reach the target of .725 or

72.5%. For example, six rows would be 75% and then two squares, or 2.5%, need to be taken away.

Solution B. Alternatively, an approach that first changes 0.725 into a fraction and then converts that fraction to an equivalent fraction with a denominator equal to the number of squares in the grid could be used, as shown in the calculations that follow.

$$.725 = {}^{725}\!/_{1,000} = {}^{29}\!/_{40} = {}^{58}\!/_{80}$$

The resulting fraction indicates that 58 out of 80 total squares should be shaded.

Problem 2

Since the grid has 8 rows and $^3\!/_8$ of the grid must be shaded, Darlene's "chunking by rows" approach (para. 40) is a common strategy for solving this problem.

FIGURE A.1. Solution for Problem 1 of the Opening Activity

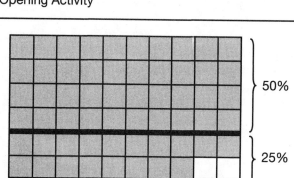

Devon's approach (paras. 37–38) illustrates an alternative way to chunk the grid into eight equal parts.

Problem 3

This problem may be the most difficult of the three problems since the grid is 8 × 9 and neither dimension suggests an obvious way to chunk the grid into subsections. However, work on Problem 2 might provide useful insight, particularly if it was solved using Darlene's chunking-by-rows approach (para. 40). As shown in Solution A, a chunking-by-rows approach can used to solve the problem as well.

Solution A. Since each row is $^1/_8$, or 0.125, or 12.5%, two rows are 25% and four rows (or half of the grid) are 50%. Adding 50%, 25%, and 12.5% equals 87.5%, as shown in Figure A.2.

Solution B. Alternatively, an approach similar to Solution B in Problem 1 also could be used to solve this problem. This would involve trying to determine an equivalent fraction with a denominator equal to the total number of squares in the grid, as shown in the calculations that follow.

$$.875 = {}^{875}/_{1,000} = {}^7/_8 = {}^{63}/_{72}$$

The resulting fraction indicates that 63 out of 72 total squares should be shaded.

FACILITATOR-GENERATED LIST OF SUPPORTING AND INHIBITING FACTORS

The list shown in Table A.1 on the next page was created by teacher educators in preparation for a group

discussion of "The Case of Randy Harris" and identifies ways in which Randy Harris's pedagogy supports and inhibits students' learning in the lesson.

TEACHER-GENERATED LIST OF SUPPORTING AND INHIBITING FACTORS

Teachers who participated in a professional development experience that focused on "The Case of Randy Harris" generated the ideas listed in Table A.2 on page 113.

FIGURE A.2. Solution A for Problem 3 of the Opening Activity

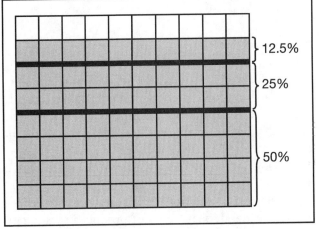

TABLE A.1. Facilitator-Generated Ideas on Ways in Which Randy Harris's Pedagogy Serves to Support and Inhibit Students' Learning

Support	Inhibit
Uses curriculum that helps develop conceptual understanding (para. 3).	
Uses problems that build on students' previous knowledge and experiences with fractions and decimals (para. 5), percents (para. 5), and relationships between fractions and decimals (para. 6).	Does not consistently—on either day—encourage students to make the connections between the diagram and each representation (i.e., fraction, decimal, percent). Once students find one way to represent the problem (e.g., percent), he allows them to use algorithms to find the decimal equivalents without any attempt to link it to the diagram (paras. 23 and 39).
Wants students to develop an understanding that moves beyond using algorithms and focuses on relationships (para. 9).	Does not consistently encourage students to use the diagrams during the first class. In particular, Problem 4 in Set A could be solved using the diagram in several ways, none of which are suggested by Mr. Harris or students. (For example, each row is 20%, which means each square is 5%. Therefore, nine squares are 45%.)
Uses appropriate tools/materials such as calculators (para. 14), transparencies of problems (para. 11), and 10 × 10 grids (para. 23).	Does not provide students with sufficient intellectual resources for solving the problems on the second day (paras. 29 and 30).
Monitors students' performance both informally and formally by reviewing their homework (paras. 13 and 27), observing the ways in which students are working in groups (para. 40—Darlene; para. 37—Devon), and giving a formal assessment at the end of the 2-day lesson (para. 41).	
Provides a summary of strategies used in problem-solving—on Day 1 he provides a written record (para. 19) and on Day 2 he provides an oral account (para. 36).	Does not provide a written record of the strategies used to solve problems on Day 2 (para. 36). Does not add Peter's visual strategy for finding the percent to the list of methods (para. 21). Success on Day 2 is due largely to the introduction of strategies by Kendra (para. 35), Devon (paras. 37–39), and Darlene (para. 40). It might have been helpful to categorize these approaches in ways that would make them accessible to other students in subsequent problem-solving.
Encourages students to work in pairs on Day 1 (para. 13) and in groups on Day 2 (para. 28).	
Introduces students to an approach that was not algorithmic when one was not forthcoming (para. 17–18).	Claims to want students to solve the problems without relying on algorithms and introduces Method 3 during the first class (para. 17–18) as a way to do so. However, in work on the subsequent two problems, this strategy is not brought up by Mr. Harris or students.

TABLE A.1. (*continued*)

Support	Inhibit
Provides support to Ramon and Marilyn, who were experiencing confusion (paras. 23–25 and 31–33).	Ignores David's comment (para. 33).
Gives students (Devon, in particular) time to think (para. 39).	Does not give students any time to think about Problem 1 before Danielle is asked to describe her method (para. 11).
Asks students to provide explanations, not just answers (paras. 12, 14, and 31).	
Encourages student-to-student interaction (para. 23).	
Asks students thought-provoking questions (para. 30).	Asks leading questions that break the problem down rather than asking more general questions that would scaffold student learning (para. 33).
	Uses examples inconsistently during the 2-day lesson. On Day 1 Mr. Harris provides two examples and one in which he models the desired strategy (paras. 11 and 17–18). Yet on Day 2 he indicates that he is concerned about doing examples because they funnel student thinking (para. 29). It is unclear why this is a concern on Day 2 but not on Day 1.
Encourages students to come up with different ways to solve the problems (para. 13).	Provides only one way to use the diagram during the first class (paras. 17–18) although other visual approaches that come up in Day 2 would have been useful and reasonable. For example, a version of Kendra's method (para. 35) would have been helpful in solving Problem 4 and, with some questioning by Mr. Harris, may have been accessible.

TABLE A.2. Teacher-Generated Ideas on Ways in Which Randy Harris's Pedagogy Supported and Inhibited Students' Learning of Mathematics

Support	Inhibit
Uses a high-level task and keeps it at a high-level.	
Wants students to feel comfortable taking risks.	
	Checks homework instead of monitoring students' progress on Day 1 (para. 13).
Wants students to solve problems in multiple ways and in ways that make use of diagrams (paras. 2, 4, and 13).	Too many solution methods could be confusing to students. Does not model what he expects of students (models memorization but expects students to explain their thinking) (para. 12). Accepts Method 2 instead of pushing students to use Method 3, which makes use of diagrams (paras. 15 and 20). Method 3 is not student-generated and was introduced to the class in a leading manner (paras. 17–18).
Asks students to explain their thinking (para. 14).	
Summarizes three methods in a chart that students can refer to (para. 19).	
Asks Denise to assume the role of teacher (para. 23).	
	Doesn't review Day 1's work on Day 2.
Uses students' misconceptions as a starting point (to push the issue of 0.45 versus .45% [para. 25]; to discuss Marilyn's and others' misconception of 72.5 squares = 72.5% [para. 33]).	Ignores David's suggestion to multiply 1¼% by 72.5% to determine the number of squares to shade (para. 33).
Asks good questions throughout the lesson. Asks leading questions to guide Marilyn (para. 33).	Assesses students' learning inconsistently (classwork is done via discussion in pairs or small groups, but the quiz is written individual work) (paras. 13, 28, and 41).
Monitors the progress of students who present solutions at the overhead.	Does not monitor the progress of students who do not present solutions at the overhead.

APPENDIX B

Sample Responses to The Case of Marie Hanson

TEACHER-GENERATED SOLUTIONS TO THE OPENING ACTIVITY

Teachers who participated in a professional development experience that focused on "The Case of Marie Hanson" generated the solutions presented in this section.

Problem 1

There are four strategies that teachers are likely to use in solving this problem: (1) factor-of-change; (2) scaling-up; (3) unit rate; and (4) cross-multiplication.

Solution A: Factor-of-change. A factor-of-change method could be implemented as used in the case by Jerry (para. 26) and Owen (para. 27). This method is common because 100 is an easily recognized multiple of 5. Thus, there should be 20 times as many Jawbreakers in the new candy jar because there are 20 times as many Jolly Ranchers.

Solution B: Scaling-up. A scaling-up strategy involves finding ratios equivalent to 5:13 and identifying a ratio that can be easily scaled-up to 100. In order to find ratios equivalent to 5:13, equivalent fractions might be generated (i.e., $^5/_{13} = {}^{10}/_{26} = {}^{100}/_{260}$) or a table similar to the one created by Jerlyn and Kamiko (para. 10) might be used.

Solution C: Unit rate. The unit rate of 1 Jolly Rancher to 2.6 Jawbreakers is equivalent to the ratio 5 Jolly Ranchers to 13 Jawbreakers. Because the new candy jar has 100 Jolly Ranchers, multiplying 100×2.6 results in 260 Jawbreakers.

Solution D: Cross-multiplication. The number of Jawbreakers could be determined using cross-multiplication, as shown in Figure B.1.

Problem 2

Teachers are likely to approach Problem 2 using strategies based on factor-of-change, scaling-up, unit rate, percentages, or algebraic solution methods.

Solution A: Factor-of-change. Because the new candy jar contains 40 times as many total candies as the original jar ($18 \times 40 = 720$), the new jar will contain 40 times as many Jolly Ranchers, or 200 Jolly Ranchers (5×40) and 40 times as many Jawbreakers, or 520 Jawbreakers (13×40). This solution is presented by Danielle in the case (para. 37). Alternatively, it might be observed that the candy jar in Problem 2 contains twice as many candies as the candy jar created in Problem 1 (720 is twice as much as 360). Thus, there also should be twice as many Jolly Ranchers and Jawbreakers.

Solution B: Scaling-up. Several values for the total number of candies are factors of 720 and provide opportunities to easily "scale-up" to the desired ratio. As described in the case (para. 36), a table that includes a third column that keeps track of the total number of candies could be used, as shown in Table B.1.

Solution C: Unit rate. Using the ratio of 5 Jolly Ranchers to 18 total candies, the unit rate of 1:3.6 can be determined. Because $3.6 \times 200 = 720$ total candies, multiplying the 1 by 200 results in 200 Jolly Ranchers. The number of Jawbreakers can be determined in a number of ways. For example, 720 total candies – 200 Jolly Ranchers = 520 Jawbreakers.

FIGURE B.1. A Solution to Problem 1 That Incorporates Cross-Multiplication

$$\frac{5 \text{ Jolly Ranchers}}{13 \text{ Jawbreakers}} = \frac{100 \text{ Jolly Ranchers}}{x \text{ Jawbreakers}}$$

$$5x = 13(100)$$

$$5x = 1{,}300$$

$$x = 260 \text{ Jawbreakers}$$

Solution D: Percentages. By focusing on the part–whole ratio of 5 Jolly Ranchers to 18 total candies, the percentage of Jolly Ranchers in the original candy jar (5 ÷ 18 = .277) can be determined. This percentage can be used to compute the number of Jolly Ranchers in the new jar (.277 × 720 = 200). This same method could be applied with the ratio of 13 Jawbreakers to 18 total candies in order to determine the number of Jawbreakers.

Solution E: Algebraic methods. Particularly if you are working with secondary teachers, you may observe an additional symbolic solution method, similar to the following, for Problem 2.

Let x = # of Jolly Ranchers and y = # of Jawbreakers.
Then $x + y = 720$ and $x = \frac{5}{13}y$
  (or, alternatively, $y = \frac{13}{5}x$).
Use substitution and solve.

Problem 3

For Problem 3, teachers' solutions might make use of equivalent ratios, a ratio table, or deductive reasoning.

TABLE B.1. "Scaling-Up" Using a Ratio Table

Jolly Ranchers	Jawbreakers	Total # of Candies
5	13	18
10	26	36
15	39	54
20	52	72
100	260	360
200	520	720

Solution A: Equivalent ratios. The ratios 5:13 and 50:125 are not equivalent ratios (50 ÷ 5 = 10 and 125 ÷ 13 = 9.61). Therefore, the most treat bags that can be made with 125 Jawbreakers is 9.

Solution B: Making a ratio table. A table such as the one shown in Table B.2 illustrates that there are enough candies for only nine treat bags.

Solution C: Deductive reasoning. Although there are enough Jolly Ranchers for 10 treat bags, that would require 130 Jawbreakers. Since there are 125 Jawbreakers, only nine treat bags can be made.

Exploring the "Consider" Question

The "Consider" portion of the Opening Activity asks teachers to think of alternative strategies for solving the problems and to find ways in which the different strategies are related. In this section, we make some of the relationships between strategies explicit. (The discussion contained in the "Case Analysis" section of Chapter 8 also may provide you with ideas on how different strategies are related. Specific mathematical ideas discussed in Chapter 8 are indicated by an asterisk [*] where appropriate.)

Relating cross-multiplication to other strategies. Cross-multiplication* is an efficient algorithm for solving missing-value proportion problems, especially those

TABLE B.2. Using a Ratio Table to Determine the Number of Treat Bags That Can Be Made

# of treat bags	Jolly Ranchers	Jawbreakers
1	5	13
2	10	26
3	15	39
4	20	52
5	25	65
6	30	78
7	35	91
8	40	104
9	45	117
10	50	130

for which both the factor-of-change* and the unit rate* are not easily recognized. Part of the efficiency of the cross-multiplication procedure is that it eliminates the need to attend to either of these relationships; rather, focusing on the factor-of-change and/or the unit rate relationship within the cross-multiplication procedure can illuminate why this algorithm works. You may want to use the article by Boston, Smith, and Hillen (2003) to explore how the factor-of-change and unit rate strategies can be used to develop an understanding of cross-multiplication. (A brief description of the article is provided in the section entitled "Connecting to Other Ideas and Issues" in Chapter 3.)

Relating ratio tables to other strategies. The "Case Analysis" in Chapter 8 provides a discussion of how ratio tables* can be used to illustrate the unit rate* and factor-of-change* relationships. A ratio table also can show the relationship between strategies based on repeated addition and multiplicative relationships*.

Relating factor-of-change strategies. Teachers might use different factor-of-change strategies* that can be related in the following ways.

- Repeated addition can be related to a factor-of-change, because multiplying by a factor of *x* will give the same result as adding the original ratio to itself *x* times.
- A "scaling-up" strategy involves multiplying by a series of factors to obtain the desired ratio rather than multiplying by the factor-of-change directly

(i.e., multiplying by 4 and then by 5 rather than multiplying directly by 20).
- The inverse relationship between multiplication and division provides different ways of identifying the factor-of-change.
- The notion of a factor-of-change can create meaning for the common algorithm for finding equivalent fractions.

Relating percents to other strategies. For part-to-whole ratios, percents can be related to unit rates by noting that percents express "how many per 100," while unit rates express "how many per 1." For example, consider Solution C to Problem 2. While a unit rate of 1 Jolly Rancher to 3.6 total candies is often useful, its reciprocal of .277 Jolly Ranchers to 1 total candy (or 27.7% Jolly Ranchers in the candy jar) also might be useful. The reciprocal of the unit rate is referred to as a *dual rate* (Lamon, 1999) and can be used to relate unit rates to percents for part-to-whole ratios.

FACILITATOR- AND TEACHER-GENERATED LIST OF WAYS IN WHICH MARIE HANSON SUPPORTED HER STUDENTS' LEARNING OF MATHEMATICS

The list shown in Table B.3 was generated by teacher educators in preparation for a discussion of "The Case of Marie Hanson." The ideas that are in italics also were identified by teachers who participated in a professional development experience that focused on "The Case of Marie Hanson."

TABLE B.3. Ways in Which Marie Hanson's Pedagogy Supported Her Students' Learning of Mathematics

Pedagogical moves that supported students' learning	How the pedagogical moves supported students' learning
Defines ratio as a "comparison between two sets of things" (para. 5). Sequences the candy jar problems (in which the unit rate is not an integer) after students explore the lollipop problem (in which the unit rate is an integer) (paras. 6 and 8). *Begins with a basic ratio problem similar in structure to earlier problems (Figure 3.3).* *Sequences the candy jar problems so that the second and third problems involve numbers in the hundreds (Figures 3.3, 3.7, and 3.9).* Selects problems that are different in structure (e.g., in the second problem, the amount of one type of candy is given and students must determine the amount of the other type of candy; in the third problem, students are given the total amount of candy and must determine the amount of each type; in the fourth problem, students create bags of candy given a total amount of candy that will result in not all of the candy being used).	Prior to this lesson, Ms. Hanson has helped her students develop an understanding of the key mathematical ideas they will need in order to make progress on the candy jar problems. During this lesson, she provides her students with opportunities to apply these understandings in new and increasingly more difficult situations. In particular, *the initial problem is accessible to a wide range of students. The other problems contain increasingly larger numbers to encourage students to use strategies based on multiplication when repeated addition becomes too tedious.*
Comments that strategies should make sense to students (in para. 36, she notes that although some students' methods are inefficient, it doesn't bother her because they appear to make sense to the students who are using them; in para. 44, she tells students that we'll "work with strategies that we can make sense of every step of the way"). The "Case Analysis" in Chapter 8 provides additional instances in which Ms. Hanson presses students to explain and make sense of their solutions.	*Ms. Hanson holds her students accountable for explaining and summarizing mathematical ideas.* She communicates that it is the students' responsibility to make sense of the mathematics.
Asks students who are struggling with the first problem to think about adding more candies while keeping the same ratio of Jawbreakers to Jolly Ranchers (para. 9). Asks questions to determine students' understanding and to help students continue to engage with the mathematical ideas, even when they are silent or do not appear to have any questions (in para. 12, she asks the class a question because she can't tell whether Kamiko and Jerlyn's explanation makes sense to the rest of the class; in para. 16, she asks the class a question because Jerry does not seem to know how to connect his work to April's; in para. 19, she asks the class a question because Kamiko isn't sure that the unit rate of 1:2.6 fits in her ratio table).	By asking questions, *Ms. Hanson encourages her students to grapple with important mathematical ideas and refrains from removing the challenging aspects of the problem.*
Students cooperatively determine the unit rate (in paras. 16–17, April, Jerry, and Sharee determine the unit rate). *Students question one another directly (in para. 25, Sarah questions Jordan; in para. 40, Danielle questions Angelica).* *Students challenge Jordan's incorrect additive strategy (in paras. 25–27, Sarah, Jerry, and Jerlyn challenge Jordan's solution).* Students solve the problems in a variety of ways, suggesting this is the norm (in para. 22, Ms. Hanson notes that she is amazed at the variety of ways in which students are attacking the second problem).	*Ms. Hanson has created a culture where students feel comfortable working together, questioning one another, and sharing alternative approaches to problems. It appears that the norm in Ms. Hanson's classroom is that you should challenge others until you understand their strategy.*

TABLE B.3. (*continued*)

Pedagogical moves that supported students' learning	How the pedagogical moves supported students' learning
Asks students to compare problems (in para. 12, students compare the first candy jar problem with the lollipop problem when Ms. Hanson asks, "What makes this problem more difficult?"). Asks students to examine and/or compare strategies (in para. 27, she asks students to compare the original jar with Jordan's new jar; in para. 32, she asks students to compare strategies for solving the second problem, by asking, "If adding doesn't work, what does?"; in para. 33 she helps students understand why the unit rate of 1:2.6 fits in Kamiko and Jerlyn's ratio table by asking them to consider what is consistent about what they're doing when they play around with the numbers in the table; in paras. 42–43, she compares Angelica's cross-multiplication strategy with Danielle's factor-of-change strategy).	By asking students to compare the problems, she helps them notice that using prior strategies might not be the most efficient endeavor. In addition, Ms. Hanson helps her students make conceptual connections between different strategies and allows students to see how multiplicative relationships surface in different strategies.
Puts Kamiko's unresolved question "on hold" until later (para. 19). *Decides to expose Jordan's incorrect additive strategy first (para. 23).* *Sets up a debate by asking, "Does everyone agree with Jordan?" (para. 26).*	*Ms. Hanson allows misconceptions to surface; and lets students work to resolve the fact that they have two different answers. By doing so, Ms. Hanson allows her students to serve as the mathematical authority in the classroom.*
Summarizes why Jordan's incorrect additive strategy does not work (paras. 28 and 33). Students discuss multiplicative relationships in the table (in para. 33, students comment that in Kamiko and Jerlyn's table, "you are always multiplying the two different sides by the same amount").	*Ms. Hanson helps her students understand the difference between correct and incorrect additive strategies and the relationships between table entries.* In addition, she helps students develop an understanding of the multiplicative relationships between equivalent ratios.
Asks Jerlyn and Kamiko to share their ratio table (para. 10). Asks Jordan to share his incorrect additive solution (para. 23).	*Ms. Hanson makes alternative strategies available to the class by selecting students who had produced them to present solutions. She purposely selects students whose ideas will contribute to her goals for the lesson.*
Participated in inservice training focusing on proportional reasoning (para. 2). Is now more attuned to how students think and reason about proportional relationships (paras. 2 and 4). Discusses how students might solve the last problem (para. 46).	Ms. Hanson has acquired both subject-matter content knowledge and pedagogical content knowledge about proportional reasoning. She has thoroughly learned the concept she wants to teach and is aware of the underlying mathematical ideas (e.g., multiplicative relationships) and of common misconceptions (e.g., using incorrect additive strategies). She is thus better able to guide students' learning toward the main mathematical ideas and to make connections between different ways of reasoning about proportional relationships.

Sample Responses to
The Case of Marcia Green

TEACHER-GENERATED SOLUTIONS TO THE OPENING ACTIVITY

Teachers who participated in a professional development experience that focused on "The Case of Marcia Green" generated the solutions presented in this section.

Responses to the "Solve" Questions

In response to the questions in the first bullet, teachers often respond that the original and enlarged figures are the same shape, have the same angle measures, and have the same number of sides. Teachers may comment that an enlargement is a transformation that preserves these properties of the original figures. Teachers also may note that the original and enlarged figures are different in size and that the figures are similar figures.

In response to the question in the second bullet, teachers often conclude that the side lengths (and thus the perimeter) of the enlarged figure have doubled and that the area has become four times larger. We have observed teachers use three general types of approaches to determine these relationships: (1) visual approaches that do not involve measuring the exact lengths of the sides; (2) numeric approaches that rely on measuring; and (3) algebraic approaches.

Solution A: Visual approaches. Cutting out the original square with scissors allows it to be compared with the enlarged image. Approximately four of the original squares will fit into the enlarged image. (The same method can be used with the equilateral triangle.)

Alternatively, the length and width of the original square could be marked off on a blank piece of paper. This could be used to informally measure the length and width of the enlarged image. The enlarged image is about twice as long and twice as wide as the original square. (The same method can be used with the equilateral triangle.)

Solution B: Numeric approaches. Measuring the linear dimensions of the figures, as suggested by Miguel (para. 17), is a common starting point. After measuring the linear dimensions of the figures, Marcia Green's students use a visual approach to discover the relationship between the areas of the figures (Alyssa's strategy in para. 22 and Bonita's strategy in para. 27). In contrast, an approach that relies solely on numeric techniques might be devised.

For example, after determining the length and width of each original square, it might be observed that the length and width of the enlarged square are about double the length and width of the original square. Using the area formula, it can be determined that the area of the original square is 4 square inches (2×2), and the area of the enlarged square is 16 square inches (4×4). Since 16 is four times four, the enlarged image's area is four times the original square's area. (The same method can be used with the equilateral triangle.)

Solution C: Algebraic approaches. Alternatively, algebraic methods that make use of the area formula might be used to generalize the relationship between the original figure and the enlarged image. In the approach illustrated in Figure C.1a, the length of each side of the original square is labeled x. The enlarged image therefore has side length $2x$. Using the formula for area of a square, the area of the original square is x^2, and the area of the enlarged image is $(2x)^2 = 4x^2$. Thus the area of the enlarged square is four times the area of the original square.

As shown in Figure C.1b, a similar approach can be used for the equilateral triangle. If the base and height

119

FIGURE C.1. (a) An Algebraic Approach to the Opening Activity Based on Generalizing the Formula for Area of a Square; (b) An Algebraic Approach to the Opening Activity Based on Generalizing the Formula for Area of a Triangle

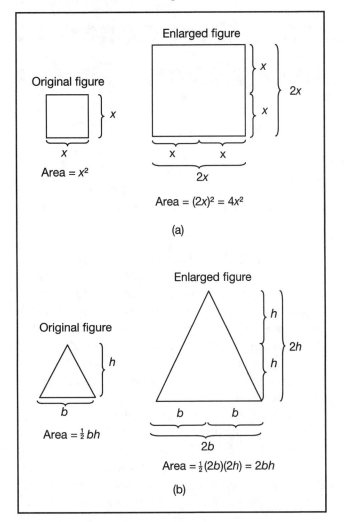

Responses to the "Consider" Question

In response to the "Consider" question, teachers may want to enlarge the square or equilateral triangle with a three-rubber-band stretcher and compare the figures using visual, numeric, or algebraic approaches before making a conjecture. Alternatively, teachers may conjecture that the three-rubber-band stretcher increases the side lengths by a factor of 3 (either by guessing or by reasoning that each rubber band displaces the original figure by one unit of length from the focal point—the knot that traces the figure is positioned at 1 unit of length and the pencil at the end of n rubber bands is positioned at n units of length) and use this information to determine that the area will increase by a factor of 9.

Comparing this information with the data obtained from the two-rubber-band stretcher, teachers then may generalize that the side lengths of the original figures and the enlargements are related by a ratio of $1:x$ (where x is the number of rubber bands) and the areas of the original figures and the enlargements are related by a ratio of $1:x^2$ (where x is the number of rubber bands), and thus conclude that the ratio of the areas of similar figures is the square of the ratio of the side lengths.

LIST OF MARCIA GREEN'S QUESTIONS

The questions that Marcia Green asked during the lesson are shown in Table C.1. The questions marked with an asterisk (*) were identified as "good questions" by teachers who participated in a discussion that focused on "The Case of Marcia Green."

TEACHER-GENERATED CRITERIA FOR GOOD QUESTIONS

A list of criteria for "good questions" that was created by teachers who participated in a discussion that focused on "The Case of Marcia Green" is shown in Table C.2. Teachers also were asked to identify the questions that Marcia Green asked that met these criteria.

of the original triangle are designated by b and h, then the base of the enlarged triangle is $2b$ and its height is $2h$. Using the formula for area of a triangle, the area of the original triangle is ½bh, and the area of the enlarged triangle is $2bh$. Thus the area of the enlarged triangle is four times the area of the original triangle.

TABLE C.1. Questions That Marcia Green Asked During the Lesson

Paragraph number	Questions that Marcia Green asked during the lesson
14	Okay, let's make some observations about what the rubber-band stretcher did to the original square and triangle.*
16	I asked for further observations or questions, and students didn't seem to have any.
17	How much larger is the image than the original figure?*
17	How might we find this out?*
17	Okay, what might we measure?
17	I would like you to think about how the original figure relates to its enlarged image.
18	Why might it be a good idea to measure all of the sides?
19	So I assume that you two are finished measuring and have this all figured out?
20	What about the other sides?
20	I asked the class if they agreed with these measurements.
20	If you got different measurements for each of the sides, how do you know that it is supposed to be a square?
21	If these are supposed to be squares, why did we get different measurement for each of the sides?
22	So if we agree that the smaller square has sides of 2½ centimeters and the larger one has sides of 5 centimeters, then how are the two squares related?*
22	I asked her [Alyssa] to continue.
22	Could you come up and show us what you mean?*
23	We seem to have two different ideas up here. Katie said, and many of you seemed to agree, that it has doubled, while Alyssa says that it is four times bigger. Any comments on that?*
24	What about the perimeter?
24	I asked her how she knew . . .
26	I put up the overhead sheet with the triangles and asked if the same relationships held for the triangles.
26	What about the area?
27	Tia looked confused, so I asked Bonita to come up and show us what she meant.
28	For homework, I asked students to write down their ideas about what would happen to the lengths of the sides, the perimeter, and the area if we enlarged the figures using three rubber bands knotted together?*

TABLE C.2. Teacher-Generated Criteria for a Good Question

Criteria	Evidence from lesson featured in "The Case of Marcia Green"
Focus on analyzing relationships	How much larger is the image than the original figure? (para. 17). So if we agree that the smaller square has sides of 2½ centimeters and the larger one has sides of 5 centimeters, then how are the two squares related? (para. 22). I asked students to write down their ideas about what would happen to the lengths of the sides, the perimeter, and the area if we enlarged the figures using three rubber bands knotted together (para. 28).
Allow students to explain their thinking; elicit student thinking	Alyssa says that the relationship is more than double, and Mrs. Green asks her to continue (para. 22). Alyssa begins to explain that "four of it will fit into the big one," and Mrs. Green asks, "Could you come up and show us what you mean?" (para. 22). Mrs. Green asks Bonita how she knew that the perimeters had doubled (para. 24). Mrs. Green asks the class about the relationship between the areas of the two triangles and allows Tia and Bonita to discuss the relationship (paras. 26–27).
Are open-ended (i.e., not yes/no questions); have multiple answers and approaches	Mrs. Green asks the class for observations about what the stretcher did to the original square and triangle (para. 14). Mrs. Green asks Katie how the two squares are related (para. 22).
Set up opportunities for mathematical debate	Mrs. Green summarizes the two different observations made by Katie and Alyssa and asks the class to comment (para. 23).
Allow students to make decisions about the way they explore mathematics	In response to Miguel's suggestion that the class measure (in order to determine how much larger the image is than the original figure), Mrs. Green asks, "Okay, what might we measure?" (para. 17). When Jared asks whether they need to measure all of the sides, Mrs. Green responds, "You decide. Why might it be a good idea to measure all of the sides?" (para. 18).

Sample Responses to The Case of Janice Patterson

TEACHER-GENERATED SOLUTIONS TO THE OPENING ACTIVITY

Teachers who participated in a professional development experience that focused on "The Case of Janice Patterson" generated the solutions presented in this section. There are two general approaches that teachers used to solve the tasks: visual-geometric approaches that focus on the use of diagrams and arithmetic-algebraic approaches that focus on numeric and/or more traditional algebraic methods. Although Janice Patterson stresses a visual approach to her students, this may not be a natural solution method for the teachers with whom you are working. The diagrams provided in the "Consider" section may help participants explore alternative solution methods that utilize diagrams.

Problem 1

A visual approach to this problem is provided by Kalla and Robin (paras. 15–16) in the case. Although this may not be the initial way that participants approach this problem, the diagram provided in the "Consider" section of the Opening Activity is intended to facilitate their understanding of this method. Teachers also may use numeric strategies to determine the scale factor, such as those presented in Solutions A through D.

Solution A. The area of a 3 × 4 rectangle is 12 square inches. The rectangle in the problem has an area of 300 square inches, which is 25 times as large as the area of a 3 × 4 rectangle (25 × 12 = 300). Thus, the scale factor for the area is 25, which means that the scale factor for the linear dimensions will be 5. In general terms, if the length and width of a rectangle increase by a factor of x, then the area of the rectangle increases by a factor of x^2.

Increasing the length and width of the 3 × 4 rectangle by a factor of 5 results in a larger rectangle that has a length of 20 inches and a width of 15 inches and an area of 300 square inches.

Solution B. In order to keep the 4:3 ratio constant, the 4 and 3 must be multiplied by the same number—call this number x. The area of the larger rectangle, 300 square inches, can be expressed as length times width, where the length is equal to $4x$, and the width is equal to $3x$. The solution for this equation follows.

$$\text{Area} = \text{Length} \times \text{Width}$$
$$300 = (4x)(3x)$$
$$300 = 12x^2$$
$$25 = x^2$$
$$5 = x$$

Therefore, the scale factor is 5, the length of the larger rectangle is 20 inches (4 × 5) and the width is 15 inches (3 × 5).

Solution C. A table similar to the one that Kevin and Maria built (paras. 12–13) also might be used. However, the table shown in Figure D.1 is more mathematically sophisticated than Kevin and Maria's because not every possible scale factor is tested. Rather, a guess (scale factor = 10) is made, which yields an area that is too big. This guess is refined and a scale factor of four is then tried, which yields an area that is too small. The guess is further refined and a scale factor of five is tried, which yields an area of 300 square inches.

Solution D. Finally, algebraic methods could be used to solve the problem. This solution differs from the previous three methods in that the unknown is one of the dimensions of the rectangle, and not the scale factor.

FIGURE D.1. A Strategy for Solving Problem 1 That Makes Use of a Table

If the width is called W, then the length will be $\frac{4}{3}$W. Therefore, the area will be $\frac{4}{3}$W × W, which is also equal to 300. The solution to this equation follows.

$$(\tfrac{4}{3}W)\,(W) = 300$$

$$\tfrac{4}{3}W^2 = 300$$

$$4W^2 = 900$$

$$W^2 = \tfrac{900}{4}$$

$$W = \tfrac{30}{2}$$

$$W = 15$$

Thus, the width of the rectangle is 15 inches. The length of the rectangle can be determined by substituting the width into the expression $\frac{4}{3}$W. Therefore, the length of the rectangle is $\frac{4}{3}(15)$, or 20 inches. (The same strategy can be used for W = ¾L.)

Problem 2

Teachers often use a visual-geometric approach to solve the problem. This approach involves dividing the string into three equal parts and then adjusting the lengths by using what they know about percent, similar to Sasha's approach (paras. 20–24).

Teachers also may use algebraic approaches to solve the problem, as presented in Solutions A and B.

Solution A. If x is the length of the first piece, then $x + 25\%$ is the length of the second piece, and $x - 25\%$ is the length of the third piece. If the length of string is divided into three equal parts, each piece is 60 cm long; 25% of 60 cm is 15 cm, so the lengths of the three pieces are: 60 cm (x), 75 cm ($x + 25\%$), and 45 cm ($x - 25\%$).

This solution can be verified by adding 60 + 75 + 45, which yields 180.

Solution B. This solution is briefly described by Janice Patterson (para. 18). Let x be the length of the first piece, then $x + .25$ is the length of the second piece, and $x - .25$ is the length of the third piece. Since the total length of string is 180 cm, adding the lengths of the three pieces together gives: $x + (x + .25x) + (x - .25x) = 180$. The solution to the equation follows.

$$x + (x + .25x) + (x - .25x) = 180$$

$$3x = 180$$

$$x = 60$$

Therefore, the length of the first piece of string is 60. The second piece is $x + .25x$, or $60 + .25(60)$, or 75 cm. The third piece is $x - .25x$, or $60 - .25(60)$, or 45 cm.

Problem 3

Teachers might attempt to solve the problem using visual-geometric approaches. We present four solutions that make use of such approaches in Solutions A through D.

Solution A. Diagrams can be used to determine the number of gallons of butterfat in each mixture, as suggested by Crystal (paras. 30–31) (shown in Figure D.2).

The rectangle shown in Figure D.2a represents the 50 gallons of cream, 20% (or $\frac{1}{5}$) of which is butterfat; therefore, 10 gallons of the cream are butterfat. The rectangle shown in Figure D.2b represents 150 gallons of milk, 4% of which is butterfat. The number of gallons of butterfat in the milk can be determined by dividing the rectangle into fifths (as shown in Figure D.2b), noticing that 20% (or each fifth) is 30 gallons, which means 2% is 3 gallons, and therefore 4% is 6 gallons.

The problem can now be completed numerically. In the total cream and milk mixture, there are 200 gallons, 16 of which are butterfat. Therefore, the cream and milk mixture is 8% butterfat ($\frac{16}{200} = \frac{8}{100} = 8\%$).

Solution B. This solution is similar to Solution A, except that it uses 10×10 grids to represent the cream and milk. However, unlike Solution A, this solution presents a third diagram in which the total mixture is shown.

As shown in Figure D.3a, for the 50 gallons of cream, each small square represents ½ gallon; 20% is 20 squares—1% each. Since each square is worth ½ gallon, 20 squares are worth 10 gallons. Similarly, for the 150

FIGURE D.2. (a) A Visual Representation of the Cream in Problem 3; (b) A Visual Representation of the Milk in Problem 3

FIGURE D.3. (a) A Visual Representation of the Cream in Problem 3 Using a 10 × 10 Grid; (b) A Visual Representation of the Milk in Problem 3 Using a 10 × 10 Grid; (c) A Visual Representation of the Cream and Milk Mixture Using a 10 × 10 Grid

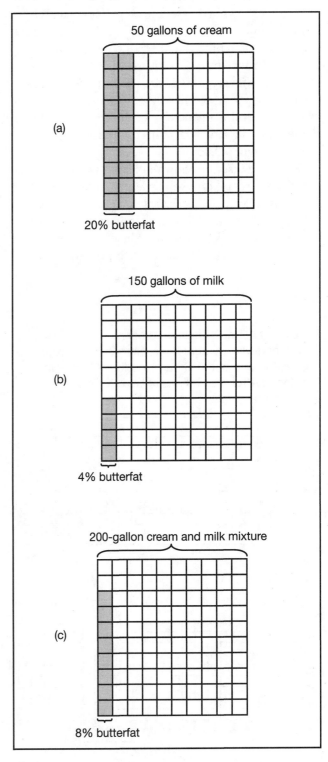

gallons of milk, each square represents 1½ gallons (shown in Figure D.3b); 4% is 4 squares—1% each. Since each square is worth 1½ gallons, 4 squares are worth 6 gallons.

In the 200-gallon cream and milk mixture, 16 gallons are butterfat. As shown in Figure D.3c, each square in the 10 × 10 grid is worth 1%, or 2 gallons. Therefore, 8 squares should be shaded. Since each square is worth 1%, the cream and milk mixture is 8% butterfat.

Solution C. This solution differs from Solutions A and B in that one diagram is used to illustrate both parts of the mixture.

The grid shown in Figure D.4a represents the 200-gallon cream and milk mixture. The 15 × 10 section represents the milk, and the 5 × 10 section represents the cream. Therefore, each square in the grid represents one gallon. The butterfat in the cream can be denoted by shading 2 rows in that section (since the cream is 20% butterfat and each row is worth 10%). Similarly, since 4% of the milk is butterfat, the shaded region should be less than 1 row (since 1 row is worth 10%). If 1 row is worth 10%, and there are 15 squares in a row, then each square is worth 1.5%. Therefore, 6 squares are worth 4%. To determine the percent of the entire grid that is shaded, the shaded squares need to be rearranged, as shown in Figure D.4b.

From the diagram shown in Figure D.4b, it is clear that the entire mixture will be less than 10% butterfat (since less than 1 row is shaded and each row is worth 10%). Sixteen of the 20 squares in the row are shaded, which is equal to $^4/_5$ of the row. Since $^4/_5$ of 10% is 8%, the cream and milk mixture is 8% butterfat.

Solution D. The "Consider" section of the Opening Activity presents a diagram that V.J. and Trina used to solve the problem. Although teachers may not spontaneously solve the problem using this approach, they should be able to make sense of this strategy. Unlike previous solutions (Solutions A, B, and C), all aspects of the problem are included in one diagram, as shown in Figure D.5.

The grid represents the 200-gallon cream and milk mixture. The left-hand side of the grid represents the cream, and the right-hand side represents the milk. Since 20%, or $^1/_5$, of the cream is butterfat, 20% of that section of the grid is shaded. To shade the amount of butterfat in the milk, the 4% mark needs to be located. This can be found by using the 20% mark and dividing the 20% into five equal parts (since 4 × 5 is 20). If the grid is thought of as a container that is holding the cream and milk mixture, imagine the 20% butterfat in the cream "leveling off" the mixture. Therefore, the 20% butterfat in the cream would be redistributed to three sections on top of the butterfat in the milk, and the entire mixture would be 8% butterfat.

As alternatives to visual-geometric approaches, teachers initially may use numeric or algebraic methods to solve the problem. Teachers often begin work on this problem by using the approaches presented in Solutions E and F.

Solution E. If 20% of the 50 gallons of cream is butterfat, then there are 10 gallons of butterfat in the cream (.20 × 50 = 10). Similarly, there are 6 gallons of butterfat in the milk (.04 × 150 = 6). Therefore, there are 16

FIGURE D.4. (a) A Visual Representation of the Cream and Milk Mixture in Problem 3; (b) A Visual Representation of the Cream and Milk Mixture in Problem 3 After the Gallons of Butterfat Have Been Rearranged

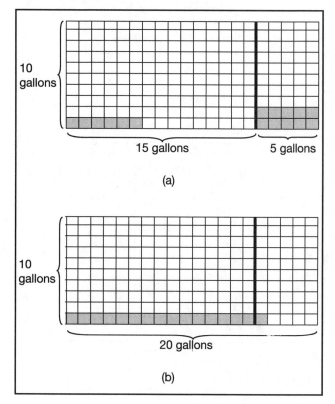

FIGURE D.5. A Solution to Problem 3 That Uses V.J. and Trina's Representation of the Cream and Milk Mixture

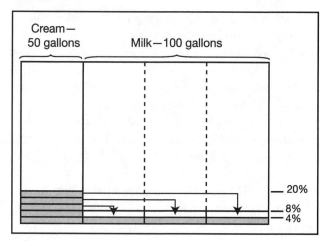

total gallons of butterfat in the 200-gallon of mixture, and the mixture is 8% butterfat ($^{16}/_{200} = 8\%$).

Solution F. Finally, a solution that you are likely to see, particularly if you are working with secondary teachers, is an algebraic approach that begins with a table (shown in Figure D.6).

$$x(200) = .20(50) + .04(150)$$

$$200x = 10 + 6$$

$$200x = 16$$

$$x = {}^{16}/_{200}$$

$$x = {}^{8}/_{100} = 8\%$$

Therefore, $x = 8\%$, which according to the table in Figure D.6 represents the percent of butterfat in the cream and milk mixture.

FIGURE D.6. A Table for Solving Problem 3 Algebraically

	Amount (Gallons)	Percent Butterfat	Amount Butterfat (Gallons)
Cream	50	20%	0.20(50)
Milk	150	4%	0.04(150)
Mixture	200	x	x(200)

FACILITATOR-GENERATED RESPONSES TO THE QUESTION, "DID JANICE PATTERSON REALLY TEACH?"

The list shown in Table D.1 was prepared by teacher educators and identifies actions taken by Janice Patterson and notes why these actions indicate that she did indeed teach.

TEACHER-GENERATED RESPONSES TO THE QUESTION, "DID JANICE PATTERSON REALLY TEACH?"

Although some teachers initially might respond that Janice Patterson did not teach because she rarely *told* her students anything, we have found that teachers identify much of the same evidence that is identified in Table

D.1. Teachers frequently characterize Mrs. Patterson as a "stage director," "facilitator," and/or "mediator." The list shown below was created by a group of teachers who participated in a discussion that focused on "The Case of Janice Patterson" and who argued that Mrs. Patterson did indeed teach. We have found it helpful to organize the evidence that teachers provide into three categories: Mrs. Patterson's teaching moves prior to the lesson, Mrs. Patterson's teaching moves during the lesson, and evidence that teaching occurred.

Actions Taken by Mrs. Patterson Prior to the Lesson

- Established classroom norms and practices (e.g., students worked in groups; student-to-student talk)
- Created a positive environment (e.g., students felt comfortable sharing, questioning, and disagreeing with each other; students felt comfortable making mistakes)
- Selected worthwhile mathematical tasks
- Built on students' prior experiences (e.g., students had explored ratio with discrete objects [black and red pieces])
- Set goals for the lesson (i.e., help students develop strategies that allow them to make sense of mathematics, students will use diagrams to solve problems)

Actions Taken by Mrs. Patterson During the Lesson

- Kept students on task
- Provided students with enough time to explore the problems
- Decided what to do next, whom to call on, how to surface disputes (e.g., Problem 3)
- Provided guidance when there was confusion (e.g., Problem 3)
- Requested additional explanation from students when needed
- Was a silent observer

Evidence That Student Learning and, Therefore, Teaching Occurred

- Met objective for students to make sense of mathematics (when students are confused by Lamont and Richard's approach to Problem 1, Mrs. Patterson invites two more groups to present

TABLE D.1. Facilitator-Generated Responses to the Question, "Did Janice Patterson Really Teach?"

Action taken by Janice Patterson	Why this action is important and provides evidence that Janice Patterson did teach
Selects three problems that build on students' prior knowledge.	The problems are intended to challenge students but not be so difficult that students have no access to the task. The problems range in difficulty, and Mrs. Patterson arranges them so that the most difficult problem is last. Hence, students experience some success before tackling the third problem.
Encourages students to talk to each other (in para. 10, students question Lamont and Richard; in para. 24, Mrs. Patterson asks the class if anyone has questions for Sasha). Also, there is evidence that student-to-student talk is becoming a part of the classroom culture (in para. 10, Tashika and Sarah question Lamont and Richard; in para. 13, Tanya and Claudia question Kevin and Maria; in para. 22, Elizabeth questions Sasha).	By inviting students to question one another, Mrs. Patterson communicates the message that each student is responsible for making sense of what is being said. In addition, she is making it clear that the person who provides the explanation is the person who can best answer the question—not necessarily the teacher.
Asks students for clarification and/or explanation rather than settling for answers or providing explanations herself (in para. 9, she asks Lamont and Richard why they multiplied 3 x 4; in para. 12, she asks Kevin and Maria to show the class what they meant; in para. 20, she asks Sasha to explain her solution while she recreates her diagram at the overhead). Also, there is evidence that students are able to communicate their thinking clearly (in paras. 15–16, Robin and Kalla provide a very clear and coherent explanation with no interruptions from the teacher; in paras. 12–13, Kevin and Maria explain their solution with no interruptions from the teacher, and two students ask Kevin and Maria for clarification, which enhances the explanation).	By doing so, Mrs. Patterson sends the message of what a good explanation looks like and that the student is capable of producing one. We see evidence throughout the class of students' ability to communicate mathematically.
Encourages multiple approaches to problems (paras. 8, 11, and 14).	By welcoming alternative solution strategies, Mrs. Patterson gives all students access to the problems at some level. Multiple approaches also provide students with new ways of thinking about problems.
Makes information available for students to consider without providing it herself (in para. 11, she solicits another solution, hoping it will be clearer than the one provided by Lamont and Richard; in para. 19, she asks Sasha to share her solution to Problem 2; in para. 27, she asks Jason and Angela to explain how they were thinking about Problem 3; in para. 29, she asks Crystal what she means by "gallon-wise").	By doing so, Mrs. Patterson is able to pursue solution paths that are mathematically productive. In addition, she is sending the message that the students' ideas are the major resource in solving the problems.
Helps students develop the ability to use pictures and diagrams as reasoning tools.	The pictures and diagrams help Mrs. Patterson's students understand the relationships involved in each problem. Without the pictures and diagrams, it is likely that students could not have solved the problems, but with these tools they were able to do very sophisticated mathematics.

solutions that make the relationships between the quantities clear; Mrs. Patterson asks the class if Angela's thinking on Problem 3 "makes sense"; Crystal uses a diagram to make sense of Angela's idea)

- Met objective for students to use diagrams (Mrs. Patterson invites several students to present solutions to Problem 1 until a visual approach is shown; Mrs. Patterson invites Sasha to present her visual solution to Problem 2)

- Students were able to apply prior knowledge to solve novel problems (students make sense of solutions to Problems 1 and 2; students work toward a starting point for Problem 3)

References

Ball, D. L., & Cohen, D. K. (1999). Developing practice, developing practitioners: Toward a practice-based theory of professional education. In G. Sykes & L. Darling-Hammond (Eds.), *Teaching as the learning profession: Handbook of policy and practice* (pp. 3–32). San Francisco: Jossey-Bass.

Barb, C., & Quinn, A. L. (1997). Problem solving does not have to be a problem. *Mathematics Teacher, 90,* 536–542.

Bennett, A. B., Maier, E., & Nelson, L. T. (1991). *Math and the mind's eye, unit VII: Modeling percentages and ratios.* Salem, OR: The Math Learning Center.

Bennett, A. B., & Nelson, L. T. (1994). A conceptual model for solving percent problems. *Mathematics Teaching in the Middle School, 1,* 20–25.

Billstein, R., & Williamson, J. (1999). *Middle grades math thematics: Book 1.* Evanston, IL: McDougal Littell.

Boston, M., Smith, M. S., & Hillen, A. F. (2003). Building on students' intuitive strategies to make sense of cross-multiplication. *Mathematics Teaching in the Middle School, 9,* 150–155.

Cramer, K., & Post, T. (1993). Proportional reasoning. *Mathematics Teacher, 86,* 404–407.

Education Development Center, Inc. (1998a). *MathScape: Buyer beware: Rates, ratios, percents, and proportions (Student guide).* Mountain View, CA: Creative Publications.

Education Development Center, Inc. (1998b). *MathScape: From zero to one and beyond: Fractions, decimals, and percents (Student guide).* Mountain View, CA: Creative Publications.

Education Development Center, Inc. (1998c). *MathScape: Gulliver's worlds: Measuring and scaling (Student guide).* Mountain View, CA: Creative Publications.

Foreman, L. C., & Bennett, A. B., Jr. (1991). *Visual mathematics course guide, Volume II.* Salem, OR: The Math Learning Center.

Foreman, L. C., & Bennett, A. B., Jr. (1996). *Visual mathematics: Course II, Lessons 21–30.* Salem, OR: The Math Learning Center.

Foreman, L. C., & Bennett, A. B., Jr. (1998). *Math alive! Course III, Lessons 13–17.* Salem, OR: The Math Learning Center.

Hart, K. (1988). Ratio and proportion. In J. Hiebert & M. Behr (Eds.), *Number concepts and operations in the middle grades* (pp. 198–219). Reston, VA: National Council of Teachers of Mathematics.

Henningsen, M., & Stein, M. K. (1997). Mathematical tasks and student cognition: Classroom-based factors that support and inhibit high-level mathematical thinking and reasoning. *Journal for Research in Mathematics Education, 29,* 524–549.

Hiebert, J., Carpenter, T. P., Fennema, E., Wearne, D., Murray, H., Olivier, A., & Human, P. (1997). *Making sense: Teaching and learning mathematics with understanding.* Portsmouth, NH: Heinemann.

Karplus, R., Pulos, S., & Stage, E. K. (1983a). Early adolescents' proportional reasoning on "rate" problems. *Educational Studies in Mathematics, 14,* 219–233.

Karplus, R., Pulos, S., & Stage, E. K. (1983b). Proportional reasoning of early adolescents. In R. Lesh & M. Landau (Eds.), *Acquisition of mathematics concepts and processes* (pp. 45–90). New York: Academic Press.

Lamon, S. (1999). *Teaching fractions and ratios for understanding: Essential content knowledge and instructional strategies for teachers.* Mahwah, NJ: Erlbaum.

Langrall, C. W., & Swafford, J. (2000). Three balloons for two dollars: Developing proportional reasoning.

Mathematics Teaching in the Middle School, 6, 254–261.

Lappan, G., Fey, J. T., Fitzgerald, W. M., Friel, S. N., & Phillips, E. D. (1997). *Connected mathematics: Stretching and shrinking: Similarity.* Palo Alto, CA: Dale Seymour.

Lappan, G., Fey, J. T., Fitzgerald, W. M., Friel, S. N., & Phillips, E. D. (1998). *Bits and pieces I: Understanding rational numbers.* Menlo Park, CA: Dale Seymour.

Lappan, G., Fey, J. T., Fitzgerald, W. M., Friel, S. N., & Phillips, E. D. (2002). *Comparing and scaling: Ratio, proportion, and percent.* Glenview, IL: Prentice Hall.

Lesh, R., Post, T., & Behr, M. (1988). Proportional reasoning. In J. Hiebert & M. Behr (Eds.), *Number concepts and operations in the middle grades* (pp. 93–118). Reston, VA: National Council of Teachers of Mathematics.

The Mathematics in Context Development Team. (1997). Mathematics in context: Per sense (Student guide). In National Center for Research in Mathematical Sciences Education & Freudenthal Institute (Eds.), *Mathematics in context.* Chicago: Encyclopaedia Britannica.

The Mathematics in Context Development Team. (1998a). Mathematics in context: Decision making (Student guide). In National Center for Research in Mathematical Sciences Education & Freudenthal Institute (Eds.), *Mathematics in context.* Chicago: Encyclopaedia Britannica.

The Mathematics in Context Development Team. (1998b). Mathematics in context: Ratios and rates (Student guide). In National Center for Research in Mathematical Sciences Education & Freudenthal Institute (Eds.), *Mathematics in context.* Chicago: Encyclopaedia Britannica.

Middleton, J. A., & van den Heuvel-Panhuizen, M. (1995). The ratio table. *Mathematics Teaching in the Middle School, 1,* 282–288.

Miller, J., & Fey, J. (2000). Proportional reasoning. *Mathematics Teaching in the Middle School, 5,* 310–313.

National Council of Teachers of Mathematics. (1989). *Curriculum and evaluation standards for school mathematics.* Reston, VA: Author.

National Council of Teachers of Mathematics. (1994). *Addenda series grades 5–8: Understanding rational numbers and proportion* (pp. 61–75). Reston, VA: Author.

National Council of Teachers of Mathematics. (2000).

Principles and standards for school mathematics. Reston, VA: Author.

Parker, M. (1999). Building on "building-up": Proportional reasoning activities for future teachers. *Mathematics Teaching in the Middle School, 4,* 286–289.

Post, T., Harel, G., Behr, M., & Lesh, R. (1991). Intermediate teachers' knowledge of rational number concepts. In E. Fennema, T. P. Carpenter, & S. J. Lamon (Eds.), *Integrating research on teaching and learning mathematics* (pp. 177–198). Madison, WI: Center for Education Research.

Shulman, J. (1992). *Case methods in teacher education.* New York: Teachers College Press.

Shulman, L. S. (1996). Just in case: Reflections on learning from experience. In J. Colbert, K. Trimble, & P. Desberg (Eds.), *The case for education: Contemporary approaches for using case methods* (pp. 197–217). Boston, MA: Allyn & Bacon.

Silver, E. A., Smith, M. S., & Nelson, B. S. (1995). The QUASAR project: Equity concerns meet mathematics education reform in the middle school. In W. G. Secada, E. Fennema, & L. B. Adajian (Eds.), *New directions in equity in mathematics education* (pp. 9–56). New York: Cambridge University Press.

Silver, E. A., & Stein, M. K. (1996). The QUASAR project: The "revolution of the possible" in mathematics instructional reform in urban middle schools. *Urban Education, 30,* 476–521.

Simon, M. A., & Blume, G. W. (1994). Mathematical modeling as a component of understanding ratio-as-measure: A study of prospective elementary teachers. *Journal of Mathematical Behavior, 13,* 183–197.

Slovin, H. (2000). Moving to proportional reasoning. *Mathematics Teaching in the Middle School, 6,* 58–60.

Smith, J. P. (1996). Efficacy and teaching mathematics by telling: A challenge for reform. *Journal for Research in Mathematics Education, 27,* 387–402.

Smith, M. S. (2000). Redefining success in mathematics teaching and learning. *Mathematics Teaching in the Middle School, 5,* 378–382, 386.

Smith, M. S. (2001a). *Practice-based professional development for teachers.* Reston, VA: National Council of Teachers of Mathematics.

Smith, M. S. (2001b). Using cases to discuss changes in mathematics teaching. *Mathematics Teaching in the Middle School, 7,* 144–149.

Sowder, J., Armstrong, B., Lamon, S., Simon, M., Sowder, L., & Thompson, A. (1998). Educating teachers to teach multiplicative structures in the middle grades.

Journal of Mathematics Teacher Education, 1, 127–155.

Stein, M. K., Grover, B. W., & Henningsen, M. (1996). Building student capacity for mathematical thinking and reasoning: An analysis of mathematical tasks used in reform classrooms. *American Educational Research Journal, 33,* 455–488.

Stein, M. K., & Lane, S. (1996). Instructional tasks and the development of student capacity to think and reason: An analysis of the relationship between teaching and learning in a reform mathematics project. *Educational Research and Evaluation, 2,* 50–80.

Stein, M. K., Smith, M. S., Henningsen, M., & Silver, E. A. (2000). *Implementing standards-based mathematics instruction: A casebook for professional development.* New York: Teachers College Press.

Sweeney, E. S., & Quinn, R. J. (2000). Concentration: Connecting fractions, decimals, & percents. *Mathematics Teaching in the Middle School, 5,* 324–328.

Thompson, C. L., & Zeuli, J. S. (1999). The frame and the tapestry: Standards-based reform and professional development. In G. Sykes & L. Darling-Hammond (Eds.), *Teaching as the learning profession: Handbook of policy and practice* (pp. 341–375). San Francisco: Jossey-Bass.

Tournaire, F., & Pulos, S. (1985). Proportional reasoning: A review of the literature. *Educational Studies in Mathematics, 16,* 181–204.

Tracy, D. M., & Hague, M. S. (1997). Toys 'R' math. *Mathematics Teaching in the Middle School, 2,* 140–145, 159.

About the Authors

Margaret Schwan Smith is an Associate Professor in the Department of Instruction and Learning in the School of Education at the University of Pittsburgh. She has a doctorate in mathematics education and has taught mathematics at the junior high, high school, and college levels. She currently works with preservice elementary, middle, and high school mathematics teachers enrolled in Master's degree programs at the University of Pittsburgh; with doctoral students in mathematics education who are interested in becoming teacher educators; and with practicing middle and high school mathematics teachers and coaches both locally and nationally. Dr. Smith is the co-author of *Implementing Standards-Based Mathematics Instruction: A Casebook for Professional Development* (Teachers College Press, 2000), which grew out of the work of the QUASAR Project. In addition, she has authored a book entitled *Practice-Based Professional Development for Teachers of Mathematics* (NCTM, 2001), which explores a particular type of professional development that connects the ongoing professional development of teachers to the actual work of teaching. Finally, she is director of two current NSF-funded projects: ASTEROID—which is studying what teachers learn from COMET cases and other practice-based professional development experiences; and the ESP project—which is focused on enhancing the preparation of secondary mathematics teachers.

Edward A. Silver is Professor of Education and Mathematics at the University of Michigan. Prior to joining the UM faculty in Fall 2000, he held a joint appointment at the University of Pittsburgh as Professor of Cognitive Studies and Mathematics Education in the School of Education and Senior Scientist at the Learning Research and Development Center. In the past, he taught mathematics at the middle school, secondary school, and community college levels in New York, and university undergraduate mathematics and graduate-level mathematics education in Illinois and California. At the University of Michigan, he teaches and advises graduate students in mathematics education, conducts research related to the teaching and learning of mathematics, and engages in a variety of professional service activities. He has published widely in books and journals in several areas, including the study of mathematical thinking, especially mathematical problem-solving and problem-posing; the design and analysis of innovative and equitable mathematics instruction for middle school students, with a special emphasis on encouraging student engagement with challenging tasks that call for mathematical reasoning and problem-solving; effective methods of assessing and reporting mathematics achievement; and the professional development of mathematics teachers. He was director of the QUASAR Project, and also has led a number of other projects in mathematics education. In addition, he was the leader of the grades 6–8 writing group for the NCTM *Principles and Standards for School Mathematics*, a member of the Mathematical Science Education Board of the National Research Council, and editor of the *Journal for Research in Mathematics Education*.

Mary Kay Stein holds a joint appointment at the University of Pittsburgh as an Associate Professor in the Administrative and Policy Department of the School of Education and Research Scientist at the Learning Research and Development Center. She has a Ph.D. in Educational Psychology from the University of Pittsburgh and has been studying the processes of educational reform for the past 18 years. Her areas of expertise are the study of classroom teaching and the investigation of ways in which educational policy, school organization, and context influence the learning of both adults and students in educational systems. Dr. Stein directed the classroom documentation effort of the QUASAR Project (1989–1996) and co-directed two follow-up, NSF-funded projects that created professional development materials for teachers (COMET, 1998–2001) and studied the impact of those materials on teacher learning (ASTEROID, 2001–2003). Dr. Stein also studies the processes of large-scale instructional improvement in districts, having directed studies of New York City's Community School District #2 (1996–2001) and the San Diego City Schools (2000–2003). Currently, she is the principal investigator of an NSF-funded, multiyear study investigating district-wide implementation of elementary mathematics curriculum (Scaling Up Mathematics: The Interface of Curricula and Human and Social Capital).

Melissa Boston is a research assistant and doctoral student in mathematics education at the University of Pittsburgh. She has taught mathematics in middle school and high school and holds a master's degree in mathematics from the University of Pittsburgh. She also has taught mathematics methods courses for prospective elementary and secondary teachers and has experience working with practicing middle and high school mathematics teachers. She served as a research assistant on the COMET project and is the project manager for the NSF-funded ESP project, which is focused on the preparation of secondary mathematics teachers. Her areas of interest include teacher learning from cases and effective case facilitation.

Marjorie A. Henningsen is an Assistant Professor of Education at the American University of Beirut, Science and Math Education Center, Beirut, Lebanon. She has a B.A. in mathematics and psychology from Benedictine College, and master's and doctorate degrees in mathematics education from the University of Pittsburgh. She has been designing and conducting professional development for preservice and inservice elementary and middle school mathematics teachers for over a decade in the United States and throughout the Middle East. She spent over 5 years designing and conducting classroom-based research with the QUASAR project. Dr. Henningsen is currently co-director of a nationwide project in Lebanon to study teaching and learning in elementary mathematics classrooms.

Amy F. Hillen is a graduate student researcher and a doctoral student in mathematics education at the University of Pittsburgh. She holds a bachelor's degree in mathematics from the University of Pittsburgh at Johnstown and has taught mathematics courses at the University of Pittsburgh. She also has taught mathematics content courses for prospective elementary teachers. She served as a graduate student researcher on the COMET project and currently works on the ASTEROID project, which is studying teacher learning from cases and other practice-based materials. Her areas of interest include preservice elementary teacher education, using student work to help teachers learn mathematics, and investigating teachers' understanding of proportionality.

Index